THE 24 MINUTE MINISTRY™ FAMILY DEVOTIONAL

THE 24 MINUTE MINISTRY

Family Devotional

JOHNNIE D. BOND, SR.

Nashville, TN

The 24 Minute Ministry™ Family Devotional
Johnnie D. Bond, Sr.
Copyright © 2008 by Johnnie D. Bond, Sr.

ISBN 978-0-9786088-1-X

Published by True Vine Publishing Company
P.O. Box 22448
Nashville, TN 37202
www.TrueVinePublishing.org

All rights reserved. No part of this book may be reproduced in any form or by any electronic or mechanical means, including information storage and retrieval or mechanical means, including information storage and retrieval systems, without permission in writing from the publisher, except by a reviewer who may quote brief passages in a review.

Unless otherwise noted, scripture quotations have been taken from the Holy Bible, King James Version.

Printed in the United States of America — First Printing

To place orders for more books or get current information; contact us at www.TrueVinePublishing.org

Cover artwork designed by Tracy Foster, Tafgraphics Design & Photography Studio 2009 . http://www.tafgraphics.com

TABLE OF CONTENTS

Acknowledgements xii
About the Author ix
The Vision and Concept xi
Introduction xiii
Instructions for the 24-Minute Ministry xvii
Explanation of Ten Categories xxi
The 24-Minute, 24/7 Plan xlv

DAILY FAMILY DEVOTIONALS

Day 1 .... 55—64
Day 2 .... 65—74
Day 3 .... 75—84
Day 4 .... 85—94
Day 5 .... 95—104
Day 6 .... 105—114
Day 7 .... 115—124
Day 8 .... 125—134
Day 9 .... 135—144
Day 10 .... 145—154
Day 11 .... 155—164
Day 12 .... 165—174
Day 13 .... 175—184
Day 14 .... 185—194
Day 15 .... 195—204
Day 16 .... 205—214
Day 17 .... 215—224
Day 18 .... 225—234
Day 19 .... 235—244
Day 20 .... 245—254
Day 21 .... 255—264
Day 22 .... 265—274
Day 23 .... 275—284
Day 24 .... 285—294
Day 25 .... 295—304
Day 26 .... 305—314
Day 27 .... 315—324
Day 28 .... 325—334

Day 29 .... 335—344
Day 30 .... 345—354

INDEX

My Service Unto the Lord 357
Daily Journal Form 359
24-Minute Prison Prayer Group 360
Consecrated Creed and Prayer of Sheep Poem 361

ACKNOWLEDGMENTS

My special thanks to all the inmates at the federal camp and officers— Malcolm "Lawman" Walker and Michael "Little Man" Hayes— for their confidence, encouragement and for the special question that they would ask all the inmates: "What does the 'B' stand for?"

A special thanks to my cellmates, Dr. Thomas Suggs and Dr. James Rodriquez, who tutored and mentored me through this entire project.

To my loving family and my extended family, James and Della Thomas.

To my lovely wife who told me long ago, "The Lord said, 'Johnnie is mine.'"

To the staff of True Vine Publishing Company who made my dream come true in the finished product of this concept. My God shall supply all of your need according to His riches in glory by our Savior Christ Jesus.

To Diana Liffengren of Finesse Proofreading & Editing Services for her gallant efforts in probing me until she truly understood my vision and concept for this ministry. I am forever grateful for her professional editing skills.

All my love and special thanks to my prayer partners in Christ.

And special recognition to Dr. Lloyd Ogilvie for his awesome inspiring book, "A Conversation with God," which helped change my life.

ABOUT THE AUTHOR

In 1999 I was sentenced to 97 months in the federal prison system. I committed errors that stemmed from my illusions of injustices deemed harmful to society. My misguided approach to fight race discrimination got the best of me. I forged forward to take matters into my own hands, which ended in my demise. Although I was a Christian, I justified my actions because I felt I was making up for all the wrong that I had witnessed in my life. Of course I could not continue on that path for long before the Lord would intervene. As a result, everything I had was destroyed. I lost my business and millions of dollars. It was devastating and embarrassing. I felt that I had let down everyone who cared about me. At times I just wanted to die.

    I was taught a very powerful lesson in this downfall. I learned I must not proceed ahead of the Lord but instead, allow Him to avenge wrongdoing in His time and in His way. As a result I suffered the greater pain. I could see the end of my life only as death while locked away in an isolated dungeon. With all the uncertainties that loomed over me as the year 2000 approached, I often felt hopeless and helpless. The thought of never being able to embrace my family or share time with them again left me very distraught and broken-spirited. I was facing a black hole. I never dreamed that the challenges I was about to experience (and eventually embrace enthusiastically) would bring about eternal euphoria.

    Rather than choose death and more hatred that would have continued to fuel my illusions, I began a fasting-and-prayer ministry. I decided to fast and pray five days per week—water only. It changed my life. Now with a renewed value of accountability, I began to re-examine the Word of God. I learned that eternal life is a test that can be aced—by those who are held accountable.

    One day an inmate that I had befriended approached me. This inmate was a doctor who, by all accounts, was a genius academically yet had received a prison sentence for becoming addicted and peddling the pain pills with which he had been entrusted. He told me, "I want to read the Bible but I do not trust myself to read and study it daily." Then he asked me to hold him accountable by joining him in daily Bible study and prayer. We began to study together from 9:30 p.m. to 10:00 p.m. At 10:00 p.m. all the lights in the prison were turned off.

One night after our session ended, even though the prayer time went well, I felt a sense of discouragement and did not know why. I knelt again to pray, now in the darkness of my prison cell, when all of a sudden I saw the glowing hand of God as it reached out to anoint my head. What did I do? I got up from my knees. Though I had been discouraged and perplexed upon kneeling, I rose rejoicing and pondering in my heart what had happened. That vision will always be ingrained and branded in my mind and spirit.

After that my prayer partner and I continued to meet daily to read scriptures and pray, and when 24 minutes was up, we went our separate ways. Every day we met for the same reason: to complete our 24-minute session. We continued this procedure for 30 days and then we changed partners and started the study all over again. In fewer than six months we had over fifty members join this ministry! From this experience emerged the 24-Minute Ministry concept. Now you hold in your hand this revolutionary new concept in ministry. This material requires partners who hold each other accountable. Partners encourage each other to achieve the goal of becoming a "Student of the Word." I did it and you can too!

My prayer for you is that you will read and listen closely as the Spirit speaks to your heart concerning this ministry. I will begin sharing my outlines of many of the great messages that God gave me during this experience. I believe if you will commit to the strict regiment of the ministry, God will open your understanding as well.

In His Service,

Johnnie Bond Sr.

THE VISION AND CONCEPT FOR THE 24-MINUTE MINISTRY

After my encounter with the Lord that night in my prison cell, it became clear that the confidence and power within each of us can only be fully realized by meditating on the words of the kingdom. When men believe God's words and act solely upon the authority of Almighty God Himself, they can conquer the world for good. Then God will be glorified.

One purpose of meditation is to first acknowledge and then visualize the divine grace of God. Through this process, we can envision how God has measured out His grace by way of three significant gifts: His Son, the Holy Ghost and eternal life.

THE GIFT OF HIS SON:

Jesus is the Son of God who lived, suffered, died, and was then raised on the third day with all power given to Him to govern heaven and earth (Matt. 28:18). Jesus was given the Spirit of God without measure, allowing Him to do many miracles which served as infallible proofs for His earthly ministry. Further proof was the sound of voices from heaven as witnessed by Christ's followers. The grace of God met all the required conditions, and receiving this grace requires that we meet His conditions. We can only access or attain this grace through faith, by reaching for and accepting the truths of the Bible as the oracles of God.

THE GIFT OF THE HOLY GHOST:

The Holy Ghost is able to interpret the perfect will of God without human assistance. Clearly, His whole mission on earth is to glorify Jesus, the Son of God Most High, and to comfort His followers. The 24-Minute Ministry provides tangible material for use in devotion and communion. This ministry is one of enlightening, daily meditation by which we enjoy the fellowship of partners and the presence of the Holy Ghost. Luke 24:45 states, "Then opened he their understanding, that they might understand the Scriptures." Daily meditation accounts for the creation of a personal relationship with God, a relationship based on love, truth, and wisdom for the prudent and creative mind. When we meditate on biblical accounts in the 24-Minute Ministry, we realize foremost that God has provided for us His divine order in the plan of salvation for mankind. Within this order we understand the necessity of the gift of His Son as a sacrifice for our sins.

THE GIFT OF ETERNAL LIFE:

Is it possible to receive the first two gifts and not this final reward? Consider what Jesus had to say to those who came to Him with this question: "Lord, Lord, have we not… in thy name done many wonderful works?" (Matt. 7:22). Jesus turned to them and said, "I never knew you: depart from me, ye that work iniquity" (v. 23). Here is proof that many design an agenda that's self-serving and miss the opportunity to build on solid rock. In this generation, many have forsaken the vineyard and harvest of our Lord for the cares of the world. Jesus has warned us, "Strait is the gate, and narrow is the way, which leadeth unto life, and few there be that find it." (Matt. 7:14).

The 24-Minute Ministry was designed to help you find the straight gate and narrow way which leads to life. The final process will assist you in your quest to receive with boldness the gifts of Jesus the Son, the Holy Ghost our Comforter, and eternal life. This daily meditation ministry will teach you how much God loves each of us; then it will teach you how to love God and how to love one another. This ministry is also God's gift to aid in your quest to understand the words of the kingdom.

INTRODUCTION
ANSWERS TO OUR QUESTIONS

There are so many unique gifts and qualities that proceed from our eternal, all-knowing, all-wise Father of lights. Though often misguided, humanity is the glory of God. We are like tarnished brass and can only be polished with His Word. Consider statements such as the following: "It pleased God by the foolishness of preaching to save them that believe." (1 Cor. 1:21); and "How shall they hear without a preacher? And how shall they preach, except they be sent?" (Rom. 10:14-15). Who are these "sent" ones? What do you think these questions mean?

Have you ever wondered why God asks questions to which He already knows the answers? For example, He asked Adam and Eve, "Who told thee that thou wast naked?" (Gen 3:11).

Insight and revelation of the Word of God will give us answers to these and many other questions. In 1 John 2:27, John declares, "But the anointing which ye have received of him abideth in you, and ye need not that any man teach you: but as the same anointing teacheth you of all things, and is truth, and is no lie, and even as it hath taught you, ye shall abide in him." Every believer must look forward to the day of maturity when he/she is filled with the Spirit daily. The 24-Minute Ministry helps answer the previous questions along with the following: How do I get the anointing? How will I know that I'm anointed? How can I begin to systematically study the tried and proven written Word and ways of God?

NO SHORT CUTS

In Old Testament times, during the detailed consecration of Aaron and his sons, the blood of a ram was put on the tip of the right ear of Aaron and his sons, then upon the thumb of the right hand and upon the great toe of the right foot. The blood was then sprinkled on the altar; then it and the anointing oil were sprinkled on Aaron and his robes and his sons and their robes (Exod. 29:20-21). At the time, all this could be visibly observed. Even today we must have spiritually anointed ears in order to hear the Word, hands to write and expound the Word, and feet with which to spread the Word. This is vital to our Christian experience and future. God has always had an orderly manner with which to bring His people into a state of unity and consecration; this method defies the philosophies of our fast-paced society that dictates quick fixes, shortcuts, hits and misses, and hocus-pocus seductions. God has always rejected anything less than our best efforts. He proved this in Leviticus, Chapter 10 when He killed Aaron's two sons for seeking a shortcut to the power of God.

The 24-Minute Ministry is a daily, systematic study approach that allows you to become a student of the Word, to inspire accountability and to gain knowledge, revelation, wisdom and understanding from the uncut, uncensored Word of God. The arrangement of Scripture under 10 categories in the family devotional session is an example. Each participant will hear and witness inspiring affirmations flowing from the lips of each partner, then proceed in prayer, asking for more enlightenment and empowerment. When this experience is shared, it brings ultimate fulfillment.

STAY STRONG IN YOUR STUDY

A brief essay was written for each category in order to define the true meaning and purpose of this ministry concept. As you read, please keep in mind that in Matthew 11:12, Jesus said, "And from the days of John the Baptist until now the kingdom of heaven suffereth violence, and the violent take it by force." I have taken the violent, "Onward Christian Soldier" approach. I believe there is an opponent who stands against the Word of God. I know that he will not prevail. He has been a murderer from the beginning. He is the father of lies (John 8:44). He will use any distraction to keep millions in darkness and in the valley of decision as they head toward self-destruction. Therefore, I have learned that the only thing he will never defeat is the power of the pure, unadulterated, incorruptible Word of God. With these words of encouragement I implore you--when it seems like you are not progressing, keep praying and reading; when you think your labor with a prayer partner is in vain, keep reading and praying; when the process seems redundant and you are reluctant to continue, remember that God is not a man—He cannot lie (Num. 23:19).

God says, "So shall my word be that goeth forth out of my mouth: it shall not return unto me void" (Isa. 55:1). Soon, you will be able to see spiritual progress toward what He has called you to do in this journey from earth to glory. Then you, too, will understand the 24-Minute Ministry as just another powerful concept—a tangible spiritual weapon to be used in the warfare of our Lord to destroy the works of the enemy. I have used this tool to win new converts to the faith; to help them develop a hunger and thirst for the Word of God; to bring them to a state of maturity; and to teach them how to pray. Remember the disciple in Luke 11:1 who came to Jesus and said, "Lord, teach us to pray, as John also taught his disciples." Jesus began to instruct His disciples, and we have the model prayer as a result.

The 24-Minute Ministry is based on a partnership concept and focuses on helping new believers and the unconverted learn that there is daily access to a loving Father—one who made each of us our brother's keeper and who said that "the elder (more mature) shall serve the younger" (Gen. 25:23, Rom. 9:12). This has always been God's plan from the beginning. Additionally, the author of the Gospel of John challenged all those who write and aspire to magnify the Father and the work of His Son through writing with these words: "And there are also many other things which Jesus did, the which, if they should be written every one, I suppose that even the world itself could not contain the books that should be written. Amen" (John 21:25). Let the 24-Minute Ministry help reveal and develop the personal gifts God has given you.

THE UNCUT AND UNCENSORED WORD

There are thousands of books by authors on prayer and the power thereof, and I commend them all. But don't miss the voice of the Spirit in this concept. The underlying theme is the power of the Word of God. Here is what we mean when we say that the 24-Minute Ministry presents the uncut and uncensored Word of God: we believe the Word of God in its purest form must be interpreted by the Holy Ghost, who determines its meaning for all humanity in every age, based on one's physical and psychological behavior and experiences in life. God's Word means not only what many people have discovered it means, but also what we discover today in a personal way—even if others have failed to be enlightened by the same Scripture. The Word is ever-evolving.

This is what is meant by the Scriptures that tell us that the Word (which is spiritual) is spiritually discerned and that the Spirit searches the deep things of God for our lives (1 Cor. 2:10). Consider this—the Spirit is the only One who can "get inside" our heads and hearts and work out life's equations, prompting the flow of life to us in a personal way. Spiritual growth will occur only when our understanding is perfected. Therefore, if the Holy Ghost gives us understanding that has been confirmed as truth by the Scriptures, our wisdom becomes limitless in regard to what we can grasp. There is no lack of understanding in any matter. Paul proclaims, "I can do all things through Christ which strengtheneth me." He could just as easily have said, "I can understand all things through Christ who enlightens me."

The 24-Minute Ministry encourages repetitive reading of the Scriptures, allowing one to revisit the uncut and uncensored Word of God during the course of each session. Then, the same words trigger more enlightenment in the spiritual realm, thus giving the Holy Ghost another opportunity to disclose the written Word of God. This takes place even if we are not conscious of what is happening. Micro-spiritual growth is taking place every moment of our lives.

This type of recollection is experienced when we hear a song for the first time. If we continue to listen, more details of the song are picked up, and we begin to participate with the artist of the song. In the verse that asks, "How shall they hear?" the emphasis is on hearing (Rom. 10:14). The 24-Minute Ministry emphasizes that the Word of God attracts the attention of the soul by speaking from God's heart to us about eternal joy and glory. The 24-Minute Ministry's deliberate usage of the Word of God as it is recorded in the King James Version will allow the Holy Ghost to be our teacher. He will patiently give us the mind of Christ as we mature. As Paul states, "We have the mind of Christ." (1 Cor. 2:16). We are able to think like Christ. This is what the Apostle had come to understand when he explained in Philippians 2:6 that Jesus "thought it not robbery to be equal with God." Jesus said that we may be "perfect, even as our Father which is in heaven is perfect" (Matt. 5:48). Jesus is the Sovereign Executor of the Word of God; therefore, God's Word is His equal in authority and recognition. However, in regard to office and operation, Jesus declared of the Father, "My Father is greater than I" (John 14:28).

I hope that the 24 Minute Ministry brings to you and yours what I have been blessed with—a clearer understanding of what it means to be a member of God's family, an heir and joint-heir with Christ (see Rom. 8:17), in a relationship freely given in the midst of our 21st-century whirlwind.

INSTRUCTIONS FOR THE 24-MINUTE MINISTRY

From the solitude of prison life, the author saw in a vision the glowing hand of his Savior reaching out to anoint him. From that lonely night in his prison cell, the author wrote over 1,000 messages that magnify Jesus as the Son of God. From those messages every Scripture was used to develop the 24-Minute Ministry.

THE FAMILY DEVOTIONAL SESSION

The family session is distinct because it requires more than 24 minutes to complete. Yet it is highly effective in bringing the family unit together in daily prayer and thanksgiving toward the Creator. It is also versatile, multifaceted and interchangeable in that all parties are represented and can be separated out to fit the occasion. Whether it is used by husband/wife, father/son, mother/daughter, etc., all Scriptures are suitable and the format can be used to pair all partners in a variety of combinations. Most of the testimonies that have been documented in regard to people's appreciation for this session, share a common theme: "My parents took me to church, but they did not teach me the Word of God."

The 24-Minute Ministry Family Devotional is a simple tool that will allow father and mother to spend time in Scripture collectively or individually with loved ones so that another generation is not lost in ignorance of the Word of God.

THE 10 PRAYER AND STUDY CATEGORIES

Prayer of Preparedness
Worship and Praise
Prayer of Confession
Prayer of Gratitude
Wisdom and Understanding

Prayer of Serenity
Prayer of Intercession
Prayer of Personal Request
Prayer of Guidance
Dedication and Consecration

It is our hope that participants in the 24-Minute Ministry use this ministry as a tool in study, and for edification, exhortation and comfort. It is essential that two or more persons participate in the prayer, praise, and intercession as well as the other Categories listed. This ministry is also used as a study and prayer session in group settings. We have discovered that each partner is encouraged and helped by the other's faith, causing all participants to be enriched by similar, yet uniquely different, petitions.

Within a 30-day period, a new habit will be formed. This will help each partner to accomplish the goal desired: to *walk in the Spirit of God by walking in the spirit of His Word*. The 24-Minute Ministry will give the congregational family (or your personal family) the fundamentals of Scripture. Add faithful Bible study to reinforce the walk in the Spirit. "Heaven and earth shall pass away: but my words shall not pass away" (Mark 13:31). This is a promise made by the Author of our faith, Jesus Himself! We have provided suggestions and comments after each Category for your convenience; however, each prayer partner will pray in his/her own way, according to the secrets of his/her heart.

DAILY STUDY BRINGS SPIRITUAL GROWTH

The 24-Minute Ministry points to Christ as the Author of our hope. He in turn shows us God's way to perfection in His sight. Daily using the repetitive reading of the Scriptures will help to do the following:

- Provide inspiration while bringing a greater enlightenment of God's Word.
- Give each partner a unique spiritual energy.

- Provide the perfect language (through God's Word, which assures that God's promises have their own timing).
- Promote confidence in each sincere participant that his/her prayers for forgiveness are heard and sins are forgiven.

There are more than 3,400 positive Scripture references every 30 days. The human soul will find one or more to live by every day. Spiritual growth is immeasurable. Why? Because our major emphasis is on the <u>Truth</u> of God's Word. It is an effective <u>Tool</u> with a unique <u>Technique</u>. In the end, it will develop you into an effective <u>Teacher</u> for this end-time harvest for our Lord. The 24-Minute Ministry allows every participant to be held accountable, which makes spiritual growth evident. As you begin this wonderful experience; remember it is based on the very Word of God as recorded in John 14:23: "Jesus answered and said unto him, If a man love me, he will keep my words: and my Father will love him, and we will come unto him, and make our abode with him." Here we only have two conditions to eternal fellowship with the Father and Son: Love Jesus and Keep His Words.

DAILY PRAYER AND STUDY TECHNIQUES
HERE IS HOW IT WORKS:

1. Each person reads their appointed Scripture, i.e., Father, Mother, Son, Daughter. If there are more children or additional adults in the household, they can take turns reading the Scriptures.
2. After everyone reads their Scripture, they each go back using the special comments or their Scripture in a prayer of thanksgiving. The latter is known as praying out of the Scriptures." This method allows God to establish true structure and order for our life in communion with Him.
3. Remember the 10 Categories will address every area and concern we will face today. It is important to use discipline to wait on the prayer of intercession before one word on prayer of intercession is uttered; to wait on the prayer of wisdom to

ask for wisdom; to wait on the prayer of guidance to ask for guidance, etc. In the end, dedicate and consecrate your life anew.
4. All 10 Categories should be read in one setting. Keep it simple and follow the same instructions as given in #'s 1 and 2 above. Read the Scripture and close in prayer.
5. There must be a prayer offered after each Category. There are two options:
   A. Everyone can choose to pray out of their Scripture as they find special nuggets or traces of wisdom found in the poetry of the inspired Word to recite.
   B. Depending on the number of people in your group, it is acceptable to alternate after each Category by having a different person address that Category using option A as their foundation. Remember, it is God's techniques we are commissioned to observe.
6. These closing prayers will help each participant perfect his/her communication with God the Father and the Lord Jesus Christ. These prayers serve as both a testimony and confession of faith before witnesses. As Philippians 1:27 states, "Ye stand fast in one spirit, with one mind striving together for the faith of the gospel."

There is no correct time to end a prayer or praise period after each Category. Remember, God knows our needs and our desires before we come to Him. We believe that God is pleased with each act of faith as well as our faithfulness to commit to being in His presence daily. Participants should hold hands during the prayer time, but especially during the final reading of dedication and consecration. When there is a Scripture that provides personal inspiration, take it into your spirit all day (See Prayer Journal Sheet). Know that God is speaking in a personal way to you in this instance. The Scriptures and setting are designed to be shared morning, noonday, and night—at all times and for all occasions.

PRAYER OF PREPAREDNESS

Preparedness differs from preparation even though it might seem they are the same thing. Where preparation is the process of making something ready for service, preparedness is a state of readiness, especially for war. Just as one would thoroughly prepare for war without limitation, there can be no limitations or reservations in regard to approaching what has been termed "the throne of grace." Scriptures that concern preparedness indicate that we are already fully prepared for the communion of prayer by the blood of Jesus, which was shed not only for the remission of our sins, but also to bring us to God the Father as His children and as members of His spiritual family. We make ourselves prepared to commune with Him—spirit to Spirit—through the Scriptures.

The Apostle Paul tells the Corinthians that they should be prepared by "having a readiness to revenge all disobedience, when their obedience is fulfilled" (2 Cor. 10:6). In a nutshell, Paul is saying that we should always be prepared to engage in spiritual warfare in order to get our requests heard and answered according to the will of God. Jesus, too, addressed why we should be prepared and what we should be prepared to do in Luke18:1-7, in the story of the widow who approached the judge who was described as unjust and lacking in regard for men or God. Jesus emphasized that the widow was prepared to pay no heed to the judge's tyrannical, ungodly attitude toward her petition. She had a readiness of mind to get her just settlement. Through this story, Christ stressed that men ought to always pray and not be timid or fearful.

The unjust judge's attitude is typical of that of our spiritual adversary, called by John in Revelation: "the accuser of our brethren," who accuses us "before our God day and night" (Rev. 12:10). Peter refers to the enemy as "a roaring lion" that "walketh about, seeking whom he may devour" (1 Pet. 5:8). Still, the widow was not hindered by him. She remained focused and ready to denounce any resistance to her desires. With God's help, she brought the judge's will into line with her will. In Luke 18:7, Jesus explains that God will certainly "avenge his own elect." Our daily prayers keep our requests before Him continually.

      The Scriptures teach us that we were once "alienated and enemies in our mind by wicked works," though now we have been "reconciled" by the blood of Jesus (Col.1:21). The 24-Minute Ministry gives us the weapon of God's Word that will prepare our hearts daily and allow each participant "to be strengthened with might by his Spirit in the inner man" (Eph. 3:16). We are able to cast out the negative thinking and mental images "that exalteth themselves against the knowledge of God" (2 Cor. 10:5). These words give us hope and faith to believe God. Remember that God makes no distinction between His Word and Himself. The more confidence we have in His Word, the more power we will have to overcome afflictions and temptations in our daily walk.

WORSHIP AND PRAISE

Most of the words translated "prayer" in the Bible, are actually close in meaning to our word "worship." Where prayer specifically means an address to God in word or thought and is an act of intimate communion of the spirit, worship is the act of expressing reverence for God. Where prayer is more a matter of private conversation, worship can be either private or public, and it involves action.

We should never be surprised that Jesus gave us so many valuable lessons through all His experiences with women, including widows, mothers, prostitutes, and those who had encountered demons. I have come to differ with those who believe that He addressed women primarily because they had more emotional insecurities than did men. I believe Jesus understood that woman, whom He had made subject to man in the Garden experience, had become victim to many unfair and misleading concepts and teachings of the day.

There is no clearer illustration to help us understand worship and praise (St. John 4) than Jesus' acquaintance with the woman at the well in Sychar, a city in Samaria. The conversation peaks in verses 20-24 as the woman explains what she had been taught all her life. She says, "Our fathers worshipped in this mountain; and ye say that in Jerusalem is the place where men ought to worship" (v. 20). In the wake of this statement, Jesus would liberate humanity with a message from heaven concerning God's desire for true worshipers—those who would not be favored or left out because of heritage or geographical location. Jesus uttered these words: "But the hour cometh, and now is, when the true worshippers shall worship the Father in spirit and in truth: for the Father seeketh such to worship him" (v. 23).

Jesus' statement is directed to all those who would worship God in response to His love and not out of duty or obligation, for He knows that those who worship out of duty or obligation will miss the intimacy of a relationship with a living and loving God. Jesus explains that worship is an action of the spirit and truth because God is Spirit. In this context, truth means "fidelity" or "constancy" and is based on faith as opposed to fact, which is based on concrete physical data. In summary, worship is an active expression of reverence to God, whom we know through faith.

Likewise, praise has a specific meaning when used within the context of worship; it means to glorify. Some have the misconception that praise simply means commending God for His good works toward mankind. Although such praise can be sincere, it is empty when compared to the active praise that can be offered. Because God's love for us is without qualification, you can share that love with others. And when you glorify God in this active manner, you praise Him in the best way. As you can see in 1 John 4, "God is love" (just as God is Spirit), and "we ought also to love one another" (vv. 8, 11).

The 24-Minute Ministry meditations on worship and praise will give you the Scriptural foundation to go forth and actively worship and praise God. You will be kindled with zeal to express your reverence, gained through faith, and to praise God by actively loving Him and everyone else.

PRAYER OF CONFESSION

To confess means to acknowledge. The Greek of the New Testament equates the word "confess" with "profess" or "affirm" in that we are to confess that Christ is Lord (1 John 4:2). Thus, confession is positive; it is not to be feared but to be welcomed. As a sacrament, confession is our opportunity to confide in God the mistakes we have made and about which He already knows. It is an intimate sharing that has been a part of humanity's relationship with God as far back as the time of Genesis. When the man into which God had breathed a living soul committed sin, he went into hiding—though hiding from an omniscient God is impossible. God called Adam, saying, "Where art thou?" but He knew where Adam was (Gen. 3:9). He gave Adam an opportunity to confess, come out of hiding, and return to the relationship. Whether spoken or unspoken, prayers of confession require the penitent to put into words the memories of sin and to acknowledge them to God. The prayer unburdens the repentant sinner and restores his or her relationship with God.

I'm reminded of what my mother tried to instill into my young mind as a child. She was always saying, "Be polite…. If you offend someone, ask for his or her forgiveness." As a kid, the difficult task for me was to confess or admit my offenses. Today, I serve a God I know is omniscient; He knows everything. Psalm 139 reveals that nothing is hidden from the Lord. While men love darkness and run from the light to their own destruction, God encourages His family members to come clean. He offers us the same love and concern, as would a mother. He simply asks us to confess, admit, and be courteous and polite— especially now that we have accepted His Son Jesus as our personal Lord and Savior.

Exodus 29:10-18, written by Moses, teaches us about two major animal sacrificial offerings made by the priests: one for sin atonement and one for a burnt offering. The first served as a sin eradicator and represented things to come; the other, which reflected God's acceptance and forgiveness toward His children, allowed humankind to remain in continual fellowship with God. Have you ever heard the phrase "two for one"? Well, within Christianity, it's "One for many."

Today we believe that Jesus was offered once for all when He took our place in death as our atonement for sin. He was then glorified through resurrection because He pleased God, accomplishing our justification and allowing for continual fellowship by being our peace offering. It is finished! It's a done deal. But what must we continue to do? We must simply confess our faults, errors, shortcomings, inconsistencies, and any other offenses for which Jesus of Nazareth was executed and sacrificed more than two thousand years ago.

The 24-Minute Ministry confession Scriptures offer a daily reminder of God's longsuffering toward us and His Son's sacrifice, which entailed the kind of suffering that we cannot even imagine. We were spared and are now witnesses of the selfless love and kindness of an awesome God, and as we experience this love, we are compelled by Him to draw nearer and nearer. Now we can keep our slates clean as we destroy the guilt complex that would keep us from living out our maximum potential in the Body of Christ.

PRAYER OF GRATITUDE

The word "gratitude" comes to us not from Hebrew or Greek but from the Latin *gratus,* which means "grateful." The Roman world, of which Latin was the language, extended to the Holy Land during the time of our Lord and His followers of the New Testament. In fact, Paul was not only a Jew, but also a Roman citizen.

To be grateful means to be appreciative of benefits received, though the meaning of the word goes much deeper than this because it also refers to the origin of those benefits: unmerited divine assistance that is given to a man for his renewal. Thus, "gratitude" and "grace" have their origins in the same Latin roots.

The 24-Minute Ministry Scriptures under the topic "Prayer of Gratitude" relate not only to being thankful but also to that for which we are thankful. God is the Creator and the origin of all things. When God set the physical universe in motion, He had you in mind. Imagine that! Fourteen billion years ago, before the universe emerged from God's Word, you were on His holy mind! Finally, all coalesced into the vast universe that surrounds you and now God helps you regenerate each day. You may not feel you deserve it, but God loves you that much!

Our thankfulness reflects how grateful we are for the continuation of His creation from the Alpha to the Omega—from the beginning to the end (Rev. 22:13)—as well as for the greatest gift of all: Jesus' sacrifice on the cross so that you might have eternal life, His gift to us all.

Sometimes it appears in our walk of faith that we have borrowed a page from a movie script and have became actors playing a part rather than people of faith who are truly experiencing a personal relationship with a living and loving Savior. God is as active in the power of His words today as He was more than two thousand years ago when His Son walked the earth. But do we really express our gratitude daily for the little things? Have we left our first love? Jesus once rebuked a group of men by asking the question, "How long shall I suffer you?" (Matt. 17:17). In essence, He was saying, "Your faith in God's Word, as written by Moses and the prophets, has become so insignificant and meaningless that you have no power in this perverse generation."

This had happened in Noah's day, and now Jesus was again calling the people a faithless and perverse generation. It's frightening to think this could happen in our generation even though Christ left this word of caution for us in Luke 18:8: "Nevertheless when the Son of man cometh, shall he find faith on the earth?" Jesus understood and taught; then He set the example for us by pleasing God with the most powerful elements of faith: a grateful heart and an obedient will.

In Luke 17:1, Jesus encountered 10 lepers. After all ten received healing, nine took off in nine different directions. We know the nine lepers did not return. In theory, one can go nine different directions even if he/she has received a miraculous touch from the Master. Among the preoccupations that can consume our attention and detract from our spiritual view—coercing us to neglect expressing genuine gratitude to our eternal God—are family, business, politics, sports, adventure, fashion, and career; these are known as the cares of the world. They can choke out gratefulness and lead to complaining. This Bible story tells us that one former leper came back to give glory to God, and he was a Samaritan. He set aside his personal ambitions long enough to say, "Thank You, Lord, for all You've done for me."

One week, I spoke to four guests on a radio program. On the last day, I brought three of my sons on the set, along with a couple of their friends. I began to interview them concerning the guests: what had impressed them the most about these various individuals? They each had an inspiring answer, but when it was my nine-year-old son's turn, he looked at me and said these words: "Dad, you have impressed me the most. I've learned a lot from what you've been doing and saying to us all." Well, I gave them the usual "Thank you" and closed the program. That was over twenty years ago. Today, that statement from a babe, my youngest son, rings out in my heart every time difficult circumstances bring me a moment of disappointment. To know that I had become the #1 choice for a moment in his life has been a lasting joy of mine through the years.

Now and then, I think about the times I've failed to express my heartfelt gratitude toward the Father and His Son for His death. The prophet Isaiah said, "It pleased the Lord to bruise him" (Isa. 53:10)—not implying that God derived pleasure or amusement or that He wanted to satisfy a need for revenge. Rather, He was a holy God who needed to show how repulsed He was by sin—no matter who bore that sin.

"The Lord hath laid on him the iniquity of us all" (Isa. 53:6). He punished Jesus accordingly; "He...spared not his own Son, but delivered him up for us all" (Rom. 8:32). The Scriptures in the 24-Minute Ministry gratitude session will inspire you to adopt a grateful attitude, with moment-by-moment expressions. The Holy Ghost will usher in rivers of living water, as the Spirit of God inhabits the praises and thanksgiving of His people.

WISDOM AND UNDERSTANDING

Wisdom is most frequently defined as deep understanding or discernment that is intellectually alert as well as the capacity for sound judgment. Solomon could have asked God for anything, but he chose wisdom—that is, to have "an understanding heart" (1 Kings 3:9). Intelligence is the ability to learn, and wisdom allowed Solomon to use his intelligence to judge God's people and to discern between good and evil.

Sometimes we confuse some of the terms that relate to wisdom, which causes unnecessary conflict. Wisdom and intelligence are both gifts from God. Assimilating facts allows the wise man to make decisions based upon sound judgment. A fact is a piece of information based upon objective reality, e.g., God created light, as recorded in Scripture (Gen 1:3). Likewise, tools of measurement confirm the fact that light travels at 186,000 miles per second; and the Greek mathematician Pythagoras established the fact that the square of the length of a hypotenuse of a right triangle equals the sum of the squares of the two sides. Armed with facts, we understand that the universe is approximately fourteen billion years old. Since the Bible is a book of the history of God's plan for man's salvation, it does not give readers a date for the creation of the universe: it only tells us that the universe has not always been, while God has always been and will always be. Wisdom allows us to recognize that there is no conflict between God's Word and facts.

Wisdom also is related to logic and reason. The word "wisdom" comes from the Greek word *eidos*, meaning "the manner of using reason to achieve understanding; a manner of thinking." It is via this very approach to understanding that John's Gospel explains the identity of our Lord Jesus Christ, the Word made flesh (John 1:1-18). Understanding is indeed a challenge, but the Scriptures in the 24-Minute Ministry equip you to pray for wisdom and understanding, gifts that God is pleased to share through your relationship with Him as your heavenly Father and the inspiration of the Holy Spirit. He gives clear and harmonious wisdom, equipping you to deal with the conflicts of the world that He so loves.

Consider the rather odd title to a message I preached years ago: "Wisdom Never Raised No Fool." This title originated from Jesus' statement of Matthew 11:19, "But wisdom is justified of her children." Jesus had just rebuked certain men who had been dissatisfied with John's style of preaching and who were now intolerant of Christ and His choice to fellowship with publicans and sinners. Wisdom was absent from their reasoning.

It is difficult to be brief while writing this section because there are so many references in regard to wisdom. I struggle to choose from among all the things that Solomon had to say, what Jesus demonstrated, the warnings of the prophets and apostles in regard to the ages to come, and the countless, essential statements and comments in the Bible that tell us how to obtain wisdom.

Since the beginning of humanity, every household has had its share of dysfunctional situations. Cain killed Abel, Noah cursed his son's child, and Abraham put out the son he had fathered with his wife's handmaid. Esau sold his birthright. Jacob tricked his father Isaac, and David was run out of his kingdom by his son. The stories go on and on. So where is the wisdom? As someone has said, "It's in there." We must all get it with understanding.

Proverbs 1:20-29 is my favorite passage of Scripture. It reads:

> Wisdom crieth without; she uttereth her voice in the streets: She crieth in the chief place of concourse, in the openings of the gates: in the city she uttereth her words, saying, How long, ye simple ones, will ye love simplicity? and the scorners delight in their scorning, and fools hate knowledge? Turn you at my reproof: behold, I will pour out my spirit unto you, I will make known my words unto you. Because I have called, and ye refused; I have stretched out my hand, and no man regarded; But ye have set at nought all my counsel, and

would none of my reproof: I also will laugh at your calaity; I will mock when your fear cometh; When your fear cometh as desolation, and your destruction cometh as a whirlwind; when distress and anguish cometh upon you. Then shall they call upon me, but I will not answer; they shall seek me early, but they shall not find me: For that they hated knowledge, and did not choose the fear of the Lord.

This passage tells me that from the White House to the lowliest outhouse, wisdom and understanding are available to even the simple ones, the scorners, and the fools. The terms of wisdom are simple: "Whoso findeth me findeth life, and shall obtain favour of the Lord" (Prov. 8:35). In Job 38:2, the Lord weighed in Job's wisdom by asking him this question: "Who is this that darkeneth counsel by words without knowledge?" One hundred eighty-three additional questions followed this one. Then Job answered; he confessed, "Therefore have I uttered that I understood not; things too wonderful for me, which I knew not" (42:3). We all must reach the same conclusion as did Job, and we must submit to James 1:5: "If any of you lack wisdom, let him ask of God, that giveth to all men liberally, and upbraideth not; and it shall be given him."

The Bible tells us that the Gospel message "is to them that perish foolishness; but unto us which are saved it is the power of God" (1 Cor. 1:18). For those of us who believe, God has made Christ our "wisdom, and righteousness, and sanctification, and redemption" (1 Cor. 1:30). What a package!

The many Scriptures that express wisdom in the 24-Minute Ministry give us the understanding we need to walk in light and not in darkness. "The wisdom that is from above is first pure, then peaceable, gentle, and easy to be intreated, full of mercy and good fruits, without partiality, and without hypocrisy" (James 3:17). Every day, as we meditate on words of wisdom, the Spirit of Truth will help each of us to be conformed into the image of God's dear Son. If there is a session and category we all should be eager to meditate upon daily, it is the one concerning wisdom and understanding.

PRAYER OF SERENITY

The truth of the matter is that human beings really don't know how to please God. Every sacrifice that God gave Moses to serve as atonement for sins committed against a holy and eternal God was God's idea. God devised the relationship that He has with those who are created in His image and likeness. Consider that what He most wanted to show us about His character was depicted through a lamb—a serene, calm, meek, tranquil sheep.

Since a lamb is easily led, confusion arises when man's pride decrees that he should do the leading. What does God think about that idea? The answer is simple. He gave us a Man—Jesus the Son of Man and Son of God, approved by God to become our righteousness—to become the Mediator between God and man. I like what the author of Hebrews says: "God, who at sundry times and in divers manners spake in time past unto the fathers by the prophets, Hath in these last days spoken unto us by his Son, whom he hath appointed heir of all things, by whom also he made the worlds" (1:1-2). Again I say, this was God's idea. He backed up this statement about Christ on many occasions. For example, He said, "This is my beloved Son, in whom I am well pleased; hear ye him" (Matt. 17:5).

The Scriptures cause us to rest—to take comfort in knowing that God gave His Son, and His Son gave His life. All we need to do is give Him our undivided attention, with only one desire and motive: to hear and obey His commands. The 24-Minute Ministry Scriptures challenge each of us to be sincere in our efforts and to say as David did in Psalm 51:10-11, "Create in me a clean heart, O God; and renew a right spirit within me. Cast me not away from thy presence; and take not thy holy spirit from me." David experienced both internal and external attacks from the fleshly mind, whose one goal is to war against the Spirit of God.

Take heed that we have been warned in ages past "they that are in the flesh cannot please God" (Rom. 8:8). "We are debtors, not to the flesh, to live after the flesh" (Rom. 8:12). The best approach to receiving God's grace is through a meek and quiet spirit. Our prayer should be, "Lord, grant us the wisdom to maintain a spirit of serenity."

Seventy years ago, Dr. Reinhold Niebuhr ascended the pulpit of the Congregational Church in Heath, Massachusetts and presented the world with "The Serenity Prayer," a single sentence that has become profoundly recognizable: "God give us grace to accept with serenity the things that cannot be changed; God give us the courage to change what should be changed; give us the wisdom to distinguish one from the other." Since most of us think of serenity as a state of peace and tranquility, it may seem strange that the word is derived from the Greek *xeros*, which means "dry." However, when used by the Greeks, this word did not describe, for example, the arid desert. Instead, it depicted a dry sky, free and clear of storms or unpleasant changes.

For the Christian, serenity means the same as the Sanskrit word *shanti*, a concept embraced and preached by Christ and expounded by Paul: "the peace of God, which passeth all understanding" (Phil. 4:7). The Scriptures of the 24-Minute Ministry which lead to The Serenity Prayer, present a path to this "peace of God" that "shall keep your hearts and minds through Christ Jesus," providing clear skies rather than cloudy as you look to Christ for serenity.

PRAYER OF INTERCESSION

When word reached King Ahasuerus about a certain people whose laws were different than those of any other (and who reportedly did not regard the king's laws), a decree was written. The king's seal was applied. In one moment a law was passed to destroy all Jews in King Ahasuerus' provinces. Mordecai, Esther's uncle, warned her that she could not take a neutral stand. "Think not with thyself that thou shalt escape in the king's house, more than all the Jews" (Esth. 4:13). Esther had to choose whether to save her people or stand by and watch her adversaries put every Jew to death at the appointed time.

In response, Esther asked her people to fast and make intercession for three days on her behalf. Then she would approach the throne and intercede on their behalf. This is a perfect illustration of effective intercession. There is always something we must do as the people of God, and then Christ will persist in His requests on our behalf. We must realize that during this journey called life, we have an enemy and he would have us all executed but for the grace of God.

True intercession involves the application of *love and deeds in the midst of conflict*. The apostle Paul interceded by frequently addressing the family of faith about the raging spiritual battles that exist within one's mind, body, and soul. There is still a war going on. Yet many believe we are engaged only in a "love fest," and they fail to recognize the battle. They feel no urgency to heed the warnings or to watch and be sober—let alone arm themselves with the whole armor of God. They are content to "armor" themselves with the world. They do not sense that there is a war for lack of physical altercations. The language of war is absent; where is the vulgarity and threatening protest? Why should someone have to die before we are drawn into intercession?

Paul explains in 2 Corinthians 10:4-5, "(For the weapons of our warfare are not carnal, but mighty through God to the pulling down of strongholds;) Casting down imaginations, and every high thing that exalteth itself against the knowledge of God, and bringing into captivity every thought to the obedience of Christ." He further states there are wild and rebellious thoughts that wreak havoc on the integrity and message of Christ's entire earthly experience and mission. I feel indignation when I hear assaults against the credibility of the Lamb of God. I acknowledge, "love is of God; and every one that loveth is born of God, and knoweth God. He that loveth not knoweth not God; for God is love"; however, these very statements reflect the conflict between "he that loveth not" and "every one that loveth" (1 John 4:7-8). One is armed with the Scriptures as he or she proclaims the Gospel message of a selfless Savior; the other is armed with the philosophies of men as he or she embraces these contradictions with equal fervor. We must intercede in this war for the hearts of humanity, for before Christ's death, He told us that "from within, out of the heart of men, proceed evil thoughts, adulteries, fornications, murders, thefts, covetousness, wickedness, deceit, lasciviousness, an evil eye, blasphemy, pride, and foolishness" (Mark 7:21-22).

Many have made the choice to believe in the Lord's resurrection and have become partakers of eternal life. Out of their hearts now proceed those things that are true, honest, just, pure, lovely, and of good report (Phil. 4:8)—all because of the awesome power in the Word of God. They have been transformed by the renewing of their minds (Rom. 12.2). When Jesus said, "the gates of hell" would "not prevail against" His church in Matthew 16:18, He was not relieving us of our responsibilities. In fact, according to many Old Testament writings, judges stood in the gates to make judgments for or against opposing parties. The gates were the

location in which judgment was rendered. Therefore, it should be no surprise that some of the most ardent opposition to Christianity is coming from the courts. The highest court opposes many of the statutes of the Church of the living God. Intercession is needed daily in matters concerning judgment. "Righteousness exalteth a nation: but sin is a reproach to any people" (Prov. 14:34).

In John 21:15-17, Peter wanted to take a neutral position, but Jesus questioned his love. It was obvious that Peter had a passion for fishing. Yet Jesus had not deviated from His original plan for Peter to be a fisher of men. Jesus questioned Peter's love, though He had interceded to the Father on behalf of Peter—just as He has interceded on behalf of every transgressor (Isa. 53:12).

In essence, Jesus said to Peter, "Will you intercede on behalf of others? Will you spend the rest of your life making persistent requests for my little ones?" There is a Scripture that justifies around-the-clock, persistent requests or intercessions—Isaiah 66:24: "They shall go forth, and look upon the carcasses of the men that have transgressed against me: for their worm shall not die, neither shall their fire be quenched; and they shall be an abhorring unto all flesh."

Humanity needs our prayers of intercession. I grieve when I think about the many fleshly, physical frames that house spirits of men and women—those who have refused to accept Jesus, God's Son, as their Sacrifice and personal Savior. This is one of my daily prayers of intercession: "Lord, John witnessed the scene as You questioned the love of Peter, and I pray that my love would be as John's was for You. I pray that my love will never be questioned because I gladly engage in intercession for many, as Jesus does so gracefully even now at the right hand of my Father. Amen."

The 24-Minute Ministry Scriptures listed under "Intercession" keep us encouraged, engaged, and about our Father's business—specifically, praying for those without and within the household of faith.

PRAYER OF PERSONAL REQUEST

The word "request" has its origin in Latin. "Quest" is the root of the word "question" and means "to ask." The prefix "re" means "again." Therefore, "request" literally means, "to ask again." This is very appropriate within the context of prayer because Jesus stated, "Your Father knoweth what things ye have need of, before ye ask him" (Matt. 6:8). So intimate is God's communion with you that He knows your every thought, your every want, and your every need—even those expressed only in the subconscious mind.

The word "personal" also comes from Latin and means "mask." A "persona" is a mask you wear for the rest of the world; it is the person that, even your closest friends and family, think you are. As you look in a mirror, you see only a dark reflection, only a partial view of the true "you" (1 Cor. 13:12). But during your prayers of personal request, you set the mask aside; God sees through it anyway. You stand before your Father as you really are, as you put into words that for which you are asking. For God, it is a "repeat performance" of sorts because He already knows your inner desires.

As you approach God with your personal requests, there is no reason to conceal the confidence that arises from knowing you are no longer considered a sinner in the eyes of God. How humbling to be called sons and daughters! This is a truth worth shouting from the rooftops from time to time. We are no longer transgressors against the Lord, nor are we willful violators of His laws or reprobates of His grace.

Focus on the scene in which John the Beloved leaned against Jesus' bosom and asked, "Lord, who is it?" (John 13:25). John was a disciple so above reproach that he was known as the disciple "whom Jesus loved" (John 13:23). If David was known as the man after God's own heart, John would own the title as the man who heard the heartbeat of God. We too can enjoy this personal intimate relationship with our savior.

Adam and Eve did not ask God to clothe them. It was the Lord God who made "coats of skins, and clothed them" (Gen. 3:21). It has been suggested that God wanted to continue the relationship as their Provider and Comforter. After all, how long could they survive with fig leaves? We are no different today; we don't know what we need, and many things that we think we need would give us the kind of security that the fig leaves offered: very temporary.

One day during a quiet moment, the Lord said to me, "Son, I love you." This was during a time when I was in a "cold shoulder" mood—that sort of mood that will prompt me to shrug off someone even when he or she pays me a compliment. But soon I realized God was speaking to me through His Spirit. He spoke words that communicated that He truly loved me. Somehow, I had forgotten He had already said this in His written Word and had demonstrated it through the death of His Son. I was inspired and awed, full of appreciation and thanksgiving, and fully aware that if He was willing to speak these words to me in His still, quiet voice, He truly understood my deepest needs and would meet them appropriately. Trust me, those words took me further than anything material I could have received.

You must use your faith to walk in God's love, knowing moment by moment that He loves with an unconditional love that cannot be compared to any earthly marital or family relationship. It can only be viewed in light of the integrity and sovereignty of a holy, almighty Father.

I respect that you have personal requests to make and that I have no business interfering, but allow me to make a few suggestions in regard to petitioning the Lord...

Our main emphasis is on prayer framed out of the Scriptures presented in the 24- Minute Ministry. Our suggestion is to look closely at each Scripture that you read and pray out of that Scripture. For example, James 1:5-6 states, "If any of you lack wisdom let him ask of God..." "Father, I ask for your wisdom today in matters concerning work..." Speaking the words that

God speaks to us is perfect communion—language that heaven easily recognizes. Remember the reason a lawyer is suggested in court is because he understands the language of the court.

- Tell God that you want your will to be consistent with His will (Matt. 26:39).
- Ask God to open your understanding to receive more of His Word and His way as well as faith to endure to the end.
- Pray a selfless prayer that concerns your personal requests as mentioned in the Bible (Matt. 6:8).
- Have an attitude of great expectation that He will give you His best, and know that His best is in line with His Word (Luke 12:32).
- Remember what Wisdom counsels: pray according to the Scriptures (Prov. 8).
- By all means, pray, believing (Matt. 21:22); even pray through the pain.
- Recognize Jesus' work on the cross and express your joy for it (Col. 2:13-14).

As part of the family of Christ, remember to share what you have, for the early Church "had all things common" (Acts 2:44). Remember that all we have is given to us by God.

The 24-Minute Ministry concept was created to reestablish the favor of God within your homes and with your neighbors as you continue steadfastly and daily in prayer and in the Word of God.

PRAYER OF GUIDANCE

One of the most sophisticated and fierce military weapons of our times is the guided missile. There are three indispensable weapons needed to guide us through our daily spiritual engagements and warfare. They include the Word of the Lord, our prayers to the Lord, and the fast of the Lord (1 Pet. 1:23-25; Rev 5:8; Isa. 58:6). (I use the term "fast" to describe self-denial and suggest that there are many ways to practice this discipline.)

During the prayer of guidance, growth is our destination. This is accomplished by the Word of God that aids us in the ability to learn more of the Father's way, which serves as reinforcement—as it did for Christ in His wilderness experience as He resisted temptation. These prayers allow believers to communicate with God as His spirit provides comfort and assurance while making decisions that cannot be avoided in an environment of law and discipline. They are designed to teach us why it is necessary to yield to the Father's right-of-way in obedience, which will accomplish His purpose and fulfill His call on our lives.

The 24-Minute Ministry concept was developed to enhance the desire of those who wish to serve the kingdom of God by way of the principles of the risen Lord, who gives us His guidance as we pursue the perfect love that is found only in His presence. It is also meant to inspire good study habits and prayerful communication time after time. The Prayer of Guidance Scripture reveals to us God's interactions with the saints of old and gives us a glimpse of their struggles and warfare. More importantly, they show that God made these saints overcomers through their faith in Him (Hebrews 11).

If you are fed up with doubts, fears, and voices from the past, commit to the 24-Minute Ministry. There is no other proven method, nor can we improvise en route to the way and the truth. Become a student of the Word. I admonish you to seek God's guidance and acquaint yourself with the liberty that is obtained in Christ alone. Then you will be able to gain through the Scriptures, day by day, the formation of new habits. A transformed mind is essential. This spiritually ordained, systematic procedure will expose you to God's abundant life. Remember what He said in regard to the guidance of the patriarchs? "I have set before you life…that both thou and thy seed (descendants) may live" (Deut. 30:19). You can rejoice forevermore because God in Christ will guide you in your decisions. The forks in the road will never again present you with a difficult choice, for you will simply choose *the path of light*.

The 24-Minute Ministry Scriptures concerning guidance will compel and empower you to rely on the Word of God; your prayers will go forth with authority as you direct your heart unto God and await the promises of the Lord.

DEDICATION AND CONSECRATION

I have learned in this spiritual war that I must pray through pain, which brings to mind the phrase "the truly dedicated play through the pain." Until recently, I was puzzled about the statement that Jesus made in Luke 18:7: "And shall not God avenge his own elect, which cry day and night unto him, though he bear long with them?" I always questioned the last five words. What did Jesus mean when He said that God bears long with us? Finally I discovered the vast difference between those who are truly devoted and consecrated and those who are not. God is longsuffering concerning my many inconsistencies, especially when I am prone to devote time to everything but the work of the Lord and even when I risk being put in jeopardy by my own iniquities. Yet, God is still willing to aid and restore me time and time again.

In every case, God has been forbearing. The songwriter penned it best when he said, "O what needless pain we bear, all because we do not carry everything to God in prayer." It has taken me fifty years—thirty of them as a professed Christian—to fully discover this truth. Though better late than never, I did not learn this until the initial phase of development of this ministry. The lesson was highlighted during a 30-day session during which I prayed with five different prayer partners daily for 24-30 minutes. Each person wanted to experience the 24-Minute Ministry concept, and they had no problem with the requirements or commitment.

I met with these individuals at separate times in the chapel or another designated place. There, we would read, and—based on the focus prayer comments—we offered prayer after each category, following the same pattern for all 10 Categories. During this month, I actually learned and understood the true meaning of dedication and consecration in my life. I also saw firsthand men who began to understand these disciplines as they gave up certain things to spend time in fellowship and daily prayer.

As I spent time alone with each person, I found that we were not timid about sharing everything that concerned us in prayer. Our compassion, our fears, our joy—we shared all without reservation. This experience taught me why God loves all men equally. I realized that there is not enough distinction in each of our requests, supplications, confessions, and vows to grant more favor to one over the other. This experience affirmed and confirmed to me why Jesus said that God "sendeth rain on the just and on the unjust" (Matt. 5:45). We would all remain helpless without His intervention.

I was blessed first of all because I reaped the benefits of the petitions of five different men on my behalf; secondly, I fully understood why David put so much emphasis on being in the sanctuary, the holy Temple, and the presence of God. In Psalm 65:4 he writes, "Blessed is the man whom thou choosest, and causest to approach unto thee, that he may dwell in thy courts: we shall be satisfied with the goodness of thy house, even of thy holy temple." I realized that God chose me to approach Him daily.

Now let's examine the resemblance between the word "dedication" (devotion to a task or purpose) and "consecration" (devotion to a sacred purpose). Two Scriptures written by Paul helped me understand the application of each meaning. Second Corinthians 5:18-19 states that God "hath given to us the ministry of reconciliation"—the ***Task***--while the "the word of reconciliation" provides the ***Terms***. In 2 Corinthians 4:7, just before telling us about the various ***Trials*** that we must endure, Paul explains how we will be sustained in this earthly mission because "we have this ***Treasure*** in earthen vessels, that the excellency of the power may be of God, and not of us." The complete package, then, consists of the ***Task***, the ***Terms***, the ***Trials***, the ***Treasure***. Shout Glory! Our consecration suits us up to yield to the power of God in Christ. Then and only then can He fully accomplish His will for humanity—His very own creation. Since we are His creatures, why can we not pray with a brother or sister—as Jesus implored His disciples—for "one hour" (Matt. 26:40)?

In conclusion, I can best describe the 24-Minute Ministry concept from the vantage point of body builders, who understand that within their muscles lies the ability to lift massive weights. But in order to be safe, they must begin by lifting minimal weight and then gradually build up to greater weight. Devotion is required—a daily commitment to a physical exercise program and to eating the proper meals along with getting plenty of rest. (We also note that most true dedicated body builders enjoy the company of a spotter or partner; one who holds him or her accountable.) Likewise, the same God who created the muscles to enable a man to endure such a program also gave him a mind that is powerful when yielded to His precious Word, to the discipline of humility, and to daily prayer.

    The anointing and guidance of the Holy Ghost allows us to function in God's wisdom and understanding. Paul tells us to "examine ourselves, whether we be in the faith" (2 Cor. 13:5). He also tells Titus to "be careful to maintain good works" (Titus 3:8). He tells Timothy in 1 Timothy 4:13, 15-16 "Till I come, give attendance to reading, to exhortation, to doctrine. Meditate upon these things; give thyself wholly to them; that thy profiting may appear to all. Take heed unto thyself, and unto the doctrine; continue in them: for in doing this thou shalt both save thyself, and them that hear thee." Christ has consecrated for us "a new and living way" (Heb. 10:20). Therefore, we should have boldness to enter into God's presence by way of Jesus' blood. The 24-Minute Ministry Scriptures remind us that we should be dedicated and consecrated daily, without excuse. According to Paul, we can maintain good works and save ourselves and those who hear us while we destroy the works of the enemy with our most powerful spiritual weapon—the Word made flesh in us daily. Enjoy this experience. It will permeate your will and cause you to walk on your "high places" (Hab. 3:19), just as it has done for many.

THE 24 MINUTE MINISTRY 24/7 PLAN

The 24 Minute Ministry is about teaching you how the word of God, alone, produces His power within. The Word is like a weight, and your mind is like a muscle. The more you meditate upon (live in) the Word, the stronger you become mentally and spiritually. "No weapon that is formed against thee shall prosper" (Isa. 54:17).

The 24 Minute Ministry Scripture truths will become drops of water that constantly beat upon stones of clay rock until a perfectly carved hole the size and diameter of those drops becomes the symbol of power and a way of life. When the Son is exalted, His life springs forth as the noonday, causing the eye to be "single" and the "whole body" to be "full of light" (Luke 11:34; see also Job 11:17).

The aim of the 24 Minute Ministry is to help you identify the Word of God as a seed that germinates, creating microspiritual energy, which causes the Holy Ghost to function as the Spirit of truth, adoption, comfort, promise, and life and the One who manifests in us the attributes of "love, joy, peace, longsuffering, gentleness, goodness, faith, meekness, and temperance" (Gal. 5:22-23).

The 24 Minute Ministry helps you understand that God will watch over His Word "to perform it" in you and your family (Jer. 1:12). The 24 Minute Ministry helps you to understand that all your desires can be consistent with the Word of God and that you will not lose any pleasures or benefits. The 24 Minute Ministry is a *Word menu smorgasbord* much like the natural diet that Daniel and his friends chose to eat, and in the end you will be wiser and more spiritually beautiful than those who indulge in the flesh. Participants do not lose their identity; they discover their purpose as designed by the living God.

The 24 Minute Ministry helps you understand why we are God's creation by choice and why all God's laws hinge on the following two commandments: "Thou shalt love the Lord thy God with all thy heart, and with all thy soul, and with all thy strength, and with all thy mind; and thy neighbour as thyself" (Luke 10:27). We are to love the Creator of all creation and the Executor of His Word—Jesus, who died for all humanity whose precious blood conquers all of our errors of ignorance and willful acts of rebellion.

Spiritual growth occurs when our understanding is perfected. To begin this growth experience, the 24 Minute Ministry introduces you to prayer partners who will hold you accountable as you reciprocate; this accountability factor serves as a witness of confession and testimony. The partners also participate together in praise, worship, and intercession before ending with dedication and consecration to the living God.

We suggest the 24/7 Plan for your family or friends: 24 minutes for seven (7) 30-day sessions. A brief outline of each session will be discussed momentarily.

Each session continues for 30 days. A day is never missed. However, if it takes an extra day to conclude a session, it should be completed. Faithfulness is a major factor of the 24 Minute Ministry. Different partners can be used during each session; in fact, this is suggested. The exception would be when a family participates.

Session I: New Beginnings (30 days)

A reflection of the creation account of Genesis Chapter 1, New Beginnings is the first 30-day session during which many of our partners lose their guilt complexes—and rightly so, as they learn how to converse with their Creator and His Son. And as their words assure us, all of our deficiencies are forgiven and cast off, and the promises of God bring grace and faith to believe. We become burden free!

Session II: Separation

This is not a boastful period but one of valuing your commitment to God's Word. Just as a child at age two makes discoveries every day, Session II makes you a "terrible two" against Satan's kingdom, as evidenced by boldness and confidence. Caution! Remain humble; there is much more to learn.

Session III: Blessings

The opening of your understanding increases the ease with which the Holy Ghost teaches you. You are now spiritually sensitive; you are developing a hearing ear as you read the Scriptures. Many of them are talking back to you. It's a wonderful experience, evidence of the blessings of God's gifts operating in you.

Session IV: Authority

Your confidence in the Word is now more powerful than ever. You are content in the Word, which has come alive. You do not shun your responsibilities, but all your cares are truly shifted to the Lord. You are being established and anchored in His Word and love.

Session V: Abundance

During this session, many of our partners have experienced such an outpouring of God's Word and spiritual enlightenment that they have asked God to slow down once the revelation knowledge and spiritual understanding are full throttle. The window of heaven is truly open and pouring out wisdom and understanding.

Session VI: Struggle

This session, which deals with trials and testing, we remind you to not allow any temptation to overcome your will and determination. Remember what the Disciple Peter asked Jesus: "Lord, to whom shall we go? thou hast the words of eternal life" (John 6:69). Know that you "shall reap, if you faint not" and you must continue to gird yourself with the truth of God's Word (Gal. 6:9; see also Eph. 6:14).

Session VII: Perfection and Completion

As a new creature and creation of God, He has developed a spiritual gift within. Begin to use it for God's glory! "I wisdom dwell with prudence, and find out knowledge of witty inventions" (Prov. 8:12). God has placed within you a special gift for use in His work.

FAMILY DEVOTIONAL

DAY 1
PRAYER OF PREPAREDNESS

FATHER—INSTRUCT: Genesis 1:1-3
In the beginning God created the heaven and the earth. And the earth was without form, and void; and darkness was upon the face of the deep. And the Spirit of God moved upon the face of the waters. And God said, Let there be light: and there was light.

MOTHER—TEACH: Genesis 1:26-27
And God said, Let us make man in our image, after our likeness: and let them have dominion over the fish of the sea, and over the fowl of the air, and over the cattle, and over all the earth, and over every creeping thing that creepeth upon the earth. So God created man in his own image, in the image of God created he him; male and female created he them.

SON(S)—LISTEN: Matthew 1:18-21
Now the birth of Jesus Christ was on this wise: When as his mother Mary was espoused to Joseph, before they came together, she was found with child of the Holy Ghost. Then Joseph her husband, being a just man, and not willing to make her a public example, was minded to put her away privily. But while he thought on these things, behold, the angel of the Lord appeared unto him in a dream, saying, Joseph, thou son of David, fear not to take unto thee Mary thy wife: for that which is conceived in her is of the Holy Ghost. And she shall bring forth a son, and thou shalt call his name JESUS: for he shall save his people from their sins.

DAUGHTER(S)—RESPOND: John 16:7, 13-14
Nevertheless I tell you the truth; It is expedient for you that I go away: for if I go not away, the Comforter will not come unto you; but if I depart, I will send him unto you. Howbeit when he, the Spirit of truth, is come, he will guide you into all truth: for he shall not speak of himself; but whatsoever he shall hear, that shall he speak: and he will show you things to come. He shall glorify me: for he shall receive of mine, and shall show it unto you.

(Our focused prayers open the window of heaven. Then, our hearts are prepared to receive God's word.)

WORSHIP AND PRAISE

FATHER—INSTRUCT: John 17:3-6
And this is life eternal, that they might know thee the only true God, and Jesus Christ, whom thou hast sent. I have glorified thee on the earth: I have finished the work which thou gavest me to do. And now, O Father, glorify thou me with thine own self with the glory which I had with thee before the world was. I have manifested thy name unto the men which thou gavest me out of the world: thine they were, and thou gavest them me; and they have kept thy word.

MOTHER—TEACH: Matthew 11:25-27
At that time Jesus answered and said, I thank thee, O Father, Lord of heaven and earth, because thou hast hid these things from the wise and prudent, and hast revealed them unto babes. Even so, Father: for so it seemed good in thy sight. All things are delivered unto me of my Father: and no man knoweth the Son, but the Father; neither knoweth any man the Father, save the Son, and he to whomsoever the Son will reveal him.

SON(S)—LISTEN: Colossians 2:6, 12-13
As ye have therefore received Christ Jesus the Lord, so walk ye in him: Buried with him in baptism, wherein also ye are risen with him through the faith of the operation of God, who hath raised him from the dead. And you, being dead in your sins and the uncircumcision of your flesh, hath he quickened together with him, having forgiven you all trespasses.

DAUGHTER(S)—RESPOND: Psalm 84:2, 4-5
My soul longeth, yea, even fainteth for the courts of the LORD: my heart and my flesh crieth out for the living God. Blessed are they that dwell in thy house: they will be still praising thee. Selah. Blessed is the man whose strength is in thee; in whose heart are the ways of them.

(Now worship the Father and His Son through the Holy Spirit: "When praises go up, blessings come down!")

PRAYER OF CONFESSION

FATHER—INSTRUCT: Romans 10:6-9
But the righteousness which is of faith speaketh on this wise, Say not in thine heart, Who shall ascend into heaven? (that is, to bring Christ down from above:) Or, Who shall descend into the deep? (that is, to bring up Christ again from the dead.) But what saith it? The word is nigh thee, even in thy mouth, and in thy heart: that is, the word of faith, which we preach; That if thou shalt confess with thy mouth the Lord Jesus, and shalt believe in thine heart that God hath raised him from the dead, thou shalt be saved.

MOTHER—TEACH: Isaiah 45:5-8
I am the LORD, and there is none else, there is no God beside me: I girded thee, though thou hast not known me: That they may know from the rising of the sun, and from the west, that there is none beside me. I am the LORD, and there is none else. I form the light, and create darkness: I make peace, and create evil: I the LORD do all these things. Drop down, ye heavens, from above, and let the skies pour down righteousness: let the earth open, and let them bring forth salvation, and let righteousness spring up together; I the LORD have created it.

SON(S)—LISTEN: Psalm 32:5-6
I acknowledged my sin unto thee, and mine iniquity have I not hid. I said, I will confess my transgressions unto the LORD; and thou forgavest the iniquity of my sin. Selah. For this shall every one that is godly pray unto thee in a time when thou mayest be found: surely in the floods of great waters they shall not come nigh unto him.

DAUGHTER(S)—RESPOND: Philippians 2:9-11
Wherefore God also hath highly exalted him, and given him a name which is above every name: That at the name of Jesus every knee should bow, of things in heaven, and things in earth, and things under the earth; And that every tongue should confess that Jesus Christ is Lord, to the glory of God the Father.

(We have a choice. We can begin confessing Jesus is Lord now or on Judgment Day. Begin now, and He will save us from our sins.)

PRAYER OF GRATITUDE

FATHER—INSTRUCT: Psalm 50:14-15
Offer unto God thanksgiving; and pay thy vows unto the most High: And call upon me in the day of trouble: I will deliver thee, and thou shalt glorify me.

MOTHER—TEACH: 1 Chronicles 16:8-11
Give thanks unto the LORD, call upon his name, make known his deeds among the people. Sing unto him, sing psalms unto him, talk ye of all his wondrous works. Glory ye in his holy name: let the heart of them rejoice that seek the LORD. Seek the LORD and his strength, seek his face continually.

SON(S)—LISTEN: Proverbs 3:5-6
Trust in the LORD with all thine heart; and lean not unto thine own understanding. In all thy ways acknowledge him, and he shall direct thy paths.

DAUGHTER(S)—RESPOND: Matthew 21:14-16
And the blind and the lame came to him in the temple; and he healed them. And when the chief priests and scribes saw the wonderful things that he did, and the children crying in the temple, and saying, Hosanna to the Son of David; they were sore displeased, And said unto him, Hearest thou what these say? And Jesus saith unto them, Yea; have ye never read, Out of the mouth of babes and sucklings thou hast perfected praise?

(Our gratitude, our thanks to God, is an example of children who are gracious; now offer thanksgiving for the wondrous work done on the cross.)

WISDOM AND UNDERSTANDING

FATHER—INSTRUCT: 1 Peter 1:22-23
Seeing ye have purified your souls in obeying the truth through the Spirit unto unfeigned loveof the brethren, see that ye love one another with a pure heart fervently: Being born again, not of corruptible seed, but of incorruptible, by the word of God, which liveth and abideth for ever.

MOTHER—TEACH: Proverbs 1:20-21, 23
Wisdom crieth without; she uttereth her voice in the streets: She crieth in the chief place of concourse, in the openings of the gates: in the city she uttereth her words, saying, Turn you at my reproof: behold, I will pour out my spirit unto you, I will make known my words unto you.

SON(S)—LISTEN: Proverbs 3:1-4
My son, forget not my law; but let thine heart keep my commandments: For length of days, and long life, and peace, shall they add to thee. Let not mercy and truth forsake thee: bind them about thy neck; write them upon the table of thine heart: So shalt thou find favour and good understanding in the sight of God and man.

DAUGHTER(S)—RESPOND: Proverbs 4:5-7
Get wisdom, get understanding: forget it not; neither decline from the words of my mouth. Forsake her not, and she shall preserve thee: love her, and she shall keep thee. Wisdom is the principal thing; therefore get wisdom: and with all thy getting get understanding.

(Remember the wisdom from God is first pure, then peaceful and He gives it without partiality to those who ask.)

PRAYER OF SERENITY

FATHER—INSTRUCT: Joshua 24:13-14
And I have given you a land for which ye did not labour, and cities which ye built not, and ye dwell in them; of the vineyards and olive-yards which ye planted not do ye eat. Now therefore fear the LORD, and serve him in sincerity and in truth: and put away the gods which your fathers served on the other side of the flood, and in Egypt; and serve ye the LORD.

MOTHER—TEACH: Joshua 24:15-16
And if it seem evil unto you to serve the LORD, choose you this day whom ye will serve; whether the gods which your fathers served that were on the other side of the flood, or the gods of the Amorites, in whose land ye dwell: but as for me and my house, we will serve the LORD. And the people answered and said, God forbid that we should forsake the LORD, to serve other gods.

SON(S)—LISTEN: Isaiah 45:22-23
Look unto me, and be ye saved, all the ends of the earth: for I am God, and there is none else. I have sworn by myself, the word is gone out of my mouth in righteousness, and shall not return, That unto me every knee shall bow, every tongue shall swear.

DAUGHTER(S)—RESPOND: Psalm 31:3-5
For thou art my rock and my fortress; therefore for thy name's sake lead me, and guide me. Pull me out of the net that they have laid privily for me: for thou art my strength. Into thine hand I commit my spirit: thou hast redeemed me, O LORD God of truth.

(Our thoughts are always open before God. He just wants to see if we will allow His Word to shape our character. Pray for His will to this end.)

PRAYER OF INTERCESSION

FATHER—INSTRUCT: Acts 8:35-37
Then Philip opened his mouth, and began at the same scripture, and preached unto him Jesus. And as they went on their way, they came unto a certain water: and the eunuch said, See, here is water; what doth hinder me to be baptized? And Philip said, If thou believest with all thine heart, thou mayest. And he answered and said, I believe that Jesus Christ is the Son of God.

MOTHER—TEACH: Hebrews 7:22-25
By so much was Jesus made a surety of a better testament. And they truly were many priests, because they were not suffered to continue by reason of death: But this man, because he continueth ever, hath an unchangeable priesthood. Wherefore he is able also to save them to the uttermost that come unto God by him, seeing he ever liveth to make intercession for them.

SON(S)—LISTEN: Hebrews 12:1-2
Wherefore seeing we also are compassed about with so great a cloud of witnesses, let us lay aside every weight, and the sin which doth so easily beset us, and let us run with patience the race that is set before us, Looking unto Jesus the author and finisher of our faith; who for the joy that was set before him endured the cross, despising the shame, and is set down at the right hand of the throne of God.

DAUGHTER(S)—RESPOND: 2 Corinthians 8:8-9
I speak not by commandment, but by occasion of the forwardness of others, and to prove the sincerity of your love. For ye know the grace of our Lord Jesus Christ, that, though he was rich, yet for your sakes he became poor, that ye through his poverty might be rich.

(Now intercede for others. God has given us this authority: "Whosoever sins you remit shall be remitted." Bring their very sickness and spiritual deprivations to God's attention.)

PRAYER OF PERSONAL REQUEST

FATHER—INSTRUCT: Proverbs 15:29, 33
The LORD is far from the wicked: but he heareth the prayer of the righteous. The fear of the LORD is the instruction of wisdom; and before honour is humility.

MOTHER—TEACH: Psalm 86:2-3
Preserve my soul; for I am holy: O thou my God, save thy servant that trusteth in thee. Be merciful unto me, O Lord: for I cry unto thee daily.

SON(S)—LISTEN: Psalm 56:1-4
Be merciful unto me, O God: for man would swallow me up; he fighting daily oppresseth me. Mine enemies would daily swallow me up: for they be many that fight against me, O thou most High. What time I am afraid, I will trust in thee. In God I will praise his word, in God I have put my trust; I will not fear what flesh can do unto me.

DAUGHTER(S)—RESPOND: Jeremiah 36:6-7
Therefore go thou, and read in the roll, which thou hast written from my mouth, the words of the LORD in the ears of the people in the LORD'S house upon the fasting day: and also thou shalt read them in the ears of all Judah that come out of their cities. It may be they will present their supplication before the LORD, and will return every one from his evil way: for great is the anger and the fury that the LORD hath pronounced against this people.

(God's love for His Son and for us prepares us for the manifestations of the Father. Now ask God to increase your faith by His Word.)

PRAYER OF GUIDANCE

FATHER—INSTRUCT: Ezekiel 36:26-27
A new heart also will I give you, and a new spirit will I put within you: and I will take away the stony heart out of your flesh, and I will give you an heart of flesh. And I will put my spirit within you, and cause you to walk in my statutes, and ye shall keep my judgments, and do them.

MOTHER—TEACH: Psalm 118:16-19
The right hand of the LORD is exalted: the right hand of the LORD doeth valiantly. I shall not die, but live, and declare the works of the LORD. The LORD hath chastened me sore: but he hath not given me over unto death. Open to me the gates of righteousness: I will go into them, and I will praise the LORD.

SON(S)—LISTEN: Psalm 119:15-16
I will meditate in thy precepts, and have respect unto thy ways. I will delight myself in thy statutes: I will not forget thy word.

DAUGHTER(S)—RESPOND: Psalm 85:10-13
Mercy and truth are met together; righteousness and peace have kissed each other. Truth shall spring out of the earth; and righteousness shall look down from heaven. Yea, the LORD shall give that which is good; and our land shall yield her increase. Righteousness shall go before him; and shall set us in the way of his steps.

(There is only one set of footprints. They were made when the "word became flesh." Our direction should be guided by God's only begotten Son. Pray for His will to this end.)

DEDICATION AND CONSECRATION

FATHER—INSTRUCT: Matthew 6:33-34
But seek ye first the kingdom of God, and his righteousness; and all these things shall be added unto you. Take therefore no thought for the morrow: for the morrow shall take thought for the things of itself. Sufficient unto the day is the evil thereof.

MOTHER—TEACH: Mark 12:30-31
And thou shalt love the Lord thy God with all thy heart, and with all thy soul, and with all thy mind, and with all thy strength: this is the first commandment. And the second is like, namely this, Thou shalt love thy neighbour as thyself. There is none other commandment greater than these.

SON(S)—LISTEN: Habakkuk 2:1-4
I will stand upon my watch, and set me upon the tower, and will watch to see what he will say unto me, and what I shall answer when I am reproved. And the LORD answered me, and said, Write the vision, and make it plain upon tables, that he may run that readeth it. For the vision is yet for an appointed time, but at the end it shall speak, and not lie: though it tarry, wait for it; because it will surely come, it will not tarry. Behold, his soul which is lifted up is not upright in him: but the just shall live by his faith.

DAUGHTER(S)—RESPOND: Micah 1:2-3
Hear, all ye people; hearken, O earth, and all that therein is: and let the Lord GOD be witness against you, the Lord from his holy temple. For, behold, the LORD cometh forth out of his place, and will come down, and tread upon the high places of the earth.

(Now dedicate your life to Christ anew! Watch and pray for the day of the Lord is near. This is an exciting time to be consecrated to the purpose of the Lord.)

DAY 2
PRAYER OF PREPAREDNESS

FATHER—INSTRUCT: Isaiah 9:6-7
For unto us a child is born, unto us a son is given: and the government shall be upon his shoulder: and his name shall be called Wonderful, Counsellor, The mighty God, The everlasting Father, The Prince of Peace. Of the increase of his government and peace there shall be no end, upon the throne of David, and upon his kingdom, to order it, and to establish it with judgment and with justice from henceforth even for ever. The zeal of the LORD of hosts will perform this.

MOTHER—TEACH: Isaiah 11:1-2
And there shall come forth a rod out of the stem of Jesse, and a Branch shall grow out of his roots: And the spirit of the LORD shall rest upon him, the spirit of wisdom and understanding, the spirit of counsel and might, the spirit of knowledge and of the fear of the LORD.

SON(S)—LISTEN: 1 Corinthians 4:1-2
Let a man so account of us, as of the ministers of Christ, and stewards of the mysteries of God. Moreover it is required in stewards, that a man be found faithful.

DAUGHTER(S)—RESPOND: Hebrews 3:1-4
Wherefore, holy brethren, partakers of the heavenly calling, consider the Apostle and High Priest of our profession, Christ Jesus; Who was faithful to him that appointed him, as also Moses was faithful in all his house. For this man was counted worthy of more glory than Moses, inasmuch as he who hath builded the house hath more honour than the house. For every house is builded by some man; but he that built all things is God.

(Faithfulness will prepare us to receive God's maximum blessing as we look to Jesus as our example. Now pray to this end.)

WORSHIP AND PRAISE

FATHER—INSTRUCT: Psalm 24:1-3
The earth is the LORD'S, and the fulness thereof; the world, and they that dwell therein. For he hath founded it upon the seas, and established it upon the floods. Who shall ascend into the hill of the LORD? or who shall stand in his holy place?

MOTHER—TEACH: Psalm 27:1-3
The LORD is my light and my salvation; whom shall I fear? the LORD is the strength of my life; of whom shall I be afraid? When the wicked, even mine enemies and my foes, came upon me to eat up my flesh, they stumbled and fell. Though an host should encamp against me, my heart shall not fear: though war should rise against me, in this will I be confident.

SON(S)—LISTEN: 1 Samuel 2:1-2
And Hannah prayed, and said, My heart rejoiceth in the LORD, mine horn is exalted in the LORD: my mouth is enlarged over mine enemies; because I rejoice in thy salvation. There is none holy as the LORD: for there is none beside thee: neither is there any rock like our God.

DAUGHTER(S)—RESPOND: 1 Samuel 2:18-19
But Samuel ministered before the LORD, being a child, girded with a linen ephod. Moreover his mother made him a little coat, and brought it to him from year to year, when she came up with her husband to offer the yearly sacrifice.

(We, too, can minister before the Lord as we offer the "Sacrifice of Praise" from the fruit of our lips. Now praise Him.)

PRAYER OF CONFESSION

FATHER—INSTRUCT: Isaiah 14:12-14
How art thou fallen from heaven, O Lucifer, son of the morning! how art thou cut down to the ground, which didst weaken the nations! For thou hast said in thine heart, I will ascend into heaven, I will exalt my throne above the stars of God: I will sit also upon the mount of the congregation, in the sides of the north: I will ascend above the heights of the clouds; I will be like the most High.

MOTHER—TEACH: John 8:42-44
Jesus said unto them, If God were your Father, ye would love me: for I proceeded forth and came from God; neither came I of myself, but he sent me. Why do ye not understand my speech? even because ye cannot hear my word. Ye are of your father the devil, and the lusts of your father ye will do. He was a murderer from the beginning, and abode not in the truth, because there is no truth in him. When he speaketh a lie, he speaketh of his own: for he is a liar, and the father of it.

SON(S)—LISTEN: Psalm 73:25-26
Whom have I in heaven but thee? and there is none upon earth that I desire beside thee. My flesh and my heart faileth: but God is the strength of my heart, and my portion for ever.

DAUGHTER(S)—RESPOND: Hebrews 4:14-15
Seeing then that we have a great high priest, that is passed into the heavens, Jesus the Son of God, let us hold fast our profession. For we have not an high priest which cannot be touched with the feeling of our infirmities; but was in all points tempted like as we are, yet without sin.

(Now confess any ungodly pride that would prevent you from honoring God's choice, Jesus, His only begotten.)

PRAYER OF GRATITUDE

FATHER—INSTRUCT: Malachi 3:1-2
Behold, I will send my messenger, and he shall prepare the way before me: and the Lord, whom ye seek, shall suddenly come to his temple, even the messenger of the covenant, whom ye delight in: behold, he shall come, saith the LORD of hosts. But who may abide the day of his coming? and who shall stand when he appeareth? for he is like a refiner's fire, and like fullers' soap.

MOTHER—TEACH: Matthew 2:10-11
When they saw the star, they rejoiced with exceeding great joy. And when they were come into the house, they saw the young child with Mary his mother, and fell down, and worshipped him: and when they had opened their treasures, they presented unto him gifts; gold, and frankincense, and myrrh.

SON(S)—LISTEN: John 1:10-12
He was in the world, and the world was made by him, and the world knew him not. He came unto his own, and his own received him not. But as many as received him, to them gave he power to become the sons of God, even to them that believe on his name.

DAUGHTER(S)—RESPOND: Matthew 8:1-3
When he was come down from the mountain, great multitudes followed him. And, behold, there came a leper and worshipped him, saying, Lord, if thou wilt, thou canst make me clean. And Jesus put forth his hand, and touched him, saying, I will; be thou clean. And immediately his leprosy was cleansed.

(Jesus is God's gift to us. Be thankful for Him and give thanks.)

WISDOM AND UNDERSTANDING

FATHER—INSTRUCT: Proverbs 4:1-4
Hear, ye children, the instruction of a father, and attend to know understanding. For I give you good doctrine, forsake ye not my law. For I was my father's son, tender and only beloved in the sight of my mother. He taught me also, and said unto me, Let thine heart retain my words: keep my commandments, and live.

MOTHER—TEACH: Psalm 25:14-15
The secret of the LORD is with them that fear him; and he will show them his covenant. Mine eyes are ever toward the LORD; for he shall pluck my feet out of the net.

SON(S)—LISTEN: Acts 28:30-31
And Paul dwelt two whole years in his own hired house, and received all that came in unto him, Preaching the kingdom of God, and teaching those things which concern the Lord Jesus Christ, with all confidence, no man forbidding him.

DAUGHTER(S)—RESPOND: 1 Timothy 1:15-17
This is a faithful saying, and worthy of all acceptation, that Christ Jesus came into the world to save sinners; of whom I am chief. Howbeit for this cause I obtained mercy, that in me first Jesus Christ might show forth all longsuffering, for a pattern to them which should hereafter believe on him to life everlasting. Now unto the King eternal, immortal, invisible, the only wise God, be honour and glory for ever and ever. Amen.

(God, open the understanding of the pure in heart. Pray now to this end.)

PRAYER OF SERENITY

FATHER—INSTRUCT: Isaiah 11:10-11
And in that day there shall be a root of Jesse, which shall stand for an ensign of the people; to it shall the Gentiles seek: and his rest shall be glorious. And it shall come to pass in that day, that the Lord shall set his hand again the second time to recover the remnant of his people, which shall be left, from Assyria, and from Egypt, and from Pathros, and from Cush, and from Elam, and from Shinar, and from Hamath, and from the islands of the sea.

MOTHER—TEACH: Luke 24:25-27
Then he said unto them, O fools, and slow of heart to believe all that the prophets have spoken: Ought not Christ to have suffered these things, and to enter into his glory? And beginning at Moses and all the prophets, he expounded unto them in all the scriptures the things concerning himself.

SON(S)—LISTEN Acts 28:25-27
And when they agreed not among themselves, they departed, after that Paul had spoken one word, Well spake the Holy Ghost by Esaias the prophet unto our fathers, Saying, Go unto this people, and say, Hearing ye shall hear, and shall not understand; and seeing ye shall see, and not perceive: For the heart of this people is waxed gross, and their ears are dull of hearing, and their eyes have they closed; lest they should see with their eyes, and hear with their ears, and understand with their heart, and should be converted, and I should heal them.

DAUGHTER(S)—RESPOND: John 3:35-36
The Father loveth the Son, and hath given all things into his hand. He that believeth on the Son hath everlasting life: and he that believeth not the Son shall not see life; but the wrath of God abideth on him.

(Our faith assures us of eternal life. Pray now to this end.)

PRAYER OF INTERCESSION

FATHER—INSTRUCT: Acts 2:32-33
This Jesus hath God raised up, whereof we all are witnesses. Therefore being by the right hand of God exalted, and having received of the Father the promise of the Holy Ghost, he hath shed forth this, which ye now see and hear.

MOTHER—TEACH: Acts 4:32-34
And the multitude of them that believed were of one heart and of one soul: neither said any of them that ought of the things which he possessed was his own; but they had all things common. And with great power gave the apostles witness of the resurrection of the Lord Jesus: and great grace was upon them all. Neither was there any among them that lacked: for as many as were possessors of lands or houses sold them, and brought the prices of the things that were sold.

SON(S)—LISTEN: Psalm 26:8-9
LORD, I have loved the habitation of thy house, and the place where thine honour dwelleth. Gather not my soul with sinners, nor my life with bloody men.

DAUGHTER(S)—RESPOND: Acts 2:29-31
Men and brethren, let me freely speak unto you of the patriarch David, that he is both dead and buried, and his sepulchre is with us unto this day. Therefore being a prophet, and knowing that God had sworn with an oath to him, that of the fruit of his loins, according to the flesh, he would raise up Christ to sit on his throne; He seeing this before spake of the resurrection of Christ, that his soul was not left in hell, neither his flesh did see corruption.

(Jesus sits at the right hand of God to make intercession for us. Show Him that you are concerned for others. Pray now to that end.)

PRAYER OF PERSONAL REQUEST

FATHER—INSTRUCT: Psalm 88:1-3
O LORD God of my salvation, I have cried day and night before thee: Let my prayer come before thee: incline thine ear unto my cry; For my soul is full of troubles: and my life draweth nigh unto the grave.

MOTHER—TEACH: Luke 1:46-48
And Mary said, My soul doth magnify the Lord, And my spirit hath rejoiced in God my Saviour. For he hath regarded the low estate of his handmaiden: for, behold, from henceforth all generations shall call me blessed.

SON(S)—LISTEN: Psalm 28:1-2
Unto thee will I cry, O LORD my rock; be not silent to me: lest, if thou be silent to me, I become like them that go down into the pit. Hear the voice of my supplications, when I cry unto thee, when I lift up my hands toward thy holy oracle.

DAUGHTER(S)—RESPOND: Luke 2:34-35
And Simeon blessed them, and said unto Mary his mother, Behold, this child is set for the fall and rising again of many in Israel; and for a sign which shall be spoken against; (Yea, a sword shall pierce through thy own soul also,) that the thoughts of many hearts may be revealed.

(Now ask the Lord to intervene on your behalf in your decisions today.)

PRAYER OF GUIDANCE

FATHER—INSTRUCT: Luke 3:4-6
As it is written in the book of the words of Esaias the prophet, saying, The voice of one crying in the wilderness, Prepare ye the way of the Lord, make his paths straight. Every valley shall be filled, and every mountain and hill shall be brought low; and the crooked shall be made straight, and the rough ways shall be made smooth; And all flesh shall see the salvation of God.

MOTHER—TEACH: John 1:19-20
And this is the record of John, when the Jews sent priests and Levites from Jerusalem to ask him, Who art thou? And he confessed, and denied not; but confessed, I am not the Christ.

SON(S)—LISTEN: John 14:6-7
Jesus saith unto him, I am the way, the truth, and the life: no man cometh unto the Father, but by me. If ye had known me, ye should have known my Father also: and from henceforth ye know him, and have seen him.

DAUGHTER(S)—RESPOND: Acts 9:17-19
And Ananias went his way, and entered into the house; and putting his hands on him said, Brother Saul, the Lord, even Jesus, that appeared unto thee in the way as thou camest, hath sent me, that thou mightest receive thy sight, and be filled with the Holy Ghost. And immediately there fell from his eyes as it had been scales: and he received sight forthwith, and arose, and was baptized. And when he had received meat, he was strengthened. Then was Saul certain days with the disciples which were at Damascus.

(Now pray for guidance and spiritual insight for your life today.)

DEDICATION AND CONSECRATION

FATHER—INSTRUCT: <u>Revelation</u> 14:1-2
And I looked, and, lo, a Lamb stood on the mount Sion, and with him an hundred forty and four thousand, having his Father's name written in their foreheads. And I heard a voice from heaven, as the voice of many waters, and as the voice of a great thunder: and I heard the voice of harpers harping with their harps.

MOTHER—TEACH: <u>2 Peter</u> 1:4-7
Whereby are given unto us exceeding great and precious promises: that by these ye might be partakers of the divine nature, having escaped the corruption that is in the world through lust. And beside this, giving all diligence, add to your faith virtue; and to virtue knowledge; And to knowledge temperance; and to temperance patience; and to patience godliness; And to godliness brotherly kindness; and to brotherly kindness charity.

SON(S)—LISTEN: <u>1 Peter</u> 5:6-7
Humble yourselves therefore under the mighty hand of God, that he may exalt you in due time: Casting all your care upon him; for he careth for you.

DAUGHTER(S)—RESPOND: <u>Acts</u> 2:36-38
Therefore let all the house of Israel know assuredly, that God hath made that same Jesus, whom ye have crucified, both Lord and Christ. Now when they heard this, they were pricked in their heart, and said unto Peter and to the rest of the apostles, Men and brethren, what shall we do? Then Peter said unto them, Repent, and be baptized every one of you in the name of Jesus Christ for the remission of sins, and ye shall receive the gift of the Holy Ghost.

(As a recipient of the precious promises, rededicate your life to God today.)
:

DAY 3
PRAYER OF PREPAREDNESS

FATHER—INSTRUCT: Matthew 5:44-45
But I say unto you, Love your enemies, bless them that curse you, do good to them that hate you, and pray for them which despitefully use you, and persecute you; That ye may be the children of your Father which is in heaven: for he maketh his sun to rise on the evil and on the good, and sendeth rain on the just and on the unjust.

MOTHER—TEACH: Matthew 5:46-48
For if ye love them which love you, what reward have ye? do not even the publicans the same? And if ye salute your brethren only, what do ye more than others? do not even the publicans so? Be ye therefore perfect, even as your Father which is in heaven is perfect.

SON(S)—LISTEN: Matthew 6:19-21
Lay not up for yourselves treasures upon earth, where moth and rust doth corrupt, and where thieves break through and steal: But lay up for yourselves treasures in heaven, where neither moth nor rust doth corrupt, and where thieves do not break through nor steal: For where your treasure is, there will your heart be also.

DAUGHTER(S)—RESPOND: Mark 10:44-45
And whosoever of you will be the chiefest, shall be servant of all. For even the Son of man came not to be ministered unto, but to minister, and to give his life a ransom for many.

(Jesus' instructions prepare us for abundant life. Now pray that his wisdom becomes our understanding.)

WORSHIP AND PRAISE

FATHER—INSTRUCT: John 9:35-38
Jesus heard that they had cast him out; and when he had found him, he said unto him, Dost thou believe on the Son of God? He answered and said, Who is he, Lord, that I might believe on him? And Jesus said unto him, Thou hast both seen him, and it is he that talketh with thee. And he said, Lord, I believe. And he worshipped him.

MOTHER—TEACH: Psalm 89:5-7
And the heavens shall praise thy wonders, O LORD: thy faithfulness also in the congregation of the saints. For who in the heaven can be compared unto the LORD? who among the sons of the mighty can be likened unto the LORD? God is greatly to be feared in the assembly of the saints, and to be had in reverence of all them that are about him.

SON(S)—LISTEN: Isaiah 12:1-2
And in that day thou shalt say, O LORD, I will praise thee: though thou wast angry with me, thine anger is turned away, and thou comfortedst me. Behold, God is my salvation; I will trust, and not be afraid: for the LORD JEHOVAH is my strength and my song; he also is become my salvation.

DAUGHTER(S)—RESPOND: John 4:24-26
God is a Spirit: and they that worship him must worship him in spirit and in truth. The woman saith unto him, I know that Messias cometh, which is called Christ: when he is come, he will tell us all things. Jesus saith unto her, I that speak unto thee am he.

(Now worship the God and father of our Lord Jesus Christ in the beauty of holiness for he is our salvation.)

PRAYER OF CONFESSION

FATHER—INSTRUCT: Psalm 85:3-4
Thou hast taken away all thy wrath: thou hast turned thyself from the fierceness of thine anger. Turn us, O God of our salvation, and cause thine anger toward us to cease.

MOTHER—TEACH: Mark 1:14-15
Now after that John was put in prison, Jesus came into Galilee, preaching the gospel of the kingdom of God, And saying, The time is fulfilled, and the kingdom of God is at hand: repent ye, and believe the gospel.

SON(S)—LISTEN: Psalm 32:1-2
Blessed is he whose transgression is forgiven, whose sin is covered. Blessed is the man unto whom the LORD imputeth not iniquity, and in whose spirit there is no guile.

DAUGHTER(S)—RESPOND: Isaiah 57:20-21
But the wicked are like the troubled sea, when it cannot rest, whose waters cast up mire and dirt. There is no peace, saith my God, to the wicked.

(Now, ask the Lord to reveal any errors or willful acts of disobedience. Then, claim his assurance of forgiveness.)

PRAYER OF GRATITUDE

FATHER—INSTRUCT: Psalm 116:8-10
For thou hast delivered my soul from death, mine eyes from tears, and my feet from falling. I will walk before the LORD in the land of the living. I believed, therefore have I spoken: I was greatly afflicted.

MOTHER—TEACH: John 2:3-5
And when they wanted wine, the mother of Jesus saith unto him, They have no wine. Jesus saith unto her, Woman, what have I to do with thee? mine hour is not yet come. His mother saith unto the servants, Whatsoever he saith unto you, do it.

SON(S)—LISTEN: Luke 11:1-4
And it came to pass, that, as he was praying in a certain place, when he ceased, one of his disciples said unto him, Lord, teach us to pray, as John also taught his disciples. And he said unto them, When ye pray, say, Our Father which art in heaven, Hallowed be thy name. Thy kingdom come. Thy will be done, as in heaven, so in earth. Give us day by day our daily bread. And forgive us our sins; for we also forgive every one that is indebted to us. And lead us not into temptation; but deliver us from evil.

DAUGHTER(S)—RESPOND: Mark 8:6-8
And he commanded the people to sit down on the ground: and he took the seven loaves, and gave thanks, and brake, and gave to his disciples to set before them; and they did set them before the people. And they had a few small fishes: and he blessed, and commanded to set them also before them. So they did eat, and were filled: and they took up of the broken meat that was left seven baskets.

(It is the Lord who provides for us daily. Now thank Him with a grateful heart.)

WISDOM AND UNDERSTANDING

FATHER—INSTRUCT: Proverbs 22:24-25
Make no friendship with an angry man; and with a furious man thou shalt not go: Lest thou learn his ways, and get a snare to thy soul.

MOTHER—TEACH: Proverbs 22:28-29
Remove not the ancient landmark, which thy fathers have set. Seest thou a man diligent in his business? he shall stand before kings; he shall not stand before mean men.

SON(S)—LISTEN: Proverbs 22:22-23
Rob not the poor, because he is poor: neither oppress the afflicted in the gate: For the LORD will plead their cause, and spoil the soul of those that spoiled them.

DAUGHTER(S)—RESPOND: Proverbs 22:5-6
Thorns and snares are in the way of the froward: he that doth keep his soul shall be far from them. Train up a child in the way he should go: and when he is old, he will not depart from it.

(The wise will hear and increase learning. Pray now for the enlightenment of God's Word.)

PRAYER OF SERENITY

FATHER—INSTRUCT: Psalm 25:20-21
O keep my soul, and deliver me: let me not be ashamed; for I put my trust in thee. Let integrity and uprightness preserve me; for I wait on thee.

MOTHER—TEACH: Isaiah 58:8-11
Then shall thy light break forth as the morning, and thine health shall spring forth speedily: and thy righteousness shall go before thee; the glory of the LORD shall be thy rereward. Then shalt thou call, and the LORD shall answer; thou shalt cry, and he shall say, Here I am. If thou take away from the midst of thee the yoke, the putting forth of the finger, and speaking vanity; And if thou draw out thy soul to the hungry, and satisfy the afflicted soul; then shall thy light rise in obscurity, and thy darkness be as the noonday: And the LORD shall guide thee continually, and
satisfy thy soul in drought, and make fat thy bones: and thou shalt be like a watered garden, and like a spring of water, whose waters fail not.

SON(S)—LISTEN: Mark 6:12-13
And they went out, and preached that men should repent. And they cast out many devils, and anointed with oil many that were sick, and healed them. And they cast out many devils, and anointed with oil many that were sick, and healed them.

DAUGHTER(S)—RESPOND: Mark 5:33-34
But the woman fearing and trembling, knowing what was done in her, came and fell down before him, and told him all the truth. And he said unto her, Daughter, thy faith hath made thee whole; go in peace, and be whole of thy plague.

(There is a work being done in each of us. Now pray that God give the boldness to share it.)

PRAYER OF INTERCESSION

FATHER—INSTRUCT: Luke 9:61-62
And another also said, Lord, I will follow thee; but let me first go bid them farewell, which are at home at my house. And Jesus said unto him, No man, having put his hand to the plough, and looking back, is fit for the kingdom of God.

MOTHER—TEACH: Luke 10:41-42
And Jesus answered and said unto her, Martha, Martha, thou art careful and troubled about many things: But one thing is needful: and Mary hath chosen that good part, which shall not be taken away from her.

SON(S)—LISTEN: John 4:34-36
Jesus saith unto them, My meat is to do the will of him that sent me, and to finish his work. Say not ye, There are yet four months, and then cometh harvest? behold, I say unto you, Lift up your eyes, and look on the fields; for they are white already to harvest. And he that reapeth receiveth wages, and gathereth fruit unto life eternal: that both he that soweth and he that reapeth may rejoice together.

DAUGHTER(S)—RESPOND: John 14:6-7, 13
Jesus saith unto him, I am the way, the truth, and the life: no man cometh unto the Father, but by me. If ye had known me, ye should have known my Father also: and from henceforth ye know him, and have seen him. And whatsoever ye shall ask in my name, that will I do, that the Father may be glorified in the Son.

(Now as part of the Lord's harvest, begin reaping through intercessory prayer for loved ones, friends, church and government leaders and world leaders.)

PRAYER OF PERSONAL REQUEST

FATHER—INSTRUCT: Psalm 27:9-11
Hide not thy face far from me; put not thy servant away in anger: thou hast been my help; leave me not, neither forsake me, O God of my salvation. When my father and my mother forsake me, then the LORD will take me up. Teach me thy way, O LORD, and lead me in a plain path, because of mine enemies.

MOTHER—TEACH: Psalm 86:6-7
Give ear, O LORD, unto my prayer; and attend to the voice of my supplications. In the day of my trouble I will call upon thee: for thou wilt answer me.

SON(S)—LISTEN: Psalm 27:13-14
I had fainted, unless I had believed to see the goodness of the LORD in the land of the living. Wait on the LORD: be of good courage, and he shall strengthen thine heart: wait, I say, on the LORD.

DAUGHTER(S)—RESPOND: Psalm 1:1-2
Blessed is the man that walketh not in the counsel of the ungodly, nor standeth in the way of sinners, nor sitteth in the seat of the scornful. But his delight is in the law of the LORD; and in his law doth he meditate day and night.

(Now turn all your concerns and decisions over to the Lord's care for He cares for us.)

PRAYER OF GUIDANCE

FATHER—INSTRUCT: Psalm 25:10-13
All the paths of the LORD are mercy and truth unto such as keep his covenant and his testimonies. For thy name's sake, O LORD, pardon mine iniquity; for it is great. What man is he that feareth the LORD? him shall he teach in the way that he shall choose. His soul shall dwell at ease; and his seed shall inherit the earth.

MOTHER—TEACH: Psalm 111:9-10
He sent redemption unto his people: he hath commanded his covenant for ever: holy and reverend is his name. The fear of the LORD is the beginning of wisdom: a good understanding have all they that do his commandments: his praise endureth for ever.

SON(S)—LISTEN: Psalm 112:1-2
Praise ye the LORD. Blessed is the man that feareth the LORD, that delighteth greatly in his commandments. His seed shall be mighty upon earth: the generation of the upright shall be blessed.

DAUGHTER(S)—RESPOND: Esther 5:1-3
Now it came to pass on the third day, that Esther put on her royal apparel, and stood in the inner court of the king's house, over against the king's house: and the king sat upon his royal throne in the royal house, over against the gate of the house. And it was so, when the king saw Esther the queen standing in the court, that she obtained favour in his sight: and the king held out to Esther the golden sceptre that was in his hand. So Esther drew near, and touched the top of the sceptre. Then said the king unto her, What wilt thou, queen Esther? and what is thy request? it shall be even given thee to the half of the kingdom.

(Our steps are made sure by the Lord's precepts. Now pray that he will guide all your decisions today.)

DEDICATION AND CONSECRATION

FATHER—INSTRUCT: Philippians 1:6-7
Being confident of this very thing, that he which hath begun a good work in you will perform it until the day of Jesus Christ: Even as it is meet for me to think this of you all, because I have you in my heart; inasmuch as both in my bonds, and in the defence and confirmation of the gospel, ye all are partakers of my grace.

MOTHER—TEACH: Luke 2:36-37
And there was one Anna, a prophetess, the daughter of Phanuel, of the tribe of Aser: she was of a great age, and had lived with an husband seven years from her virginity; And she was a widow of about fourscore and four years, which departed not from the temple, but served God with fastings and prayers night and day.

SON(S)—LISTEN: Luke 2:21-23
And when eight days were accomplished for the circumcising of the child, his name was called JESUS, which was so named of the angel before he was conceived in the womb. And when the days of her purification according to the law of Moses were accomplished, they brought him to Jerusalem, to present him to the Lord; (As it is written in the law of the Lord, Every male that openeth the womb shall be called holy to the Lord).

DAUGHTER(S)—RESPOND: Matthew 3:14-17
But John forbad him, saying, I have need to be baptized of thee, and comest thou to me? And Jesus answering said unto him, Suffer it to be so now: for thus it becometh us to fulfil all righteousness. Then he suffered him. And Jesus, when he was baptized, went up straightway out of the water: and, lo, the heavens were opened unto him, and he saw the Spirit of God descending like a dove, and lighting upon him: And lo a voice from heaven, saying, This is my beloved Son, in whom I am well pleased.

(Just as John, Anna, and Paul, our dedication to God will not go unnoticed. Now consecrate your life to this end.)

DAY 4
PRAYER OF PREPAREDNESS

FATHER—INSTRUCT: Malachi 3:17-18
And they shall be mine, saith the LORD of hosts, in that day when I make up my jewels; and I will spare them, as a man spareth his own son that serveth him. Then shall ye return, and discern between the righteous and the wicked, between him that serveth God and him that serveth him not.

MOTHER—TEACH: Proverbs 16:1-2
The preparations of the heart in man, and the answer of the tongue, is from the LORD. All the ways of a man are clean in his own eyes; but the LORD weigheth the spirits.

SON(S)—LISTEN: 1 Peter 2:9-10
But ye are a chosen generation, a royal priesthood, an holy nation, a peculiar people; that ye should show forth the praises of him who hath called you out of darkness into his marvelous light: Which in time past were not a people, but are now the people of God: which had not obtained mercy, but now have obtained mercy.

DAUGHTER(S)—RESPOND: Hebrews 3:12-14
Take heed, brethren, lest there be in any of you an evil heart of unbelief, in departing from the living God. But exhort one another daily, while it is called To day; lest any of you be hardened through the deceitfulness of sin. For we are made partakers of Christ, if we hold the beginning of our confidence stedfast unto the end.

(Now ask the Lord to prepare your heart to praise Him today with lips that speak only what please Him.)

WORSHIP AND PRAISE

FATHER—INSTRUCT: Psalm 24:8-10
Who is this King of glory? The LORD strong and mighty, the LORD mighty in battle. Lift up your heads, O ye gates; even lift them up, ye everlasting doors; and the King of glory shall come in. Who is this King of glory? The LORD of hosts, he is the King of glory. Selah

MOTHER—TEACH: Isaiah 57:18-19
I have seen his ways, and will heal him: I will lead him also, and restore comforts unto him and to his mourners. I create the fruit of the lips; Peace, peace to him that is far off, and to him that is near, saith the LORD; and I will heal him.

SON(S)—LISTEN: Psalm 108:1-3
O God, my heart is fixed; I will sing and give praise, even with my glory. Awake, psaltery and harp: I myself will awake early. I will praise thee, O LORD, among the people: and I will sing praises unto thee among the nations.

DAUGHTER(S)—RESPOND: John 16:25-27
These things have I spoken unto you in proverbs: but the time cometh, when I shall no more speak unto you in proverbs, but I shall show you plainly of the Father. At that day ye shall ask in my name: and I say not unto you, that I will pray the Father for you: For the Father himself loveth you, because ye have loved me, and have believed that I came out from God.

(Praise the King of glory in your words of adoration.)

PRAYER OF CONFESSION

FATHER—INSTRUCT: 1 Peter 3:8-10
Finally, be ye all of one mind, having compassion one of another, love as brethren, be pitiful, be courteous: Not rendering evil for evil, or railing for railing: but contrariwise blessing; knowing that ye are thereunto called, that ye should inherit a blessing. For he that will love life, and see good days, let him refrain his tongue from evil, and his lips that they speak no guile.

MOTHER—TEACH: Psalm 25:7-9
Remember not the sins of my youth, nor my transgressions: according to thy mercy remember thou me for thy goodness' sake, O LORD. Good and upright is the LORD: therefore will he teach sinners in the way. The meek will he guide in judgment: and the meek will he teach his way.

SON(S)—LISTEN: 1 John 1:8-10
If we say that we have no sin, we deceive ourselves, and the truth is not in us. If we confess our sins, he is faithful and just to forgive us our sins, and to cleanse us from all unrighteousness. If we say that we have not sinned, we make him a liar, and his word is not in us.

DAUGHTER(S)—RESPOND: Isaiah 5:20-21
Woe unto them that call evil good, and good evil; that put darkness for light, and light for darkness; that put bitter for sweet, and sweet for bitter! Woe unto them that are wise in their own eyes, and prudent in their own sight!

(Our thoughts are transparent before the Lord. Now confess any error that has disconnected your fellowship with the Lord and your brethren.)

PRAYER OF GRATITUDE

FATHER—INSTRUCT: 1 John 5:5-8
Who is he that overcometh the world, but he that believeth that Jesus is the Son of God? This is he that came by water and blood, even Jesus Christ; not by water only, but by water and blood. And it is the Spirit that beareth witness, because the Spirit is truth. For there are three that bear record in heaven, the Father, the Word, and the Holy Ghost: and these three are one. And there are three that bear witness in earth, the Spirit, and the water, and the blood: and these three agree in one.

MOTHER—TEACH: Philemon 3-5
Grace to you, and peace, from God our Father and the Lord Jesus Christ. I thank my God, making mention of thee always in my prayers, Hearing of thy love and faith, which thou hast toward the Lord Jesus, and toward all saints.

SON(S)—LISTEN: Psalm 116:16-18
O LORD, truly I am thy servant; I am thy servant, and the son of thine handmaid: thou hast loosed my bonds. I will offer to thee the sacrifice of thanksgiving, and will call upon the name of the LORD. I will pay my vows unto the LORD now in the presence of all his people.

DAUGHTER(S)—RESPOND: 1 Thessalonians 1:2-3
We give thanks to God always for you all, making mention of you in our prayers; Remembering without ceasing your work of faith, and labour of love, and patience of hope in our Lord Jesus Christ, in the sight of God and our Father.

(Express your gratitude to God for Christ's overcoming power in this world; He is our example.)

WISDOM AND UNDERSTANDING

FATHER—INSTRUCT: Proverbs 23:19, 22
Hear thou, my son, and be wise, and guide thine heart in the way. Hearken unto thy father that begat thee, and despise not thy mother when she is old.

MOTHER—TEACH: Proverbs 23:23-25
Buy the truth, and sell it not; also wisdom, and instruction, and understanding. The father of the righteous shall greatly rejoice: and he that begetteth a wise child shall have joy of him. Thy father and thy mother shall be glad, and she that bare thee shall rejoice.

SON(S)—LISTEN: Proverbs 25:2-3
It is the glory of God to conceal a thing: but the honour of kings is to search out a matter. The heaven for height, and the earth for depth, and the heart of kings is unsearchable.

DAUGHTER(S)—RESPOND: Proverbs 25:11-12
A word fitly spoken is like apples of gold in pictures of silver. As an earring of gold, and an ornament of fine gold, so is a wise reprover upon an obedient ear.

(God's wisdom today will guide our lives now and forever.)

PRAYER OF SERENITY

FATHER—INSTRUCT: 1 John 5:18-20
We know that whosoever is born of God sinneth not; but he that is begotten of God keepeth himself, and that wicked one toucheth him not.

MOTHER—TEACH: Titus 3:7-8
That being justified by his grace, we should be made heirs according to the hope of eternal life. This is a faithful saying, and these things I will that thou affirm constantly, that they which have believed in God might be careful to maintain good works. These things are good and profitable unto men.

SON(S)—LISTEN: 2 Timothy 4:1-2
I charge thee therefore before God, and the Lord Jesus Christ, who shall judge the quick and the dead at his appearing and his kingdom; Preach the word; be instant in season, out of season; reprove, rebuke, exhort with all longsuffering and doctrine.

DAUGHTER(S)—RESPOND: 1 John 4:17-19
Herein is our love made perfect, that we may have boldness in the day of judgment: because as he is, so are we in this world. There is no fear in love; but perfect love casteth out fear: because fear hath torment. He that feareth is not made perfect in love. We love him, because he first loved us.

(Now express your love for God in sincerity.)

PRAYER OF INTERCESSION

FATHER—INSTRUCT: 1 Timothy 2:1-3
I exhort therefore, that, first of all, supplications, prayers, intercessions, and giving of thanks, be made for all men; For kings, and for all that are in authority; that we may lead a quiet and peaceable life in all godliness and honesty. For this is good and acceptable in the sight of God our Saviour.

MOTHER—TEACH: Acts 16:14-16
And a certain woman named Lydia, a seller of purple, of the city of Thyatira, which worshipped God, heard us: whose heart the Lord opened, that she attended unto the things which were spoken of Paul. And when she was baptized, and her household, she besought us, saying, If ye have judged me to be faithful to the Lord, come into my house, and abide there. And she constrained us. And it came to pass, as we went to prayer, a certain damsel possessed with a spirit of divination met us, which brought her masters much gain by soothsaying.

SON(S)—LISTEN: 2 Thessalonians 3:1-3
Finally, brethren, pray for us, that the word of the Lord may have free course, and be glorified, even as it is with you: And that we may be delivered from unreasonable and wicked men: for all men have not faith. But the Lord is faithful, who shall stablish you, and keep you from evil.

DAUGHTER(S)—RESPOND: 1 Timothy 1:5-6
Now the end of the commandment is charity out of a pure heart, and of a good conscience, and of faith unfeigned: From which some having swerved have turned aside unto vain jangling.

(Now intercede for loved ones and those in authority.)

PRAYER OF PERSONAL REQUEST

FATHER—INSTRUCT: 2 Peter 1:2-4
Grace and peace be multiplied unto you through the knowledge of God, and of Jesus our Lord, According as his divine power hath given unto us all things that pertain unto life and godliness, through the knowledge of him that hath called us to glory and virtue: Whereby are given unto us exceeding great and precious promises: that by these ye might be partakers of the divine nature, having escaped the corruption that is in the world through lust.

MOTHER—TEACH: John 14:26-27
But the Comforter, which is the Holy Ghost, whom the Father will send in my name, he shall teach you all things, and bring all things to your remembrance, whatsoever I have said unto you. Peace I leave with you, my peace I give unto you: not as the world giveth, give I unto you. Let not your heart be troubled, neither let it be afraid.

SON(S)—LISTEN: Proverbs 16:21-23
The wise in heart shall be called prudent: and the sweetness of the lips increaseth learning. Understanding is a wellspring of life unto him that hath it: but the instruction of fools is folly. The heart of the wise teacheth his mouth, and addeth learning to his lips.

DAUGHTER(S)—RESPOND: 2 Timothy 3:16-17
All scripture is given by inspiration of God, and is profitable for doctrine, for reproof, for correction, for instruction in righteousness: That the man of God may be perfect, throughly furnished unto all good works.

(The comforter has come to comfort us. Now give the Lord your concerns and experience why he was sent by the Father. Pray to this end.)

PRAYER FOR GUIDANCE

FATHER—INSTRUCT: Psalm 112:5-7
A good man showeth favour, and lendeth: he will guide his affairs with discretion. Surely he shall not be moved for ever: the righteous shall be in everlasting remembrance. He shall not be afraid of evil tidings: his heart is fixed, trusting in the LORD.

MOTHER—TEACH: 1 Thessalonians 3:11-12
Now God himself and our Father, and our Lord Jesus Christ, direct our way unto you. And the Lord make you to increase and abound in love one toward another, and toward all men, even as we do toward you.

SON(S)—LISTEN: Hebrews 1:1-2
God, who at sundry times and in divers manners spake in time past unto the fathers by the prophets, Hath in these last days spoken unto us by his Son, whom he hath appointed heir of all things, by whom also he made the worlds.

DAUGHTER(S)—RESPOND: Hebrews 1:3-4
Who being the brightness of his glory, and the express image of his person, and upholding all things by the word of his power, when he had by himself purged our sins, sat down on the right hand of the Majesty on high; Being made so much better than the angels, as he hath by inheritance obtained a more excellent name than they.

(Trust the Lord in all your decisions. Today he will guide your steps.)

DEDICATION AND CONSECRATION

FATHER—INSTRUCT: Micah 1:2-3
Hear, all ye people; hearken, O earth, and all that therein is: and let the Lord GOD be witness against you, the Lord from his holy temple. For, behold, the LORD cometh forth out of his place, and will come down, and tread upon the high places of the earth.

MOTHER—TEACH: Daniel 12:1-2
And at that time shall Michael stand up, the great prince which standeth for the children of thy people: and there shall be a time of trouble, such as never was since there was a nation even to that same time: and at that time thy people shall be delivered, every one that shall be found written in the book. And many of them that sleep in the dust of the earth shall awake, some to everlasting life, and some to shame and everlasting contempt.

SON(S)—LISTEN: Joel 2:11-14
And the LORD shall utter his voice before his army: for his camp is very great: for he is strong that executeth his word: for the day of the LORD is great and very terrible; and who can abide it? Therefore also now, saith the LORD, turn ye even to me with all your heart, and with fasting, and with weeping, and with mourning: And rend your heart, and not your garments, and turn unto the LORD your God: for he is gracious and merciful, slow to anger, and of great kindness, and repenteth him of the evil. Who knoweth if he will return and repent, and leave a blessing behind him; even a meat offering and a drink offering unto the LORD your God?

DAUGHTER(S)—RESPOND: Psalm 115:14-16
The LORD shall increase you more and more, you and your children. Ye are blessed of the LORD which made heaven and earth. The heaven, even the heavens, are the LORD'S: but the earth hath he given to the children of men.

(Now rejoice. This is going to be a great day. Live it with freedom and praise to our God.)

DAY 5
PRAYER OF PREPAREDNESS

FATHER—INSTRUCT: Galatians 5:1, 5-6
Stand fast therefore in the liberty wherewith Christ hath made us free, and be not entangled again with the yoke of bondage. For we through the Spirit wait for the hope of righteousness by faith. For in Jesus Christ neither circumcision availeth any thing, nor uncircumcision; but faith which worketh by love.

MOTHER—TEACH: 2 Corinthians 10:3-5
For though we walk in the flesh, we do not war after the flesh: (For the weapons of our warfare are not carnal, but mighty through God to the pulling down of strongholds;) Casting down imaginations, and every high thing that exalteth itself against the knowledge of God, and bringing into captivity every thought to the obedience of Christ.

SON(S)—LISTEN: John 15:7-11
If ye abide in me, and my words abide in you, ye shall ask what ye will, and it shall be done unto you. Herein is my Father glorified, that ye bear much fruit; so shall ye be my disciples. As the Father hath loved me, so have I loved you: continue ye in my love. If ye keep my commandments, ye shall abide in my love; even as I have kept my Father's commandments, and abide in his love. These things have I spoken unto you, that my joy might remain in you, and that your joy might be full.

DAUGHTER(S)—RESPOND: Luke 4:18-19
The Spirit of the Lord is upon me, because he hath anointed me to preach the gospel to the poor; he hath sent me to heal the brokenhearted, to preach deliverance to the captives, and recovering of sight to the blind, to set at liberty them that are bruised, To preach the acceptable year of the Lord.

(Our God through faith in Jesus Christ prepares us for battle in spiritual warfare.)

WORSHIP AND PRAISE

FATHER—INSTRUCT: Psalm 103:1-4
Bless the LORD, O my soul: and all that is within me, bless his holy name. Bless the LORD, O my soul, and forget not all his benefits: Who forgiveth all thine iniquities; who healeth all thy diseases; Who redeemeth thy life from destruction; who crowneth thee with lovingkindness and tender mercies.

MOTHER—TEACH: Psalm 138:1-3
I will praise thee with my whole heart: before the gods will I sing praise unto thee. I will worship toward thy holy temple, and praise thy name for thy lovingkindness and for thy truth: for thou hast magnified thy word above all thy name. In the day when I cried thou answeredst me, and strengthenedst me with strength in my soul.

SON(S)—LISTEN: Exodus 34:8-10
And Moses made haste, and bowed his head toward the earth, and worshipped. And he said, If now I have found grace in thy sight, O Lord, let my Lord, I pray thee, go among us; for it is a stiffnecked people; and pardon our iniquity and our sin, and take us for thine inheritance. And he said, Behold, I make a covenant: before all thy people I will do marvels, such as have not been done in all the earth, nor in any nation: and all the people among which thou art shall see the work of the LORD: for it is a terrible thing that I will do with thee.

DAUGHTER(S)—RESPOND: Ecclesiastes 12:1-2
Remember now thy Creator in the days of thy youth, while the evil days come not, nor the years draw nigh, when thou shalt say, I have no pleasure in them; While the sun, or the light, or the moon, or the stars, be not darkened, nor the clouds return after the rain.

(Now bless the Lord with all your strength; He is worthy.)

PRAYER OF CONFESSION

FATHER—INSTRUCT: Acts 8:35-37
Then Philip opened his mouth, and began at the same scripture, and preached unto him Jesus. And as they went on their way, they came unto a certain water: and the eunuch said, See, here is water; what doth hinder me to be baptized? And Philip said, If thou believest with all thine heart, thou mayest. And he answered and said, I believe that Jesus Christ is the Son of God.

MOTHER—TEACH: 1 Peter 4:1-3
Forasmuch then as Christ hath suffered for us in the flesh, arm yourselves likewise with the same mind: for he that hath suffered in the flesh hath ceased from sin; That he no longer should live the rest of his time in the flesh to the lusts of men, but to the will of God. For the time past of our life may suffice us to have wrought the will of the Gentiles, when we walked in lasciviousness, lusts, excess of wine, revellings, banquetings, and abominable idolatries.

SON(S)—LISTEN: Isaiah 59:1-2
Behold, the LORD'S hand is not shortened, that it cannot save; neither his ear heavy, that it cannot hear: But your iniquities have separated between you and your God, and your sins have hid his face from you, that he will not hear.

DAUGHTER(S)—RESPOND: Ecclesiastes 11:7-8
Truly the light is sweet, and a pleasant thing it is for the eyes to behold the sun: But if a man live many years, and rejoice in them all; yet let him remember the days of darkness; for they shall be many. All that cometh is vanity.

(We are a work in progress. God understands our weaknesses. Now confess them and receive assurance that he has forgiven you.)

PRAYER OF GRATITUDE

FATHER—INSTRUCT: Colossians 2:13-14
And you, being dead in your sins and the uncircumcision of your flesh, hath he quickened together with him, having forgiven you all trespasses; Blotting out the handwriting of ordinances that was against us, which was contrary to us, and took it out of the way, nailing it to his cross.

MOTHER—TEACH: John 1:12-13
But as many as received him, to them gave he power to become the sons of God, even to them that believe on his name: Which were born, not of blood, nor of the will of the flesh, nor of the will of man, but of God.

SON(S)—LISTEN: John 1:14-15
And the Word was made flesh, and dwelt among us, (and we beheld his glory, the glory as of the only begotten of the Father,) full of grace and truth. John bare witness of him, and cried, saying, This was he of whom I spake, He that cometh after me is preferred before me: for he was before me.

DAUGHTER(S)—RESPOND: John 1:16-17
And of his fulness have all we received, and grace for grace. For the law was given by Moses, but grace and truth came by Jesus Christ.

(The work on the cross guaranteed our sonship.)

WISDOM AND UNDERSTANDING

FATHER—INSTRUCT: Deuteronomy 18:17-19
And the LORD said unto me, They have well spoken that which they have spoken. I will raise them up a Prophet from among their brethren, like unto thee, and will put my words in his mouth; and he shall speak unto them all that I shall command him. And it shall come to pass, that whosoever will not hearken unto my words which he shall speak in my name, I will require it of him.

MOTHER—TEACH: Exodus 35:10, 25
And every wise hearted among you shall come, and make all that the LORD hath commanded; And all the women that were wise hearted did spin with their hands, and brought that which they had spun, both of blue, and of purple, and of scarlet, and of fine linen.

SON(S)—LISTEN: Proverbs 27:1-2
Boast not thyself of tomorrow; for thou knowest not what a day may bring forth. Let another man praise thee, and not thine own mouth; a stranger, and not thine own lips.

DAUGHTER(S)—RESPOND: Proverbs 20:14-15, 24
It is naught, it is naught, saith the buyer: but when he is gone his way, then he boasteth. There is gold, and a multitude of rubies: but the lips of knowledge are a precious jewel. Man's goings are of the LORD; how can a man then understand his own way?

(God's wisdom helps us to recognize Jesus Christ as the prophet spoken of in Deuteronomy, Chapter 18. Praise Him now for your understanding.)

PRAYER OF SERENITY

FATHER—INSTRUCT: John 5:39-40
Search the scriptures; for in them ye think ye have eternal life: and they are they which testify of me. And ye will not come to me, that ye might have life.

MOTHER—TEACH: John 7:16-17
Jesus answered them, and said, My doctrine is not mine, but his that sent me. If any man will do his will, he shall know of the doctrine, whether it be of God, or whether I speak of myself.

SON(S)—LISTEN: John 8:45-47
And because I tell you the truth, ye believe me not. Which of you convinceth me of sin? And if I say the truth, why do ye not believe me? He that is of God heareth God's words: ye therefore hear them not, because ye are not of God.

DAUGHTER(S)—RESPOND: John 10:1-4
Verily, verily, I say unto you, He that entereth not by the door into the sheepfold, but climbeth up some other way, the same is a thief and a robber. But he that entereth in by the door is the shepherd of the sheep. To him the porter openeth; and the sheep hear his voice: and he calleth his own sheep by name, and leadeth them out. And when he putteth forth his own sheep, he goeth before them, and the sheep follow him: for they know his voice.

(We abandon all selfish motives when we see what Christ endured. Now pray to this end.)

PRAYER OF INTERCESSION

FATHER—INSTRUCT: Psalm 116:12-14
What shall I render unto the LORD for all his benefits toward me? I will take the cup of salvation, and call upon the name of the LORD. I will pay my vows unto the LORD now in the presence of all his people.

MOTHER—TEACH: 2 Corinthians 8:16-18
But thanks be to God, which put the same earnest care into the heart of Titus for you. For indeed he accepted the exhortation; but being more forward, of his own accord he went unto you. And we have sent with him the brother, whose praise is in the gospel throughout all the churches.

SON(S)—LISTEN: James 51-3
Go to now, ye rich men, weep and howl for your miseries that shall come upon you. Your riches are corrupted, and your garments are mot-heaten. Your gold and silver is cankered; and the rust of them shall be a witness against you, and shall eat your flesh as it were fire. Ye have heaped treasure together for the last days.

DAUGHTERS(S)—RESPOND: Romans 15:1-3
We then that are strong ought to bear the infirmities of the weak, and not to please ourselves. Let every one of us please his neighbour for his good to edification. For even Christ pleased not himself; but, as it is written, The reproaches of them that reproached thee fell on me.

(Bearing our brother's weaknesses helps us to love our neighbors as ourselves. This is the will of God. Pray for this enlightenment.)

PRAYER OF PERSONAL REQUEST

FATHER—INSTRUCT: Psalm 23:1-6
The LORD is my shepherd; I shall not want. He maketh me to lie down in green pastures: he leadeth me beside the still waters. He restoreth my soul: he leadeth me in the paths of righteousness for his name's sake. Yea, though I walk through the valley of the shadow of death, I will fear no evil: for thou art with me; thy rod and thy staff they comfort me. Thou preparest a table before me in the presence of mine enemies: thou anointest my head with oil; my cup runneth over. Surely goodness and mercy shall follow me all the days of my life: and I will dwell in the house of the LORD for ever.

MOTHER—TEACH: Psalm 116:4-5
Then called I upon the name of the LORD; O LORD, I beseech thee, deliver my soul. Gracious is the LORD, and righteous; yea, our God is merciful.

SON(S)—LISTEN: James 1:5-6
If any of you lack wisdom, let him ask of God, that giveth to all men liberally, and upbraideth not; and it shall be given him. But let him ask in faith, nothing wavering. For he that wavereth is like a wave of the sea driven with the wind and tossed.

DAUGHTER(S)—RESPOND: Romans 15:5-7
Now the God of patience and consolation grant you to be likeminded one toward another according to Christ Jesus: That ye may with one mind and one mouth glorify God, even the Father of our Lord Jesus Christ. Wherefore receive ye one another, as Christ also received us to the glory of God.

(The God of patience will comfort your hearts today. Only believe, then make your request known.)

PRAYER FOR GUIDANCE

FATHER—INSTRUCT: 2 Peter 1:16-18
Because it is written, Be ye holy; for I am holy. And if ye call on the Father, who without respect of persons judgeth according to every man's work, pass the time of your sojourning here in fear: Forasmuch as ye know that ye were not redeemed with corruptible things, as silver and gold, from your vain conversation received by tradition from your fathers.

MOTHER—TEACH: Luke 19:9-10
And Jesus said unto him, This day is salvation come to this house, forsomuch as he also is a son of Abraham. For the Son of man is come to seek and to save that which was lost.

SON(S)—LISTEN: Matthew 16:24-26
Then said Jesus unto his disciples, If any man will come after me, let him deny himself, and take up his cross, and follow me. For whosoever will save his life shall lose it: and whosoever will lose his life for my sake shall find it. For what is a man profited, if he shall gain the whole world, and lose his own soul? or what shall a man give in exchange for his soul?

DAUGHTER(S)—RESPOND: Ruth 1:16-17
And Ruth said, Entreat me not to leave thee, or to return from following after thee: for whither thou goest, I will go; and where thou lodgest, I will lodge: thy people shall be my people, and thy God my God: Where thou diest, will I die, and there will I be buried: the LORD do so to me, and more also, if aught but death part thee and me.

(The voice through God's Word is speaking out of heaven these words "be ye holy." Pray for the path of Christ to be made plain for you.)

DEDICATION AND CONSECRATION

FATHER—INSTRUCT: Isaiah 48:17-18
Thus saith the LORD, thy Redeemer, the Holy One of Israel; I am the LORD thy God which teacheth thee to profit, which leadeth thee by the way that thou shouldest go. O that thou hadst hearkened to my commandments! then had thy peace been as a river, and thy righteousness as the waves of the sea.

MOTHER—TEACH: Psalm 118:5-7
I called upon the LORD in distress: the LORD answered me, and set me in a large place. The LORD is on my side; I will not fear: what can man do unto me? The LORD taketh my part with them that help me: therefore shall I see my desire upon them that hate me.

SON(S)—LISTEN: James 1:12-13
Blessed is the man that endureth temptation: for when he is tried, he shall receive the crown of life, which the Lord hath promised to them that love him. Let no man say when he is tempted, I am tempted of God: for God cannot be tempted with evil, neither tempteth he any man.

DAUGHTER(S)—RESPOND: 2 Thessalonians 2:16-17
Now our Lord Jesus Christ himself, and God, even our Father, which hath loved us, and hath given us everlasting consolation and good hope through grace, Comfort your hearts, and stablish you in every good word and work.

(The Lord will bless those who bless you. Continue to dedicate your effort and labor to Him.)

DAY 6
PRAYER OF PREPAREDNESS

FATHER—INSTRUCT: Isaiah 57:1-2
The righteous perisheth, and no man layeth it to heart: and merciful men are taken away, none considering that the righteous is taken away from the evil to come. He shall enter into peace: they shall rest in their beds, each one walking in his uprightness.

MOTHER—TEACH: Job 13:1-3
Lo, mine eye hath seen all this, mine ear hath heard and understood it. What ye know, the same do I know also: I am not inferior unto you. Surely I would speak to the Almighty, and I desire to reason with God.

SON(S)—LISTEN: 1 Peter 2:2-4
As newborn babes, desire the sincere milk of the word, that ye may grow thereby: If so be ye have tasted that the Lord is gracious. To whom coming, as unto a living stone, disallowed indeed of men, but chosen of God, and precious.

DAUGHTER(S)—RESPOND: Song of Solomon 6:9-10
My dove, my undefiled is but one; she is the only one of her mother, she is the choice one of her that bare her. The daughters saw her, and blessed her; yea, the queens and the concubines, and they praised her. Who is she that looketh forth as the morning, fair as the moon, clear as the sun, and terrible as an army with banners?

(The righteous are strengthened and prepared through various forms of meditation, one such is the sincere milk of the word. Now pray for a greater enlightenment of the word.)

WORSHIP AND PRAISE

FATHER—INSTRUCT: Genesis 24:26-27
And the man bowed down his head, and worshipped the LORD. And he said, Blessed be the LORD God of my master Abraham, who hath not left destitute my master of his mercy and his truth: I being in the way, the LORD led me to the house of my master's brethren.

MOTHER—TEACH: Isaiah 12:4-5
And in that day shall ye say, Praise the LORD, call upon his name, declare his doings among the people, make mention that his name is exalted. Sing unto the LORD; for he hath done excellent things: this is known in all the earth.

SON(S)—LISTEN: Psalm 69:16-17
Hear me, O LORD; for thy lovingkindness is good: turn unto me according to the multitude of thy tender mercies. And hide not thy face from thy servant; for I am in trouble: hear me speedily.

DAUGHTER(S)—RESPOND: Psalm 9:1-2
I will praise thee, O LORD, with my whole heart; I will show forth all thy marvellous works. I will be glad and rejoice in thee: I will sing praise to thy name, O thou most High.

(We are marvelous works of God. Now praise Him for your existence with your whole heart.)

PRAYER OF CONFESSION

FATHER—INSTRUCT: Psalm 25:17-20
The troubles of my heart are enlarged: O bring thou me out of my distresses. Look upon mine affliction and my pain; and forgive all my sins. Consider mine enemies; for they are many; and they hate me with cruel hatred. O keep my soul, and deliver me: let me not be ashamed; for I put my trust in thee.

MOTHER—TEACH: Psalm 119:10-12
With my whole heart have I sought thee: O let me not wander from thy commandments. Thy word have I hid in mine heart, that I might not sin against thee. Blessed art thou, O LORD: teach me thy statutes.

SON(S)—LISTEN: Psalm 69:18-19
Draw nigh unto my soul, and redeem it: deliver me because of mine enemies. Thou hast known my reproach, and my shame, and my dishonour: mine adversaries are all before thee.

DAUGHTER(S)—RESPOND: Psalm 15:1-3
LORD, who shall abide in thy tabernacle? who shall dwell in thy holy hill? He that walketh uprightly, and worketh righteousness, and speaketh the truth in his heart. He that backbiteth not with his tongue, nor doeth evil to his neighbour, nor taketh up a reproach against his neighbour.

(Remember, it's the "heart of the matter." Now confess any conditions that may be influencing your heart to disobey God's word.)

PRAYER OF GRATITUDE

FATHER—INSTRUCT: 2 Thessalonians 1:11-12
Wherefore also we pray always for you, that our God would count you worthy of this calling, and fulfil all the good pleasure of his goodness, and the work of faith with power: That the name of our Lord Jesus Christ may be glorified in you, and ye in him, according to the grace of our God and the Lord Jesus Christ.

MOTHER—TEACH: 1 Thessalonians 5:21-23
Prove all things; hold fast that which is good. Abstain from all appearance of evil. And the very God of peace sanctify you wholly; and I pray God your whole spirit and soul and body be preserved blameless unto the coming of our Lord Jesus Christ.

SON(S)—LISTEN: John 9:4-6
I must work the works of him that sent me, while it is day: the night cometh, when no man can work. As long as I am in the world, I am the light of the world. When he had thus spoken, he spat on the ground, and made clay of the spittle, and he anointed the eyes of the blind man with the clay.

DAUGHTER(S)—RESPOND: Philippians 4:6-7
Be careful for nothing; but in every thing by prayer and supplication with thanksgiving let your requests be made known unto God. And the peace of God, which passeth all understanding, shall keep your hearts and minds through Christ Jesus.

(Now express your gratitude for a pure heart because we shall see God.)

WISDOM AND UNDERSTANDING

FATHER—INSTRUCT: Proverbs 24:20-21
For there shall be no reward to the evil man; the candle of the wicked shall be put out. My son, fear thou the LORD and the king: and meddle not with them that are given to change.

MOTHER—TEACH: Proverbs 24:15-16
Lay not wait, O wicked man, against the dwelling of the righteous; spoil not his resting place: For a just man falleth seven times, and riseth up again: but the wicked shall fall into mischief.

SON(S)—LISTEN: Proverbs 24:5-7
A wise man is strong; yea, a man of knowledge increaseth strength. For by wise counsel thou shalt make thy war: and in multitude of counsellors there is safety. Wisdom is too high for a fool: he openeth not his mouth in the gate.

DAUGHTER(S)—RESPOND: Proverbs 24:10, 17-18
If thou faint in the day of adversity, thy strength is small. Rejoice not when thine enemy falleth, and let not thine heart be glad when he stumbleth: Lest the LORD see it, and it displease him, and he turn away his wrath from him.

(With the promptings of the Holy Spirit, our hearts study the wisdom of our savior. Now praise the Father for this gift to us.)

PRAYER OF SERENITY

FATHER—INSTRUCT: Psalm 26:1-3
Judge me, O LORD; for I have walked in mine integrity: I have trusted also in the LORD; therefore I shall not slide. Examine me, O LORD, and prove me; try my reins and my heart. For thy lovingkindness is before mine eyes: and I have walked in thy truth.

MOTHER—TEACH: John 5:12-13
Then asked they him, What man is that which said unto thee, Take up thy bed, and walk? And he that was healed wist not who it was: for Jesus had conveyed himself away, a multitude being in that place.

SON(S)—LISTEN: Philippians 4:8-9
Finally, brethren, whatsoever things are true, whatsoever things are honest, whatsoever things are just, whatsoever things are pure, whatsoever things are lovely, whatsoever things are of good report; if there be any virtue, and if there be any praise, think on these things. Those things, which ye have both learned, and received, and heard, and seen in me, do: and the God of peace shall be with you.

DAUGHTER(S)—RESPOND: Ephesians 2:13-14
But now in Christ Jesus ye who sometimes were far off are made nigh by the blood of Christ. For he is our peace, who hath made both one, and hath broken down the middle wall of partition between us.

(Now boldly approach the throne of grace, expressing your heartfelt need for inner strength.)

PRAYER OF INTERCESSION

FATHER—INSTRUCT: Hebrews 13:1-3
Let brotherly love continue. Be not forgetful to entertain strangers: for thereby some have entertained angels unawares. Remember them that are in bonds, as bound with them; and them which suffer adversity, as being yourselves also in the body.

MOTHER—TEACH: 1 Corinthians 9:19-20
For though I be free from all men, yet have I made myself servant unto all, that I might gain the more. And unto the Jews I became as a Jew, that I might gain the Jews; to them that are under the law, as under the law, that I might gain them that are under the law.

SON(S)—LISTEN: Daniel 2:19-21
Then was the secret revealed unto Daniel in a night vision. Then Daniel blessed the God of heaven. Daniel answered and said, Blessed be the name of God for ever and ever: for wisdom and might are his: And he changeth the times and the seasons: he removeth kings, and setteth up kings: he giveth wisdom unto the wise, and knowledge to them that know understanding.

DAUGHTER(S)—RESPOND: 2 Peter 3:3-4
Knowing this first, that there shall come in the last days scoffers, walking after their own lusts, And saying, Where is the promise of his coming? for since the fathers fell asleep, all things continue as they were from the beginning of the creation.

(Now intercede for those who need encouragement, guidance, and those who may be weary awaiting the manifestation.)

PRAYER OF PERSONAL REQUEST

FATHER—INSTRUCT: Matthew 13:57-58
And they were offended in him. But Jesus said unto them, A prophet is not without honour, save in his own country, and in his own house. And he did not many mighty works there because of their unbelief.

MOTHER—TEACH: Psalm 16:1-3
Preserve me, O God: for in thee do I put my trust. O my soul, thou hast said unto the LORD, Thou art my Lord: my goodness extendeth not to thee; But to the saints that are in the earth, and to the excellent, in whom is all my delight.

SON(S)—LISTEN: Ephesians 5:13-14
But all things that are reproved are made manifest by the light: for whatsoever doth make manifest is light. Wherefore he saith, Awake thou that sleepest, and arise from the dead, and Christ shall give thee light.

DAUGHTER(S)—RESPOND: Hebrews 13:7-8
Remember them which have the rule over you, who have spoken unto you the word of God: whose faith follow, considering the end of their conversation. Jesus Christ the same yesterday, and to day, and for ever.

(Remember, we will reap if we faint not. Now ask the Lord to increase your faith for faithfulness.)

PRAYER OF GUIDANCE

FATHER—INSTRUCT: Romans 6:1-3
What shall we say then? Shall we continue in sin, that grace may abound? God forbid. How shall we, that are dead to sin, live any longer therein? Know ye not, that so many of us as were baptized into Jesus Christ were baptized into his death?

MOTHER—TEACH: Philippians 2:14-15
Do all things without murmurings and disputings: That ye may be blameless and harmless, the sons of God, without rebuke, in the midst of a crooked and perverse nation, among whom ye shine as lights in the world.

SON(S)—LISTEN: Psalm 18:20-21
The LORD rewarded me according to my righteousness; according to the cleanness of my hands hath he recompensed me. For I have kept the ways of the LORD, and have not wickedly departed from my God.

DAUGHTER(S)—RESPOND: Psalm 17:7-8
Show thy marvellous lovingkindness, O thou that savest by thy right hand them which put their trust in thee from those that rise up against them. Keep me as the apple of the eye, hide me under the shadow of thy wings.

(Our relationship with our Savior will guide us by the spirit of truth. Now pray for unity and a clear pathway.)

DEDICATION AND CONSECRATION

FATHER—INSTRUCT: Revelation 15:3-4
And they sing the song of Moses the servant of God, and the song of the Lamb, saying, Great and marvellous are thy works, Lord God Almighty; just and true are thy ways, thou King of saints. Who shall not fear thee, O Lord, and glorify thy name? for thou only art holy: for all nations shall come and worship before thee; for thy judgments are made manifest.

MOTHER—TEACH: Luke 9:46-48
Then there arose a reasoning among them, which of them should be greatest. And Jesus, perceiving the thought of their heart, took a child, and set him by him, And said unto them, Whosoever shall receive this child in my name receiveth me: and whosoever shall receive me receiveth him that sent me: for he that is least among you all, the same shall be great.

SON(S)—LISTEN: John 12:26-28
If any man serve me, let him follow me; and where I am, there shall also my servant be: if any man serve me, him will my Father honour. Now is my soul troubled; and what shall I say? Father, save me from this hour: but for this cause came I unto this hour. Father, glorify thy name. Then came there a voice from heaven, saying, I have both glorified it, and will glorify it again.

DAUGHTER(S)—RESPOND: Joel 2:28-30
And it shall come to pass afterward, that I will pour out my spirit upon all flesh; and your sons and your daughters shall prophesy, your old men shall dream dreams, your young men shall see visions: And also upon the servants and upon the handmaids in those days will I pour out my spirit. And I will show wonders in the heavens and in the earth, blood, and fire, and pillars of smoke.

(The King of saints is committed to us. He proved it with His life. Now rededicate yours. This is a day to rejoice in the Lord always.)

DAY 7
PRAYER OF PREPAREDNESS

FATHER—INSTRUCT: Galatians 3:26-28
For ye are all the children of God by faith in Christ Jesus. For as many of you as have been baptized into Christ have put on Christ. There is neither Jew nor Greek, there is neither bond nor free, there is neither male nor female: for ye are all one in Christ Jesus.

MOTHER—TEACH: Proverbs 31:10-12
Who can find a virtuous woman? for her price is far above rubies. The heart of her husband doth safely trust in her, so that he shall have no need of spoil. She will do him good and not evil all the days of her life.

SON(S)—LISTEN: Ecclesiastes 7:16-17
Be not righteous over much; neither make thyself over wise: why shouldest thou destroy thyself? Be not over much wicked, neither be thou foolish: why shouldest thou die before thy time?

DAUGHTER(S)—RESPOND: Proverbs 30:5-6
Every word of God is pure: he is a shield unto them that put their trust in him. Add thou not unto his words, lest he reprove thee, and thou be found a liar.

(The preparation of the heart in all mankind is from the Lord. Pray, believing that He will prepare your heart today to understand His purpose.)

WORSHIP AND PRAISE

FATHER—INSTRUCT: Psalm 113:2-6
Blessed be the name of the LORD from this time forth and for evermore. From the rising of the sun unto the going down of the same the LORD'S name is to be praised. The LORD is high above all nations, and his glory above the heavens. Who is like unto the LORD our God, who dwelleth on high, Who humbleth himself to behold the things that are in heaven, and in the earth!

MOTHER—TEACH: Psalm 121:1-3
I will lift up mine eyes unto the hills, from whence cometh my help. My help cometh from the LORD, which made heaven and earth. He will not suffer thy foot to be moved: he that keepeth thee will not slumber.

SON(S)—LISTEN: Ecclesiastes 5:19-20
Every man also to whom God hath given riches and wealth, and hath given him power to eat thereof, and to take his portion, and to rejoice in his labour; this is the gift of God. For he shall not much remember the days of his life; because God answereth him in the joy of his heart.

DAUGHTER(S)—RESPOND: Psalm 18:1-3
I will love thee, O LORD, my strength. The LORD is my rock, and my fortress, and my deliverer; my God, my strength, in whom I will trust; my buckler, and the horn of my salvation, and my high tower. I will call upon the LORD, who is worthy to be praised: so shall I be saved from mine enemies.

(Now express your love and praise to the Father of all creation and His Son.)

PRAYER OF CONFESSION

FATHER—INSTRUCT: 1 John 4:15-16
Whosoever shall confess that Jesus is the Son of God, God dwelleth in him, and he in God. And we have known and believed the love that God hath to us. God is love; and he that dwelleth in love dwelleth in God, and God in him.

MOTHER—TEACH: John 8:53-54
Art thou greater than our father Abraham, which is dead? and the prophets are dead: whom makest thou thyself? Jesus answered, If I honour myself, my honour is nothing: it is my Father that honoureth me; of whom ye say, that he is your God.

SON(S)—LISTEN: Philippians 3:13-15
Brethren, I count not myself to have apprehended: but this one thing I do, forgetting those things which are behind, and reaching forth unto those things which are before, I press toward the mark for the prize of the high calling of God in Christ Jesus. Let us therefore, as many as be perfect, be thus minded: and if in any thing ye be otherwise minded, God shall reveal even this unto you.

DAUGHTER(S)—RESPOND: Romans 8:1-2
There is therefore now no condemnation to them which are in Christ Jesus, who walk not after the flesh, but after the Spirit. For the law of the Spirit of life in Christ Jesus hath made me free from the law of sin and death.

(Our faith in Christ voids our condemnation. Now confess any reflection in thought that causes us to live in the past.)

PRAYER OF GRATITUDE

FATHER—INSTRUCT: Daniel 2:22-23
He revealeth the deep and secret things: he knoweth what is in the darkness, and the light dwelleth with him. I thank thee, and praise thee, O thou God of my fathers, who hast given me wisdom and might, and hast made known unto me now what we desired of thee: for thou hast now made known unto us the king's matter.

MOTHER—TEACH: Psalm 138:7-8
Though I walk in the midst of trouble, thou wilt revive me: thou shalt stretch forth thine hand against the wrath of mine enemies, and thy right hand shall save me. The LORD will perfect that which concerneth me: thy mercy, O LORD, endureth for ever: forsake not the works of thine own hands.

SON(S)—LISTEN: Psalm 140:12-13
I know that the LORD will maintain the cause of the afflicted, and the right of the poor. Surely the righteous shall give thanks unto thy name: the upright shall dwell in thy presence.

DAUGHTER(S)—RESPOND: John 8:50-51
And I seek not mine own glory: there is one that seeketh and judgeth. Verily, verily, I say unto you, If a man keep my saying, he shall never see death.

(Now thank the Lord for the wisdom and might that satisfy your desire.)

WISDOM AND UNDERSTANDING

FATHER—INSTRUCT: Proverbs 21:21, 30
He that followeth after righteousness and mercy findeth life, righteousness, and honour. There is no wisdom nor understanding nor counsel against the LORD.

MOTHER—TEACH: Proverbs 19:19-20
A man of great wrath shall suffer punishment: for if thou deliver him, yet thou must do it again. Hear counsel, and receive instruction, that thou mayest be wise in thy latter end.

SON(S)—LISTEN: Proverbs 20:20-21
Whoso curseth his father or his mother, his lamp shall be put out in obscure darkness. An inheritance may be gotten hastily at the beginning; but the end thereof shall not be blessed.

DAUGHTER(S)—RESPOND: Proverbs 19:21-23
There are many devices in a man's heart; nevertheless the counsel of the LORD, that shall stand. The desire of a man is his kindness: and a poor man is better than a liar. The fear of the LORD tendeth to life: and he that hath it shall abide satisfied; he shall not be visited with evil.

(Now pray asking God to help you stand only in the counsel of the Lord.)

PRAYER OF SERENITY

FATHER—INSTRUCT: Psalm 4:1-4
Hear me when I call, O God of my righteousness: thou hast enlarged me when I was in distress; have mercy upon me, and hear my prayer. O ye sons of men, how long will ye turn my glory into shame? how long will ye love vanity, and seek after leasing? Selah. But know that the LORD hath set apart him that is godly for himself: the LORD will hear when I call unto him. Stand in awe, and sin not: commune with your own heart upon your bed, and be still. Selah

MOTHER—TEACH: Ecclesiastes 7:13-14
Consider the work of God: for who can make that straight, which he hath made crooked? In the day of prosperity be joyful, but in the day of adversity consider: God also hath set the one over against the other, to the end that man should find nothing after him.

SON(S)—LISTEN: Psalm 103:11-13
For as the heaven is high above the earth, so great is his mercy toward them that fear him. As far as the east is from the west, so far hath he removed our transgressions from us. Like as a father pitieth his children, so the LORD pitieth them that fear him.

DAUGHTER(S)—RESPOND: Psalm 18:16-18
He sent from above, he took me, he drew me out of many waters. He delivered me from my strong enemy, and from them which hated me: for they were too strong for me. They prevented me in the day of my calamity: but the LORD was my stay.

(Recognize that the strength of our spiritual enemy is too strong for us. Now pray for the strength that comes through Jesus and God's Word.)

PRAYER OF INTERCESSION

FATHER—INSTRUCT: Psalm 14:2-3
The LORD looked down from heaven upon the children of men, to see if there were any that did understand, and seek God. They are all gone aside, they are all together become filthy: there is none that doeth good, no, not one.

MOTHER—TEACH: Acts 28:23-24
And when they had appointed him a day, there came many to him into his lodging; to whom he expounded and testified the kingdom of God, persuading them concerning Jesus, both out of the law of Moses, and out of the prophets, from morning till evening. And some believed the things which were spoken, and some believed not.

SON(S)—LISTEN: 1 John 3:14-16
We know that we have passed from death unto life, because we love the brethren. He that loveth not his brother abideth in death. Whosoever hateth his brother is a murderer: and ye know that no murderer hath eternal life abiding in him. Hereby perceive we the love of God, because he laid down his life for us: and we ought to lay down our lives for the brethren.

DAUGHTER(S)—RESPOND: Hebrews 11:1-2, 6
Now faith is the substance of things hoped for, the evidence of things not seen. For by it the elders obtained a good report. But without faith it is impossible to please him: for he that cometh to God must believe that he is, and that he is a rewarder of them that diligently seek him.

(Now intercede on behalf of brothers, sisters, and your neighbors. Pray to God for their salvation.)

PRAYER OF PERSONAL REQUEST

FATHER—INSTRUCT: <u>Psalm</u> 116:1-4
I love the LORD, because he hath heard my voice and my supplications. Because he hath inclined his ear unto me, therefore will I call upon him as long as I live. The sorrows of death compassed me, and the pains of hell gat hold upon me: I found trouble and sorrow. Then called I upon the name of the LORD; O LORD, I beseech thee, deliver my soul.

MOTHER—TEACH: <u>Hebrews</u> 9:11-14
But Christ being come an high priest of good things to come, by a greater and more perfect tabernacle, not made with hands, that is to say, not of this building; Neither by the blood of goats and calves, but by his own blood he entered in once into the holy place, having obtained eternal redemption for us. For if the blood of bulls and of goats, and the ashes of an heifer sprinkling the unclean, sanctifieth to the purifying of the flesh: How much more shall the blood of Christ, who through the eternal Spirit offered himself without spot to God, purge your conscience from dead works to serve the living God?

SON(S)—LISTEN: <u>2 Corinthians</u> 10:17-18
But he that glorieth, let him glory in the Lord. For not he that commendeth himself is approved, but whom the Lord commendeth.

DAUGHTER(S)—RESPOND: <u>Ephesians</u> 6:1-4
Children, obey your parents in the Lord: for this is right. Honour thy father and mother; (which is the first commandment with promise;) That it may be well with thee, and thou mayest live long on the earth. And, ye fathers, provoke not your children to wrath: but bring them up in the nurture and admonition of the Lord.

(Parents, pray for your children; call each name. Now children, pray for your parents.)

PRAYER OF GUIDANCE

FATHER—INSTRUCT: Psalm 17:3-5
Thou hast proved mine heart; thou hast visited me in the night; thou hast tried me, and shalt find nothing; I am purposed that my mouth shall not transgress. Concerning the works of men, by the word of thy lips I have kept me from the paths of the destroyer. Hold up my goings in thy paths, that my footsteps slip not.

MOTHER—TEACH: Psalm 139:1-4
O LORD, thou hast searched me, and known me. Thou knowest my downsitting and mine uprising, thou understandest my thought afar off. Thou compassest my path and my lying down, and art acquainted with all my ways. For there is not a word in my tongue, but, lo, O LORD, thou knowest it altogether.

SON(S)—LISTEN: Romans 15:18-19
For I will not dare to speak of any of those things which Christ hath not wrought by me, to make the Gentiles obedient, by word and deed, Through mighty signs and wonders, by the power of the Spirit of God; so that from Jerusalem, and round about unto Illyricum, I have fully preached the gospel of Christ.

DAUGHTER(S)—RESPOND: Luke 19:5-6
And when Jesus came to the place, he looked up, and saw him, and said unto him, Zacchaeus, make haste, and come down; for to day I must abide at thy house. And he made haste, and came down, and received him joyfully.

(Ask the Lord to search your ways and reveal any new direction that you should take today.)

DEDICATION AND CONSECRATION

FATHER—INSTRUCT: Isaiah 62:10-12
Go through, go through the gates; prepare ye the way of the people; cast up, cast up the highway; gather out the stones; lift up a standard for the people. Behold, the LORD hath proclaimed unto the end of the world, Say ye to the daughter of Zion, Behold, thy salvation cometh; behold, his reward is with him, and his work before him. And they shall call them, The holy people, The redeemed of the LORD: and thou shalt be called, Sought out, A city not forsaken.

MOTHER—TEACH: Acts 6:2-4
Then the twelve called the multitude of the disciples unto them, and said, It is not reason that we should leave the word of God, and serve tables. Wherefore, brethren, look ye out among you seven men of honest report, full of the Holy Ghost and wisdom, whom we may appoint over this business. But we will give ourselves continually to prayer, and to the ministry of the word.

SON(S)—LISTEN: Matthew 18:19-20
Again I say unto you, That if two of you shall agree on earth as touching any thing that they shall ask, it shall be done for them of my Father which is in heaven. For where two or three are gathered together in my name, there am I in the midst of them.

DAUGHTER(S)—RESPOND: John 16:23-24
And in that day ye shall ask me nothing. Verily, verily, I say unto you, Whatsoever ye shall ask the Father in my name, he will give it you. Hitherto have ye asked nothing in my name: ask, and ye shall receive, that your joy may be full.

(Now pray in agreement trusting in the Lord and dedicate this day to His purpose.)

DAY 8
PRAYER OF PREPAREDNESS

FATHER—INSTRUCT: Jeremiah 33:2-3
Thus saith the LORD the maker thereof, the LORD that formed it, to establish it; the LORD is his name; Call unto me, and I will answer thee, and show thee great and mighty things, which thou knowest not.

MOTHER—TEACH: Psalm 11:3-5
If the foundations be destroyed, what can the righteous do? The LORD is in his holy temple, the LORD'S throne is in heaven: his eyes behold, his eyelids try, the children of men. The LORD trieth the righteous: but the wicked and him that loveth violence his soul hateth.

SON(S)—LISTEN: Romans 1:24-25
Wherefore God also gave them up to uncleanness through the lusts of their own hearts, to dishonour their own bodies between themselves: Who changed the truth of God into a lie, and worshipped and served the creature more than the Creator, who is blessed for ever.

DAUGHTER(S)—RESPOND: Ephesians 4:1, 4-6
I therefore, the prisoner of the Lord, beseech you that ye walk worthy of the vocation wherewith ye are called. There is one body, and one Spirit, even as ye are called in one hope of your calling; One Lord, one faith, one baptism, One God and Father of all, who is above all, and through all, and in you all.

(It is God's will to prepare our hearts to be righteous. His words today focus on His righteousness; now begin with a prayer of great expectation.)

WORSHIP AND PRAISE

FATHER—INSTRUCT: John 6:28-29
Then said they unto him, What shall we do, that we might work the works of God? Jesus answered and said unto them, This is the work of God, that ye believe on him whom he hath sent.

MOTHER—TEACH: Psalm 87:2-3, 6-7
The LORD loveth the gates of Zion more than all the dwellings of Jacob. Glorious things are spoken of thee, O city of God. The LORD shall count, when he writeth up the people, that this man was born there. As well the singers as the players on instruments shall be there: all my springs are in thee.

SON(S)—LISTEN: Psalm 61:5, 8
For thou, O God, hast heard my vows: thou hast given me the heritage of those that fear thy name. So will I sing praise unto thy name for ever, that I may daily perform my vows.

DAUGHTER(S)—RESPOND: Psalm 80:17-19
Let thy hand be upon the man of thy right hand, upon the son of man whom thou madest strong for thyself. So will not we go back from thee: quicken us, and we will call upon thy name. Turn us again, O LORD God of hosts, cause thy face to shine; and we shall be saved.

(Now praise the God and Father of our Lord Jesus Christ that your name is written in heaven.)

PRAYER OF CONFESSION

FATHER—INSTRUCT: Psalm 130:1-4
Out of the depths have I cried unto thee, O LORD. Lord, hear my voice: let thine ears be attentive to the voice of my supplications. If thou, LORD, shouldest mark iniquities, O Lord, who shall stand? But there is forgiveness with thee, that thou mayest be feared.

MOTHER—TEACH: Lamentation 3:58-60
O Lord, thou hast pleaded the causes of my soul; thou hast redeemed my life. O LORD, thou hast seen my wrong: judge thou my cause. Thou hast seen all their vengeance and all their imaginations against me.

SON(S)—LISTEN: Romans 3:10-12
As it is written, There is none righteous, no, not one: There is none that understandeth, there is none that seeketh after God. They are all gone out of the way, they are together become unprofitable; there is none that doeth good, no, not one.

DAUGHTER(S)—RESPOND: John 5:26-27
For as the Father hath life in himself; so hath he given to the Son to have life in himself; And hath given him authority to execute judgment also, because he is the Son of man.

(All have sinned; but the blood of Jesus cleanses us of our unrighteousness. Now confess anything that needs His forgiveness.)

PRAYER OF GRATITUDE

FATHER—INSTRUCT: 1 Thessalonians 4:7-9
For God hath not called us unto uncleanness, but unto holiness. He therefore that despiseth, despiseth not man, but God, who hath also given unto us his holy Spirit. But as touching brotherly love ye need not that I write unto you: for ye yourselves are taught of God to love one another.

MOTHER—TEACH: Revelation 7:11-14
And all the angels stood round about the throne, and about the elders and the four beasts, and fell before the throne on their faces, and worshipped God, Saying, Amen: Blessing, and glory, and wisdom, and thanksgiving, and honour, and power, and might, be unto our God for ever and ever. Amen. And one of the elders answered, saying unto me, What are these which are arrayed in white robes? and whence came they? And I said unto him, Sir, thou knowest. And he said to me, These are they which came out of great tribulation, and have washed their robes, and made them white in the blood of the Lamb.

SON(S)—LISTEN: Romans 1:8-9
First, I thank my God through Jesus Christ for you all, that your faith is spoken of throughout the whole world. For God is my witness, whom I serve with my spirit in the gospel of his Son, that without ceasing I make mention of you always in my prayers.

DAUGHTER(S)—RESPOND: John 9:35-38
Jesus heard that they had cast him out; and when he had found him, he said unto him, Dost thou believe on the Son of God? He answered and said, Who is he, Lord, that I might believe on him? And Jesus said unto him, Thou hast both seen him, and it is he that talketh with thee. And he said, Lord, I believe. And he worshipped him.

(Just as the blind man of John Chapter 9, worship the Lord for your spiritual sight.)

WISDOM AND UNDERSTANDING

FATHER—INSTRUCT: Proverbs 21:2-4
Every way of a man is right in his own eyes: but the LORD pondereth the hearts. To do justice and judgment is more acceptable to the LORD than sacrifice. An high look, and a proud heart, and the plowing of the wicked, is sin.

MOTHER—TEACH: Proverbs 20:7-9
The just man walketh in his integrity: his children are blessed after him. A king that sitteth in the throne of judgment scattereth away all evil with his eyes. Who can say, I have made my heart clean, I am pure from my sin?

SON(S)—LISTEN: Proverbs 19:26-27
He that wasteth his father, and chaseth away his mother, is a son that causeth shame, and bringeth reproach. Cease, my son, to hear the instruction that causeth to err from the words of knowledge.

DAUGHTER(S)—RESPOND: Proverbs 20:11-14
Even a child is known by his doings, whether his work be pure, and whether it be right. The hearing ear, and the seeing eye, the LORD hath made even both of them. Love not sleep, lest thou come to poverty; open thine eyes, and thou shalt be satisfied with bread. It is naught, it is naught, saith the buyer: but when he is gone his way, then he boasteth.

(Now pray for the wisdom from above. Remember, it is first pure then peaceable.)

PRAYER OF SERENITY

FATHER—INSTRUCT: <u>Philippians</u> 4:4-6
Rejoice in the Lord alway: and again I say, Rejoice. Let your moderation be known unto all men. The Lord is at hand. Be careful for nothing; but in every thing by prayer and supplication with thanksgiving let your requests be made known unto God.

MOTHER—TEACH: <u>Ephesians</u> 2:8-10
For by grace are ye saved through faith; and that not of yourselves: it is the gift of God: Not of works, lest any man should boast. For we are his workmanship, created in Christ Jesus unto good works, which God hath before ordained that we should walk in them.

SON(S)—LISTEN: <u>Romans</u> 1:16-17
For I am not ashamed of the gospel of Christ: for it is the power of God unto salvation to every one that believeth; to the Jew first, and also to the Greek. For therein is the righteousness of God revealed from faith to faith: as it is written, The just shall live by faith.

DAUGHTER(S)—RESPOND: <u>Romans</u> 12:1-2
I beseech you therefore, brethren, by the mercies of God, that ye present your bodies a living sacrifice, holy, acceptable unto God, which is your reasonable service. And be not conformed to this world: but be ye transformed by the renewing of your mind, that ye may prove what is that good, and acceptable, and perfect, will of God.

(Now pray that God's words complete His transformation within your hearts.)

PRAYER OF INTERCESSION

FATHER—INSTRUCT: Song of Solomon 4:1-2
Behold, thou art fair, my love; behold, thou art fair; thou hast doves' eyes within thy locks: thy hair is as a flock of goats, that appear from mount Gilead. Thy teeth are like a flock of sheep that are even shorn, which came up from the washing; whereof every one bear twins, and none is barren among them.

MOTHER—TEACH: Hebrews 11:6-7
But without faith it is impossible to please him: for he that cometh to God must believe that he is, and that he is a rewarder of them that diligently seek him. By faith Noah, being warned of God of things not seen as yet, moved with fear, prepared an ark to the saving of his house; by the which he condemned the world, and became heir of the righteousness which is by faith.

SON(S)—LISTEN: Psalm 13:3-5
Consider and hear me, O LORD my God: lighten mine eyes, lest I sleep the sleep of death; Lest mine enemy say, I have prevailed against him; and those that trouble me rejoice when I am moved. But I have trusted in thy mercy; my heart shall rejoice in thy salvation.

DAUGHTER(S)—RESPOND: 1 Timothy 2:1-2
I exhort therefore, that, first of all, supplications, prayers, intercessions, and giving of thanks, be made for all men; For kings, and for all that are in authority; that we may lead a quiet and peaceable life in all godliness and honesty.

(It takes faith to see the beauty in every situation in our lives and others. Pray now to this end.)

PRAYER OF PERSONAL REQUEST

FATHER—INSTRUCT: 1 Corinthians 9:24-27
Know ye not that they which run in a race run all, but one receiveth the prize? So run, that ye may obtain. And every man that striveth for the mastery is temperate in all things. Now they do it to obtain a corruptible crown; but we an incorruptible. I therefore so run, not as uncertainly; so fight I, not as one that beateth the air: But I keep under my body, and bring it into subjection: lest that by any means, when I have preached to others, I myself should be a castaway.

MOTHER—TEACH: Philippians 1:12-14
But I would ye should understand, brethren, that the things which happened unto me have fallen out rather unto the furtherance of the gospel; So that my bonds in Christ are manifest in all the palace, and in all other places; And many of the brethren in the Lord, waxing confident by my bonds, are much more bold to speak the word without fear.

SON(S)—LISTEN: 2 Corinthians 5:17-19
Therefore if any man be in Christ, he is a new creature: old things are passed away; behold, all things are become new. And all things are of God, who hath reconciled us to himself by Jesus Christ, and hath given to us the ministry of reconciliation; To wit, that God was in Christ, reconciling the world unto himself, not imputing their trespasses unto them; and hath committed unto us the word of reconciliation.

DAUGHTER(S)—RESPOND: Romans 15:2-4
Let every one of us please his neighbour for his good to edification. For even Christ pleased not himself; but, as it is written, The reproaches of them that reproached thee fell on me. For whatsoever things were written aforetime were written for our learning, that we through patience and comfort of the Scriptures might have hope.

(Pray that God will keep you on pace in the race to your abundant life in Christ.)

PRAYER OF GUIDANCE

FATHER—INSTRUCT: Romans 3:20-22
Therefore by the deeds of the law there shall no flesh be justified in his sight: for by the law is the knowledge of sin. But now the righteousness of God without the law is manifested, being witnessed by the law and the prophets; Even the righteousness of God which is by faith of Jesus Christ unto all and upon all them that believe: for there is no difference.

MOTHER—TEACH: Luke 24:13-16
And, behold, two of them went that same day to a village called Emmaus, which was from Jerusalem about threescore furlongs. And they talked together of all these things which had happened. And it came to pass, that, while they communed together and reasoned, Jesus himself drew near, and went with them. But their eyes were holden that they should not know him.

SON(S)—LISTEN: Acts 8:29-31
Then the Spirit said unto Philip, Go near, and join thyself to this chariot. And Philip ran thither to him, and heard him read the prophet Esaias, and said, Understandest thou what thou readest? And he said, How can I, except some man should guide me? And he desired Philip that he would come up and sit with him.

DAUGHTER(S)—RESPOND: John 17:13-17
And now come I to thee; and these things I speak in the world, that they might have my joy fulfilled in themselves. I have given them thy word; and the world hath hated them, because they are not of the world, even as I am not of the world. I pray not that thou shouldest take them out of the world, but that thou shouldest keep them from the evil. They are not of the world, even as I am not of the world. Sanctify them through thy truth: thy word is truth.

(Now pray to God that we can see Christ in the Word beside and near us to guide us.)

DEDICATION AND CONSECRATION

FATHER—INSTRUCT: Luke 7:37-38
And, behold, a woman in the city, which was a sinner, when she knew that Jesus sat at meat in the Pharisee's house, brought an alabaster box of ointment, And stood at his feet behind him weeping, and began to wash his feet with tears, and did wipe them with the hairs of her head, and kissed his feet, and anointed them with the ointment.

MOTHER—TEACH: Luke 5:33-35
And they said unto him, Why do the disciples of John fast often, and make prayers, and likewise the disciples of the Pharisees; but thine eat and drink? And he said unto them, Can ye make the children of the bridechamber fast, while the bridegroom is with them? But the days will come, when the bridegroom shall be taken away from them, and then shall they fast in those days.

SON(S)—LISTEN: John 15:1-4
I am the true vine, and my Father is the husbandman. Every branch in me that beareth not fruit he taketh away: and every branch that beareth fruit, he purgeth it, that it may bring forth more fruit. Now ye are clean through the word which I have spoken unto you. Abide in me, and I in you. As the branch cannot bear fruit of itself, except it abide in the vine; no more can ye, except ye abide in me.

DAUGHTER(S)—RESPOND: Luke 9:44-46
Let these sayings sink down into your ears: for the Son of man shall be delivered into the hands of men. But they understood not this saying, and it was hid from them, that they perceived it not: and they feared to ask him of that saying. Then there arose a reasoning among them, which of them should be greatest.

(Jesus gave all for our salvation! Live in it today with the joy of the Lord.)

DAY 9
PRAYER OF PREPAREDNESS

FATHER—INSTRUCT: Matthew 21:21-22
Jesus answered and said unto them, Verily I say unto you, If ye have faith, and doubt not, ye shall not only do this which is done to the fig tree, but also if ye shall say unto this mountain, Be thou removed, and be thou cast into the sea; it shall be done. And all things, whatsoever ye shall ask in prayer, believing, ye shall receive.

MOTHER—TEACH: John 3:17-18
For God sent not his Son into the world to condemn the world; but that the world through him might be saved. He that believeth on him is not condemned: but he that believeth not is condemned already, because he hath not believed in the name of the only begotten Son of God.

SON(S)—LISTEN: Romans 10:14-15
How then shall they call on him in whom they have not believed? and how shall they believe in him of whom they have not heard? and how shall they hear without a preacher? And how shall they preach, except they be sent? as it is written, How beautiful are the feet of them that preach the gospel of peace, and bring glad tidings of good things!

DAUGHTER(S)—RESPOND: Isaiah 53:1-2
Who hath believed our report? and to whom is the arm of the LORD revealed? For he shall grow up before him as a tender plant, and as a root out of a dry ground: he hath no form nor comeliness; and when we shall see him, there is no beauty that we should desire him.

(The Author of our faith will prepare us for greater opportunities that lie ahead; pray to this end.)

WORSHIP AND PRAISE

FATHER—INSTRUCT: Psalm 107:19-21
Then they cry unto the LORD in their trouble, and he saveth them out of their distresses. He sent his word, and healed them, and delivered them from their destructions. Oh that men would praise the LORD for his goodness, and for his wonderful works to the children of men!

MOTHER—TEACH: Matthew 21:8-9
And a very great multitude spread their garments in the way; others cut down branches from the trees, and strawed them in the way. And the multitudes that went before, and that followed, cried, saying, Hosanna to the Son of David: Blessed is he that cometh in the name of the Lord; Hosanna in the highest.

SON(S)—LISTEN: Revelation 5:13-14
And every creature which is in heaven, and on the earth, and under the earth, and such as are in the sea, and all that are in them, heard I saying, Blessing, and honour, and glory, and power, be unto him that sitteth upon the throne, and unto the Lamb for ever and ever. And the four beasts said, Amen. And the four and twenty elders fell down and worshipped him that liveth for ever and ever.

DAUGHTER(S)—RESPOND: Matthew 15:25-28
Then came she and worshipped him, saying, Lord, help me. But he answered and said, It is not meet to take the children's bread, and to cast it to dogs. And she said, Truth, Lord: yet the dogs eat of the crumbs which fall from their masters' table. Then Jesus answered and said unto her, O woman, great is thy faith: be it unto thee even as thou wilt. And her daughter was made whole from that very hour.

(If God's first answer does not satisfy you, continue to worship and praise Him which gives Him another reason to answer your requests.)

PRAYER OF CONFESSION

FATHER—INSTRUCT: Isaiah 53:3-4
He is despised and rejected of men; a man of sorrows, and acquainted with grief: and we hid as it were our faces from him; he was despised, and we esteemed him not. Surely he hath borne our griefs, and carried our sorrows: yet we did esteem him stricken, smitten of God, and afflicted.

MOTHER—TEACH: Matthew 19:21-22
Jesus said unto him, If thou wilt be perfect, go and sell that thou hast, and give to the poor, and thou shalt have treasure in heaven: and come and follow me. But when the young man heard that saying, he went away sorrowful: for he had great possessions.

SON(S)—LISTEN: Psalm 32:1-2
Blessed is he whose transgression is forgiven, whose sin is covered. Blessed is the man unto whom the LORD imputeth not iniquity, and in whose spirit there is no guile.

DAUGHTER(S)—RESPOND: Proverbs 16:2-4
All the ways of a man are clean in his own eyes; but the LORD weigheth the spirits. Commit thy works unto the LORD, and thy thoughts shall be established. The LORD hath made all things for himself: yea, even the wicked for the day of evil.

(God has given us absolute grace uncut and uncensored by the suffering of Christ. Now confess any bitter resentments or sins that He has already suffered for.)

PRAYER OF GRATITUDE

FATHER—INSTRUCT: Psalm 107:22-24
And let them sacrifice the sacrifices of thanksgiving, and declare his works with rejoicing. They that go down to the sea in ships, that do business in great waters; These see the works of the LORD, and his wonders in the deep.

MOTHER—TEACH: John 1:17-18
For the law was given by Moses, but grace and truth came by Jesus Christ. No man hath seen God at any time; the only begotten Son, which is in the bosom of the Father, he hath declared him.

SON(S)—LISTEN: Isaiah 46:9-10
Remember the former things of old: for I am God, and there is none else; I am God, and there is none like me, Declaring the end from the beginning, and from ancient times the things that are not yet done, saying, My counsel shall stand, and I will do all my pleasure.

DAUGHTER(S)—RESPOND: Psalm 147:9-11
He giveth to the beast his food, and to the young ravens which cry. He delighteth not in the strength of the horse: he taketh not pleasure in the legs of a man. The LORD taketh pleasure in them that fear him, in those that hope in his mercy.

(Your end from the beginning has already been declared. Now thank God with a grateful heart.)

WISDOM AND UNDERSTANDING

FATHER—INSTRUCT: Romans 5:1-3
Therefore being justified by faith, we have peace with God through our Lord Jesus Christ: By whom also we have access by faith into this grace wherein we stand, and rejoice in hope of the glory of God. And not only so, but we glory in tribulations also: knowing that tribulation worketh patience.

MOTHER—TEACH: Isaiah 50:7-9
For the Lord GOD will help me; therefore shall I not be confounded: therefore have I set my face like a flint, and I know that I shall not be ashamed. He is near that justifieth me; who will contend with me? let us stand together: who is mine adversary? let him come near to me. Behold,
the Lord GOD will help me; who is he that shall condemn me? lo, they all shall wax old as a garment; the moth shall eat them up.

SON(S)—LISTEN: Proverbs 8:6, 17
Hear; for I will speak of excellent things; and the opening of my lips shall be right things. I love them that love me; and those that seek me early shall find me.

DAUGHTER(S)—RESPOND: Proverbs 8:34-36
Blessed is the man that heareth me, watching daily at my gates, waiting at the posts of my doors. For whoso findeth me findeth life, and shall obtain favour of the LORD. But he that sinneth against me wrongeth his own soul: all they that hate me love death.

(The open door to approach the throne of grace was unlocked by love. Now tell God how much you love Him and His wisdom.)

PRAYER OF SERENITY

FATHER—INSTRUCT: John 4:34-36
Jesus saith unto them, My meat is to do the will of him that sent me, and to finish his work. Say not ye, There are yet four months, and then cometh harvest? behold, I say unto you, Lift up your eyes, and look on the fields; for they are white already to harvest. And he that reapeth receiveth wages, and gathereth fruit unto life eternal: that both he that soweth and he that reapeth may rejoice together.

MOTHER—TEACH: Philippians 1:9-10
And this I pray, that your love may abound yet more and more in knowledge and in all judgment; That ye may approve things that are excellent; that ye may be sincere and without offence till the day of Christ.

SON(S)—LISTEN: Isaiah 45:18-20
For thus saith the LORD that created the heavens; God himself that formed the earth and made it; he hath established it, he created it not in vain, he formed it to be inhabited: I am the LORD; and there is none else. I have not spoken in secret, in a dark place of the earth: I said not unto the seed of Jacob, Seek ye me in vain: I the LORD speak righteousness, I declare things that are right. Assemble yourselves and come; draw near together, ye that are escaped of the nations: they have no knowledge that set up the wood of their graven image, and pray unto a god that
cannot save.

DAUGHTER(S)—RESPOND: Ephesians 2:7-8
That in the ages to come he might show the exceeding riches of his grace in his kindness toward us through Christ Jesus. For by grace are ye saved through faith; and that not of yourselves: it is the gift of God.

(Our goal is to glorify the Father by laboring in the harvest of His Son. Now pray that you can be an effective witness.)

PRAYER OF INTERCESSION

FATHER—INSTRUCT: John 4:13-15
Jesus answered and said unto her, Whosoever drinketh of this water shall thirst again: But whosoever drinketh of the water that I shall give him shall never thirst; but the water that I shall give him shall be in him a well of water springing up into everlasting life. The woman saith unto him, Sir, give me this water, that I thirst not, neither come hither to draw.

MOTHER—TEACH: Psalm 24:6-7
This is the generation of them that seek him, that seek thy face, O Jacob. Lift up your heads, O ye gates; and be ye lift up, ye everlasting doors; and the King of glory shall come in.

SON(S)—LISTEN: Isaiah 63:7-8
I will mention the lovingkindnesses of the LORD, and the praises of the LORD, according to all that the LORD hath bestowed on us, and the great goodness toward the house of Israel, which he hath bestowed on them according to his mercies, and according to the multitude of his lovingkindnesses. For he said, Surely they are my people, children that will not lie: so he was their Saviour.

DAUGHTER(S)—RESPOND: John 5:19-21
Then answered Jesus and said unto them, Verily, verily, I say unto you, The Son can do nothing of himself, but what he seeth the Father do: for what things soever he doeth, these also doeth the Son likewise. For the Father loveth the Son, and showeth him all things that himself doeth: and he will show him greater works than these, that ye may marvel. For as the Father raiseth up the dead, and quickeneth them; even so the Son quickeneth whom he will.

(We can do all things through Christ who strengthens us. Now pray for those who have not made this discovery.)

PRAYER OF PERSONAL REQUEST

FATHER—INSTRUCT: Matthew 20:32-34
And Jesus stood still, and called them, and said, What will ye that I shall do unto you? They say unto him, Lord, that our eyes may be opened. So Jesus had compassion on them, and touched their eyes: and immediately their eyes received sight, and they followed him.

MOTHER—TEACH: Philippians 1:3-6
I thank my God upon every remembrance of you, Always in every prayer of mine for you all making request with joy, For your fellowship in the gospel from the first day until now; Being confident of this very thing, that he which hath begun a good work in you will perform it until the day of Jesus Christ.

SON(S)—LISTEN: John 3:5-7
Jesus answered, Verily, verily, I say unto thee, Except a man be born of water and of the Spirit, he cannot enter into the kingdom of God. That which is born of the flesh is flesh; and that which is born of the Spirit is spirit. Marvel not that I said unto thee, Ye must be born again.

DAUGHTER(S)—RESPOND: Psalm 27:13-14
I had fainted, unless I had believed to see the goodness of the LORD in the land of the living. Wait on the LORD: be of good courage, and he shall strengthen thine heart: wait, I say, on the LORD.

(There are some newborn animals that follow the first thing they see. Pray that Jesus answers your prayers and that you see Him.)

PRAYER OF GUIDANCE

FATHER—INSTRUCT: Isaiah 53:6-8
All we like sheep have gone astray; we have turned every one to his own way; and the LORD hath laid on him the iniquity of us all. He was oppressed, and he was afflicted, yet he opened not his mouth: he is brought as a lamb to the slaughter, and as a sheep before her shearers is dumb, so he openeth not his mouth. He was taken from prison and from judgment: and who shall declare his generation? for he was cut off out of the land of the living: for the transgression of my people was he stricken.

MOTHER—TEACH: Acts 8:32-35
The place of the scripture which he read was this, He was led as a sheep to the slaughter; and like a lamb dumb before his shearer, so opened he not his mouth: In his humiliation his judgment was taken away: and who shall declare his generation? for his life is taken from the earth. And the eunuch answered Philip, and said, I pray thee, of whom speaketh the prophet this? of himself, or of some other man? Then Philip opened his mouth, and began at the same scripture,
and preached unto him Jesus.

SON(S)—LISTEN: Psalm 25:4-6
Show me thy ways, O LORD; teach me thy paths. Lead me in thy truth, and teach me: for thou art the God of my salvation; on thee do I wait all the day. Remember, O LORD, thy tender mercies and thy lovingkindnesses; for they have been ever of old.

DAUGHTER(S)—RESPOND: John 2:22-25
When therefore he was risen from the dead, his disciples remembered that he had said this unto them; and they believed the scripture, and the word which Jesus had said. Now when he was in Jerusalem at the passover, in the feast day, many believed in his name, when they saw the miracles which he did. But Jesus did not commit himself unto them, because he knew all men, And needed not that any should testify of man: for he knew what was in man.

(The great Shepherd gives us guidance, strength, help, and understanding sufficient for our needs. Praise Him for his care.)

DEDICATION AND CONSECRATION

FATHER—INSTRUCT: Proverbs 10:23-24, 27
It is as sport to a fool to do mischief: but a man of understanding hath wisdom. The fear of the wicked, it shall come upon him: but the desire of the righteous shall be granted. The fear of the LORD prolongeth days: but the years of the wicked shall be shortened.

MOTHER—TEACH: Proverbs 10:25, 28
As the whirlwind passeth, so is the wicked no more: but the righteous is an everlasting foundation. The hope of the righteous shall be gladness: but the expectation of the wicked shall perish.

SON(S)—LISTEN: Proverbs 10:29-30
The way of the LORD is strength to the upright: but destruction shall be to the workers of iniquity. The righteous shall never be removed: but the wicked shall not inhabit the earth.

DAUGHTER(S)—RESPOND: Proverbs 10:31-32
The mouth of the just bringeth forth wisdom: but the froward tongue shall be cut out. The lips of the righteous know what is acceptable: but the mouth of the wicked speaketh frowardness.

(As we study, as we meditate, as we seek to act on God's Word, our consecration allows us to grow. Pray to this end. This is going to be a great day.)

DAY 10
PRAYER OF PREPAREDNESS

FATHER—INSTRUCT: Matthew 10:40-42
He that receiveth you receiveth me, and he that receiveth me receiveth him that sent me. He that receiveth a prophet in the name of a prophet shall receive a prophet's reward; and he that receiveth a righteous man in the name of a righteous man shall receive a righteous man's reward. And whosoever shall give to drink unto one of these little ones a cup of cold water only in the name of a disciple, verily I say unto you, he shall in no wise lose his reward.

MOTHER—TEACH: 2 Samuel 22:21-22
The LORD rewarded me according to my righteousness: according to the cleanness of my hands hath he recompensed me. For I have kept the ways of the LORD, and have not wickedly departed from my God.

SON(S)—LISTEN: Romans 11:33-36
O the depth of the riches both of the wisdom and knowledge of God! how unsearchable are his judgments, and his ways past finding out! For who hath known the mind of the Lord? or who hath been his counsellor? Or who hath first given to him, and it shall be recompensed unto him again? For of him, and through him, and to him, are all things: to whom be glory for ever.

DAUGHTER(S)—RESPOND: Philippians 4:19-20
But my God shall supply all your need according to his riches in glory by Christ Jesus. Now unto God and our Father be glory for ever and ever.

(The Word of God prepared the disciples, righteous men, and prophets. Now pray that He prepares you for His purpose.)

WORSHIP AND PRAISE

FATHER—INSTRUCT: Psalm 40:4-5
Blessed is that man that maketh the LORD his trust, and respecteth not the proud, nor such as turn aside to lies. Many, O LORD my God, are thy wonderful works which thou hast done, and thy thoughts which are to us-ward: they cannot be reckoned up in order unto thee: if I would declare and speak of them, they are more than can be numbered.

MOTHER—TEACH: Psalm 104:24, 30
O LORD, how manifold are thy works! in wisdom hast thou made them all: the earth is full of thy riches. Thou sendest forth thy spirit, they are created: and thou renewest the face of the earth.

SON(S)—LISTEN: Colossians 1:16-17
For by him were all things created, that are in heaven, and that are in earth, visible and invisible, whether they be thrones, or dominions, or principalities, or powers: all things were created by him, and for him: And he is before all things, and by him all things consist.

DAUGHTER(S)—RESPOND: Colossians 1:18-19
And he is the head of the body, the church: who is the beginning, the firstborn from the dead; that in all things he might have the preeminence. For it pleased the Father that in him should all fulness dwell.

(Now worship and praise the Father for Jesus, the firstborn from the dead.)

PRAYER OF CONFESSION

FATHER—INSTRUCT: Romans 6:15-16
What then? shall we sin, because we are not under the law, but under grace? God forbid. Know ye not, that to whom ye yield yourselves servants to obey, his servants ye are to whom ye obey; whether of sin unto death, or of obedience unto righteousness?

MOTHER—TEACH: Psalm 119: 65-67
Thou hast dealt well with thy servant, O LORD, according unto thy word. Teach me good judgment and knowledge: for I have believed thy commandments. Before I was afflicted I went astray: but now have I kept thy word.

SON(S)—LISTEN: Jeremiah 10:23-24
O LORD, I know that the way of man is not in himself: it is not in man that walketh to direct his steps. O LORD, correct me, but with judgment; not in thine anger, lest thou bring me to nothing.

DAUGHTER(S)—RESPOND: Psalm 39:12-13
Hear my prayer, O LORD, and give ear unto my cry; hold not thy peace at my tears: for I am a stranger with thee, and a sojourner, as all my fathers were. O spare me, that I may recover strength, before I go hence, and be no more.

(Now allow the Lord to show you any errors to confess and trust Him for forgiveness as you forgive others.)

PRAYER OF GRATITUDE

FATHER—INSTRUCT: Isaiah 25:8-9
He will swallow up death in victory; and the Lord GOD will wipe away tears from off all faces; and the rebuke of his people shall he take away from off all the earth: for the LORD hath spoken it. And it shall be said in that day, Lo, this is our God; we have waited for him, and he will save us: this is the LORD; we have waited for him, we will be glad and rejoice in his salvation.

MOTHER—TEACH: Romans 8:10-11
And if Christ be in you, the body is dead because of sin; but the Spirit is life because of righteousness. But if the Spirit of him that raised up Jesus from the dead dwell in you, he that raised up Christ from the dead shall also quicken your mortal bodies by his Spirit that dwelleth in you.

SON(S)—LISTEN: 2 Corinthians 2:14-15
Now thanks be unto God, which always causeth us to triumph in Christ, and maketh manifest the savour of his knowledge by us in every place. For we are unto God a sweet savour of Christ, in them that are saved, and in them that perish.

DAUGHTER(S)—RESPOND: Ruth 2:12-13
The LORD recompense thy work, and a full reward be given thee of the LORD God of Israel, under whose wings thou art come to trust. Then she said, Let me find favour in thy sight, my lord; for that thou hast comforted me, and for that thou hast spoken friendly unto thine handmaid, though I be not like unto one of thine handmaidens.

(Because Christ is in you, express your gratitude to God.)

WISDOM AND UNDERSTANDING

FATHER—INSTRUCT: 1 Timothy 6:5-7
Perverse disputings of men of corrupt minds, and destitute of the truth, supposing that gain is godliness: from such withdraw thyself. But godliness with contentment is great gain. For we brought nothing into this world, and it is certain we can carry nothing out.

MOTHER—TEACH: Colossians 1:9-10
For this cause we also, since the day we heard it, do not cease to pray for you, and to desire that ye might be filled with the knowledge of his will in all wisdom and spiritual understanding; That ye might walk worthy of the Lord unto all pleasing, being fruitful in every good work, and increasing in the knowledge of God.

SON(S)—LISTEN: Proverbs 11:17-18
The merciful man doeth good to his own soul: but he that is cruel troubleth his own flesh. The wicked worketh a deceitful work: but to him that soweth righteousness shall be a sure reward.

DAUGHTER(S)—RESPOND: Proverbs 25:21-22
If thine enemy be hungry, give him bread to eat; and if he be thirsty, give him water to drink: For thou shalt heap coals of fire upon his head, and the LORD shall reward thee.

(Praise God for contentment, and pray that His knowledge become your wisdom.)

PRAYER OF SERENITY

FATHER—INSTRUCT: 2 Corinthians 6:17-18
Wherefore come out from among them, and be ye separate, saith the Lord, and touch not the unclean thing; and I will receive you, And will be a Father unto you, and ye shall be my sons and daughters, saith the Lord Almighty.

MOTHER—TEACH: 1 Peter 3:14-15
But and if ye suffer for righteousness' sake, happy are ye: and be not afraid of their terror, neither be troubled; But sanctify the Lord God in your hearts: and be ready always to give an answer to every man that asketh you a reason of the hope that is in you with meekness and fear.

SON(S)—LISTEN: Romans 13:7-8
Render therefore to all their dues: tribute to whom tribute is due; custom to whom custom; fear to whom fear; honour to whom honour. Owe no man any thing, but to love one another: for he that loveth another hath fulfilled the law.

DAUGHTER(S)—RESPOND: Micah 4:12-13
But they know not the thoughts of the LORD, neither understand they his counsel: for he shall gather them as the sheaves into the floor. Arise and thresh, O daughter of Zion: for I will make thine horn iron, and I will make thy hoofs brass: and thou shalt beat in pieces many people: and I will consecrate their gain unto the LORD, and their substance unto the Lord of the whole earth.

(A broken and sincere heart God will not despise. Now pray for His will to be accomplished in your life.)

PRAYER OF INTERCESSION

FATHER—INSTRUCT: Psalm 40:15-16
Let them be desolate for a reward of their shame that say unto me, Aha, aha. Let all those that seek thee rejoice and be glad in thee: let such as love thy salvation say continually, The LORD be magnified.

MOTHER—TEACH: Psalm 31:23-24
O love the LORD, all ye his saints: for the LORD preserveth the faithful, and plentifully rewardeth the proud doer. Be of good courage, and he shall strengthen your heart, all ye that hope in the LORD.

SON(S)—LISTEN: Matthew 11:28-30
Come unto me, all ye that labour and are heavy laden, and I will give you rest. Take my yoke upon you, and learn of me; for I am meek and lowly in heart: and ye shall find rest unto your souls. For my yoke is easy, and my burden is light.

DAUGHTER(S)—RESPOND: Psalm 30:10-12
Hear, O LORD, and have mercy upon me: LORD, be thou my helper. Thou hast turned for me my mourning into dancing: thou hast put off my sackcloth, and girded me with gladness; To the end that my glory may sing praise to thee, and not be silent. O LORD my God, I will give thanks unto thee for ever.

(Now intercede for family, friends, church leaders, the President, government leaders, and your enemies.)

PRAYER FOR PERSONAL REQUEST

FATHER—INSTRUCT: 1 Peter 3:8-11
Finally, be ye all of one mind, having compassion one of another, love as brethren, be pitiful, be courteous: Not rendering evil for evil, or railing for railing: but contrariwise blessing; knowing that ye are thereunto called, that ye should inherit a blessing. For he that will love life, and see good days, let him refrain his tongue from evil, and his lips that they speak no guile: Let him eschew evil, and do good; let him seek peace, and ensue it.

MOTHER—TEACH: Colossians 1:3-5
We give thanks to God and the Father of our Lord Jesus Christ, praying always for you, Since we heard of your faith in Christ Jesus, and of the love which ye have to all the saints, For the hope which is laid up for you in heaven, whereof ye heard before in the word of the truth of the gospel.

SON(S)—LISTEN: Psalm 19:9-11
The fear of the LORD is clean, enduring for ever: the judgments of the LORD are true and righteous altogether. More to be desired are they than gold, yea, than much fine gold: sweeter also than honey and the honeycomb. Moreover by them is thy servant warned: and in keeping of them there is great reward.

DAUGHTER(S)—RESPOND: Psalm 40:7-10
Then said I, Lo, I come: in the volume of the book it is written of me, I delight to do thy will, O my God: yea, thy law is within my heart. I have preached righteousness in the great congregation: lo, I have not refrained my lips, O LORD, thou knowest. I have not hid thy righteousness within my heart; I have declared thy faithfulness and thy salvation: I have not concealed thy lovingkindness and thy truth from the great congregation.

(Trust all your decisions to the Lord today and rely totally on His answers.)

PRAYER OF GUIDANCE

FATHER—INSTRUCT: Psalm 18:20-22
The LORD rewarded me according to my righteousness; according to the cleanness of my hands hath he recompensed me. For I have kept the ways of the LORD, and have not wickedly departed from my God. For all his judgments were before me, and I did not put away his statutes from me.

MOTHER—TEACH: Psalm 127:1-2
Except the LORD build the house, they labour in vain that build it: except the LORD keep the city, the watchman waketh but in vain. It is vain for you to rise up early, to sit up late, to eat the bread of sorrows: for so he giveth his beloved sleep.

SON(S)—LISTEN: Matthew 5:11-12
Blessed are ye, when men shall revile you, and persecute you, and shall say all manner of evil against you falsely, for my sake. Rejoice, and be exceeding glad: for great is your reward in heaven: for so persecuted they the prophets which were before you.

DAUGHTER(S)—RESPOND: Ecclesiastes 4:9-10
Two are better than one; because they have a good reward for their labour. For if they fall, the one will lift up his fellow: but woe to him that is alone when he falleth; for he hath not another to help him up.

(Pray now that the guidance of the Lord leads you to His rewards.)

DEDICATION AND CONSECRATION

FATHER—INSTRUCT: <u>1 Timothy</u> 4:13-16
Till I come, give attendance to reading, to exhortation, to doctrine. Neglect not the gift that is in thee, which was given thee by prophecy, with the laying on of the hands of the presbytery. Meditate upon these things; give thyself wholly to them; that thy profiting may appear to all. Take heed unto thyself, and unto the doctrine; continue in them: for in doing this thou shalt both save thyself, and them that hear thee.

MOTHER—TEACH: <u>Hebrews</u> 10:35-38
Cast not away therefore your confidence, which hath great recompence of reward. For ye have need of patience, that, after ye have done the will of God, ye might receive the promise. For yet a little while, and he that shall come will come, and will not tarry. Now the just shall live by faith: but if any man draw back, my soul shall have no pleasure in him.

SON(S)—LISTEN: <u>2 John</u> 7-10
For many deceivers are entered into the world, who confess not that Jesus Christ is come in the flesh. This is a deceiver and an antichrist. Look to yourselves, that we lose not those things which we have wrought, but that we receive a full reward. Whosoever transgresseth, and abideth not in the doctrine of Christ, hath not God. He that abideth in the doctrine of Christ, he hath both the Father and the Son. If there come any unto you, and bring not this doctrine, receive him not into your house, neither bid him God speed.

DAUGHTER (S)—RESPOND: <u>Revelation</u> 22:11-13
He that is unjust, let him be unjust still: and he which is filthy, let him be filthy still: and he that is righteous, let him be righteous still: and he that is holy, let him be holy still. And, behold, I come quickly; and my reward is with me, to give every man according as his work shall be. I am Alpha and Omega, the beginning and the end, the first and the last.

(Now consecrate your life anew today and live victoriously.)

DAY 11
PRAYER OF PREPAREDNESS

FATHER—INSTRUCT: John 1:3-5
All things were made by him; and without him was not any thing made that was made. In him was life; and the life was the light of men. And the light shineth in darkness; and the darkness comprehended it not.

MOTHER—TEACH: Ephesians 5:13-15
But all things that are reproved are made manifest by the light: for whatsoever doth make manifest is light. Wherefore he saith, Awake thou that sleepest, and arise from the dead, and Christ shall give thee light. See then that ye walk circumspectly, not as fools, but as wise.

SON(S)—LISTEN: Psalm 36:9-11
For with thee is the fountain of life: in thy light shall we see light. O continue thy lovingkindness unto them that know thee; and thy righteousness to the upright in heart. Let not the foot of pride come against me, and let not the hand of the wicked remove me.

DAUGHTER(S)—RESPOND: Psalm 43:3-4
O send out thy light and thy truth: let them lead me; let them bring me unto thy holy hill, and to thy tabernacles. Then will I go unto the altar of God, unto God my exceeding joy: yea, upon the harp will I praise thee, O God my God.

(The Light of the world shines to prepare us for the dark paths ahead. Jesus is the Light. Now praise God for Light.)

WORSHIP AND PRAISE

FATHER—INSTRUCT: Psalm 104:1-2, 27
Bless the LORD, O my soul. O LORD my God, thou art very great; thou art clothed with honour and majesty. Who coverest thyself with light as with a garment: who stretchest out the heavens like a curtain: These wait all upon thee; that thou mayest give them their meat in due season.

MOTHER—TEACH: Psalm 45:2-4
Thou art fairer than the children of men: grace is poured into thy lips: therefore God hath blessed thee for ever. Gird thy sword upon thy thigh, O most mighty, with thy glory and thy majesty. And in thy majesty ride prosperously because of truth and meekness and righteousness; and thy right hand shall teach thee terrible things.

SON(S)—LISTEN: Psalm 118:27-29
God is the LORD, which hath shown us light: bind the sacrifice with cords, even unto the horns of the altar. Thou art my God, and I will praise thee: thou art my God, I will exalt thee. O give thanks unto the LORD; for he is good: for his mercy endureth for ever.

DAUGHTER(S)—RESPOND: Isaiah 42:12-13
Let them give glory unto the LORD, and declare his praise in the islands. The LORD shall go forth as a mighty man, he shall stir up jealousy like a man of war: he shall cry, yea, roar; he shall prevail against his enemies.

(Now continue to worship the Father for His true Light.)

PRAYER OF CONFESSION

FATHER—INSTRUCT: Titus 2:11-13
For the grace of God that bringeth salvation hath appeared to all men, Teaching us that, denying ungodliness and worldly lusts, we should live soberly, righteously, and godly, in this present world; Looking for that blessed hope, and the glorious appearing of the great God and our Saviour Jesus Christ.

MOTHER—TEACH: Romans 8:5-8
For they that are after the flesh do mind the things of the flesh; but they that are after the Spirit the things of the Spirit. For to be carnally minded is death; but to be spiritually minded is life and peace. Because the carnal mind is enmity against God: for it is not subject to the law of God, neither indeed can be. So then they that are in the flesh cannot please God.

SON(S)—LISTEN: Ezekiel 33:11-12
Say unto them, As I live, saith the Lord GOD, I have no pleasure in the death of the wicked; but that the wicked turn from his way and live: turn ye, turn ye from your evil ways; for why will ye die, O house of Israel? Therefore, thou son of man, say unto the children of thy people, The righteousness of the righteous shall not deliver him in the day of his transgression: as for the wickedness of the wicked, he shall not fall thereby in the day that he turneth from his wickedness; neither shall the righteous be able to live for his righteousness in the day that he sinneth.

DAUGHTER(S)—RESPOND: Psalm 38:21-22
Forsake me not, O LORD: O my God, be not far from me. Make haste to help me, O Lord my salvation.

(Disobedience is failure "to hear perfectly." Now confess any disobedience in your life. Then thank Him for forgiveness.)

PRAYER OF GRATITUDE

FATHER—INSTRUCT: 1 John 4:7-10
Beloved, let us love one another: for love is of God; and every one that loveth is born of God, and knoweth God. He that loveth not knoweth not God; for God is love. In this was manifested the love of God toward us, because that God sent his only begotten Son into the world, that we might live through him. Herein is love, not that we loved God, but that he loved us, and sent his Son to be the propitiation for our sins.

MOTHER—TEACH: 2 Corinthians 4:14-16
Knowing that he which raised up the Lord Jesus shall raise up us also by Jesus, and shall present us with you. For all things are for your sakes, that the abundant grace might through the thanksgiving of many redound to the glory of God. For which cause we faint not; but though our outward man perish, yet the inward man is renewed day by day.

SON(S)—LISTEN: Psalm 136:7-9
To him that made great lights: for his mercy endureth for ever: The sun to rule by day: for his mercy endureth for ever: The moon and stars to rule by night: for his mercy endureth for ever.

DAUGHTER(S)—RESPOND: 2 Corinthians 9:10-12
Now he that ministereth seed to the sower both minister bread for your food, and multiply your seed sown, and increase the fruits of your righteousness;) Being enriched in every thing to all bountifulness, which causeth through us thanksgiving to God. For the administration of this service not only supplieth the want of the saints, but is abundant also by many thanksgivings unto God.

(Love suffers long. Now ask the Lord to renew and teach you how to be longsuffering in love for others.)

WISDOM AND UNDERSTANDING

FATHER—INSTRUCT: 1 Thessalonians 5:4-6
But ye, brethren, are not in darkness, that that day should overtake you as a thief. Ye are all the children of light, and the children of the day: we are not of the night, nor of darkness. Therefore let us not sleep, as do others; but let us watch and be sober.

MOTHER—TEACH: 2 Corinthians 4:3-5
But if our gospel be hid, it is hid to them that are lost: In whom the god of this world hath blinded the minds of them which believe not, lest the light of the glorious gospel of Christ, who is the image of God, should shine unto them. For we preach not ourselves, but Christ Jesus the Lord; and ourselves your servants for Jesus' sake.

SON(S)—LISTEN: Psalm 119:8-11
I will keep thy statutes: O forsake me not utterly. Wherewithal shall a young man cleanse his way? by taking heed thereto according to thy word. With my whole heart have I sought thee: O let me not wander from thy commandments. Thy word have I hid in mine heart, that I might not sin against thee.

DAUGHTER(S)—RESPOND: Proverbs 4:18-21
But the path of the just is as the shining light, that shineth more and more unto the perfect day. The way of the wicked is as darkness: they know not at what they stumble. My son, attend to my words; incline thine ear unto my sayings. Let them not depart from thine eyes; keep them in the midst of thine heart.

(Now pray that the Lord's words in wisdom become your shining light.)

PRAYER OF SERENITY

FATHER—INSTRUCT: <u>1 Timothy</u> 6:13-16
I give thee charge in the sight of God, who quickeneth all things, and before Christ Jesus, who before Pontius Pilate witnessed a good confession; That thou keep this commandment without spot, unrebukeable, until the appearing of our Lord Jesus Christ: Which in his times he shall show, who is the blessed and only Potentate, the King of kings, and Lord of lords; Who only hath immortality, dwelling in the light which no man can approach unto; whom no man hath seen, nor can see: to whom be honour and power everlasting.

MOTHER—TEACH: <u>John</u> 8:12, 32
Then spake Jesus again unto them, saying, I am the light of the world: he that followeth me shall not walk in darkness, but shall have the light of life. And ye shall know the truth, and the truth shall make you free.

SON(S)—LISTEN: <u>Luke</u> 8:15-16
But that on the good ground are they, which in an honest and good heart, having heard the word, keep it, and bring forth fruit with patience. No man, when he hath lighted a candle, covereth it with a vessel, or putteth it under a bed; but setteth it on a candlestick, that they which enter in may see the light.

DAUGHTER(S)—RESPOND: <u>Matthew</u> 12:36-37
But I say unto you, That every idle word that men shall speak, they shall give account thereof in the day of judgment. For by thy words thou shalt be justified, and by thy words thou shalt be condemned.

(As an heir of God and a joint heir with Christ, you do not walk in darkness. Praise God.)

PRAYER OF INTERCESSION

FATHER—INSTRUCT: Psalm 40:10-11
I have not hid thy righteousness within my heart; I have declared thy faithfulness and thy salvation: I have not concealed thy lovingkindness and thy truth from the great congregation. Withhold not thou thy tender mercies from me, O LORD: let thy lovingkindness and thy truth continually preserve me.

MOTHER—TEACH: Psalm 38:9-10
Lord, all my desire is before thee; and my groaning is not hid from thee. My heart panteth, my strength faileth me: as for the light of mine eyes, it also is gone from me.

SON(S)—LISTEN: Isaiah 42:5-8
Thus saith God the LORD, he that created the heavens, and stretched them out; he that spread forth the earth, and that which cometh out of it; he that giveth breath unto the people upon it, and spirit to them that walk therein: I the LORD have called thee in righteousness, and will hold thine hand, and will keep thee, and give thee for a covenant of the people, for a light of the Gentiles; To open the blind eyes, to bring out the prisoners from the prison, and them that sit in darkness out of the prison house. I am the LORD: that is my name: and my glory will I not give to another, neither my praise to graven images.

DAUGHTER(S)—RESPOND: Matthew 5:14-16
Ye are the light of the world. A city that is set on an hill cannot be hid. Neither do men light a candle, and put it under a bushel, but on a candlestick; and it giveth light unto all that are in the house. Let your light so shine before men, that they may see your good works, and glorify your Father which is in heaven.

(Now intercede for those in authority and who carry heavy responsibilities. The entire family should pray for each other.)

PRAYER OF PERSONAL REQUEST

FATHER—INSTRUCT: John 19:28-30
After this, Jesus knowing that all things were now accomplished, that the scripture might be fulfilled, saith, I thirst. Now there was set a vessel full of vinegar: and they filled a spunge with vinegar, and put it upon hyssop, and put it to his mouth. When Jesus therefore had received the vinegar, he said, It is finished: and he bowed his head, and gave up the ghost.

MOTHER—TEACH: 1 John 5:6-8
This is he that came by water and blood, even Jesus Christ; not by water only, but by water and blood. And it is the Spirit that beareth witness, because the Spirit is truth. For there are three that bear record in heaven, the Father, the Word, and the Holy Ghost: and these three are one. And there are three that bear witness in earth, the spirit, and the water, and the blood: and these three agree in one.

SON(S)—LISTEN: Acts 9:3-6
And as he journeyed, he came near Damascus: and suddenly there shined round about him a light from heaven: And he fell to the earth, and heard a voice saying unto him, Saul, Saul, why persecutest thou me? And he said, Who art thou, Lord? And the Lord said, I am Jesus whom thou persecutest: it is hard for thee to kick against the pricks. And he trembling and astonished said, Lord, what wilt thou have me to do? And the Lord said unto him, Arise, and go into the city, and it shall be told thee what thou must do.

DAUGHTER(S)—RESPOND: Acts 9:11, 16-17
And the Lord said unto him, Arise, and go into the street which is called Straight, and enquire in the house of Judas for one called Saul, of Tarsus: for, behold, he prayeth, For I will show him how great things he must suffer for my name's sake. And Ananias went his way, and entered into the house; and putting his hands on him said, Brother Saul, the Lord, even Jesus, that appeared unto thee in the way as thou camest, hath sent me, that thou mightest receive thy sight, and be filled with the Holy Ghost.

(Now ask the Lord to help you finish the work that you began for His glory.)

PRAYER OF GUIDANCE

FATHER—INSTRUCT: Isaiah 42:16-17
And I will bring the blind by a way that they knew not; I will lead them in paths that they have not known: I will make darkness light before them, and crooked things straight. These things will I do unto them, and not forsake them. They shall be turned back, they shall be greatly ashamed, that trust in graven images, that say to the molten images, Ye are our gods.

MOTHER—TEACH: Psalm 119:4-6
Thou hast commanded us to keep thy precepts diligently. O that my ways were directed to keep thy statutes! Then shall I not be ashamed, when I have respect unto all thy commandments.

SON(S)—LISTEN: Psalm 119:129-130
Thy testimonies are wonderful: therefore doth my soul keep them. The entrance of thy words giveth light; it giveth understanding unto the simple.

DAUGHTER(S)—RESPOND: John 12:35-38
Then Jesus said unto them, Yet a little while is the light with you. Walk while ye have the light, lest darkness come upon you: for he that walketh in darkness knoweth not whither he goeth. While ye have light, believe in the light, that ye may be the children of light. These things spake Jesus, and departed, and did hide himself from them. But though he had done so many miracles before them, yet they believed not on him: That the saying of Esaias the prophet might be fulfilled, which he spake, Lord, who hath believed our report? and to whom hath the arm of the Lord been revealed?

(The Lord's steps are our pathway. Pray for His guidance today.)

DEDICATION AND CONSECRATION

FATHER—INSTRUCT: I Timothy 6:17-19
Charge them that are rich in this world, that they be not highminded, nor trust in uncertain riches, but in the living God, who giveth us richly all things to enjoy; That they do good, that they be rich in good works, ready to distribute, willing to communicate; Laying up in store for themselves a good foundation against the time to come, that they may lay hold on eternal life.

MOTHER—TEACH: Revelation 21:22-24
And I saw no temple therein: for the Lord God Almighty and the Lamb are the temple of it. And the city had no need of the sun, neither of the moon, to shine in it: for the glory of God did lighten it, and the Lamb is the light thereof. And the nations of them which are saved shall walk in the light of it: and the kings of the earth do bring their glory and honour into it.

SON(S)—LISTEN: Revelation 22:5-6
And there shall be no night there; and they need no candle, neither light of the sun; for the Lord God giveth them light: and they shall reign for ever and ever. And he said unto me, These sayings are faithful and true: and the Lord God of the holy prophets sent his angel to show unto his servants the things which must shortly be done.

DAUGHTER(S)—RESPOND: Revelation 22:16-17
I Jesus have sent mine angel to testify unto you these things in the churches. I am the root and the offspring of David, and the bright and morning star. And the Spirit and the bride say, Come. And let him that heareth say, Come. And let him that is athirst come. And whosoever will, let him take the water of life freely.

(Our strength and manifested attributes of God overcome our weaknesses. Then, we have the Light of lights. Now commit this day to Jesus our Savior.)

DAY 12
PRAYER OF PREPAREDNESS

FATHER—INSTRUCT: Romans 5:8-11
But God commendeth his love toward us, in that, while we were yet sinners, Christ died for us. Much more then, being now justified by his blood, we shall be saved from wrath through him. For if, when we were enemies, we were reconciled to God by the death of his Son, much more, being reconciled, we shall be saved by his life. And not only so, but we also joy in God through our Lord Jesus Christ, by whom we have now received the atonement.

MOTHER—TEACH: 1 Peter 1:8-10
Whom having not seen, ye love; in whom, though now ye see him not, yet believing, ye rejoice with joy unspeakable and full of glory: Receiving the end of your faith, even the salvation of your souls. Of which salvation the prophets have enquired and searched diligently, who prophesied of the grace that should come unto you.

SON(S)—LISTEN: 1 Thessalonians 1:5-6
For our gospel came not unto you in word only, but also in power, and in the Holy Ghost, and in much assurance; as ye know what manner of men we were among you for your sake. And ye became followers of us, and of the Lord, having received the word in much affliction, with joy of the Holy Ghost.

DAUGHTER(S)—RESPOND: Hebrews 12:1-2
Wherefore seeing we also are compassed about with so great a cloud of witnesses, let us lay aside every weight, and the sin which doth so easily beset us, and let us run with patience the race that is set before us, Looking unto Jesus the author and finisher of our faith; who for the joy that was set before him endured the cross, despising the shame, and is set down at the right hand of the throne of God.

(Love prompted the activity when God prepared His Son to die for our sins. Now exalt the Prince of peace.)

WORSHIP AND PRAISE

FATHER—INSTRUCT: Psalm 98:4-6
Make a joyful noise unto the LORD, all the earth: make a loud noise, and rejoice, and sing praise. Sing unto the LORD with the harp; with the harp, and the voice of a psalm. With trumpets and sound of cornet make a joyful noise before the LORD, the King.

MOTHER—TEACH: Luke 19:36-38
And as he went, they spread their clothes in the way. And when he was come nigh, even now at the descent of the mount of Olives, the whole multitude of the disciples began to rejoice and praise God with a loud voice for all the mighty works that they had seen; Saying, Blessed be the King that cometh in the name of the Lord: peace in heaven, and glory in the highest.

SON(S)—LISTEN: Psalm 100:4-5
Enter into his gates with thanksgiving, and into his courts with praise: be thankful unto him, and bless his name. For the LORD is good; his mercy is everlasting; and his truth endureth to all generations.

DAUGHTER(S)—RESPOND: Acts 8:6-8
And the people with one accord gave heed unto those things which Philip spake, hearing and seeing the miracles which he did. For unclean spirits, crying with loud voice, came out of many that were possessed with them: and many taken with palsies, and that were lame, were healed. And there was great joy in that city.

(Now with a joyful noise rejoice in the glory of the Father.)

PRAYER OF CONFESSION

FATHER—INSTRUCT: 2 Peter 3:8-9
But, beloved, be not ignorant of this one thing, that one day is with the Lord as a thousand years, and a thousand years as one day. The Lord is not slack concerning his promise, as some men count slackness; but is longsuffering to us-ward, not willing that any should perish, but that all should come to repentance.

MOTHER—TEACH: 1 Peter 3:12-14
For the eyes of the Lord are over the righteous, and his ears are open unto their prayers: but the face of the Lord is against them that do evil. And who is he that will harm you, if ye be followers of that which is good? But and if ye suffer for righteousness' sake, happy are ye: and be not afraid of their terror, neither be troubled.

SON(S)—LISTEN: 2 Corinthians 7:10-11
For godly sorrow worketh repentance to salvation not to be repented of: but the sorrow of the world worketh death. For behold this selfsame thing, that ye sorrowed after a godly sort, what carefulness it wrought in you, yea, what clearing of yourselves, yea, what indignation, yea, what fear, yea, what vehement desire, yea, what zeal, yea, what revenge! In all things ye have approved yourselves to be clear in this matter.

DAUGHTER(S)—RESPOND: Titus 1:15-16
Unto the pure all things are pure: but unto them that are defiled and unbelieving is nothing pure; but even their mind and conscience is defiled. They profess that they know God; but in works they deny him, being abominable, and disobedient, and unto every good work reprobate.

(The sin of unbelief is the most deadly. Now confess any doubts or fears that grip you today.)

PRAYER OF GRATITUDE

FATHER—INSTRUCT: Hebrews 3:17-18
But with whom was he grieved forty years? was it not with them that had sinned, whose carcases fell in the wilderness? And to whom sware he that they should not enter into his rest, but to them that believed not?

MOTHER—TEACH: Isaiah 51:11-13
Therefore the redeemed of the LORD shall return, and come with singing unto Zion; and everlasting joy shall be upon their head: they shall obtain gladness and joy; and sorrow and mourning shall flee away. I, even I, am he that comforteth you: who art thou, that thou shouldest be afraid of a man that shall die, and of the son of man which shall be made as grass; And forgettest the LORD thy maker, that hath stretched forth the heavens, and laid the foundations of the earth; and hast feared continually every day because of the fury of the oppressor, as if he were ready to destroy? and where is the fury of the oppressor?

SON(S)—LISTEN: Psalm 2:10-12
Be wise now therefore, O ye kings: be instructed, ye judges of the earth. Serve the LORD with fear, and rejoice with trembling. Kiss the Son, lest he be angry, and ye perish from the way, when his wrath is kindled but a little. Blessed are all they that put their trust in him.

DAUGHTER(S)—RESPOND: Psalm 4:7-8
Thou hast put gladness in my heart, more than in the time that their corn and their wine increased. I will both lay me down in peace, and sleep: for thou, LORD, only makest me dwell in safety.

(Begin to thank God for His comfort that comes out of the depths of His love.)

WISDOM AND UNDERSTANDING

FATHER—INSTRUCT: Proverbs 15:20-23
A wise son maketh a glad father: but a foolish man despiseth his mother. Folly is joy to him that is destitute of wisdom: but a man of understanding walketh uprightly. Without counsel purposes are disappointed: but in the multitude of counsellors they are established. A man hath joy by the answer of his mouth: and a word spoken in due season, how good is it!

MOTHER—TEACH: Proverbs 23:24-25
The father of the righteous shall greatly rejoice: and he that begetteth a wise child shall have joy of him. Thy father and thy mother shall be glad, and she that bare thee shall rejoice.

SON(S)—LISTEN: Psalm 35:27-28
Let them shout for joy, and be glad, that favour my righteous cause: year, let them say continually, Let the LORD by magnified, which hath pleasure in the prosperity of his servant. And my tongue shall speak of thy righteousness [and] of thy praise all the day long.

DAUGHTER(S)—RESPOND: Psalm 50:22-23
Now consider this, ye that forget God, lest I tear you in pieces, and there be none to deliver. Whoso offereth praise glorifieth me: and to him that ordereth his conversation aright will I show the salvation of God.

(Spiritual growth occurs when our understanding is made perfect. Now pray that God will help you to order your conversation aright.)

PRAYER OF SERENITY

FATHER—INSTRUCT: Isaiah 45:11-13
Thus saith the LORD, the Holy One of Israel, and his Maker, Ask me of things to come concerning my sons, and concerning the work of my hands command ye me. I have made the earth, and created man upon it: I, even my hands, have stretched out the heavens, and all their host have I commanded. I have raised him up in righteousness, and I will direct all his ways: he shall build my city, and he shall let go my captives, not for price nor reward, saith the LORD of hosts.

MOTHER—TEACH: Luke 11:42-44
But woe unto you, Pharisees! for ye tithe mint and rue and all manner of herbs, and pass over judgment and the love of God: these ought ye to have done, and not to leave the other undone. Woe unto you, Pharisees! for ye love the uppermost seats in the synagogues, and greetings in the markets. Woe unto you, scribes and Pharisees, hypocrites! for ye are as graves which appear not, and the men that walk over them are not aware of them.

SON(S)—LISTEN: John 3:29-31
He that hath the bride is the bridegroom: but the friend of the bridegroom, which standeth and heareth him, rejoiceth greatly because of the bridegroom's voice: this my joy therefore is fulfilled. He must increase, but I must decrease. He that cometh from above is above all: he that is of the earth is earthly, and speaketh of the earth: he that cometh from heaven is above all.

DAUGHTER(S)—RESPOND: Matthew 13:20-21
But he that received the seed into stony places, the same is he that heareth the word, and anon with joy receiveth it; Yet hath he not root in himself, but dureth for a while: for when tribulation or persecution ariseth because of the word, by and by he is offended.

(Now pray that the Lord will raise you up in righteousness and that He will direct all your ways.)

PRAYER OF INTERCESSION

FATHER—INSTRUCT: Isaiah 53:10-12
Yet it pleased the LORD to bruise him; he hath put him to grief: when thou shalt make his soul an offering for sin, he shall see his seed, he shall prolong his days, and the pleasure of the LORD shall prosper in his hand. He shall see of the travail of his soul, and shall be satisfied: by his knowledge shall my righteous servant justify many; for he shall bear their iniquities. Therefore will I divide him a portion with the great, and he shall divide the spoil with the strong; because he hath poured out his soul unto death: and he was numbered with the transgressors; and he bare the sin of many, and made intercession for the transgressors.

MOTHER—TEACH: Romans 8:24-26
For we are saved by hope: but hope that is seen is not hope: for what a man seeth, why doth he yet hope for? But if we hope for that we see not, then do we with patience wait for it. Likewise the Spirit also helpeth our infirmities: for we know not what we should pray for as we ought: but the Spirit itself maketh intercession for us with groanings which cannot be uttered.

SON(S)—LISTEN: Romans 8:27-28
And he that searcheth the hearts knoweth what is the mind of the Spirit, because he maketh intercession for the saints according to the will of God. And we know that all things work together for good to them that love God, to them who are the called according to his purpose.

DAUGHTER(S)—RESPOND: Matthew 6:28-30
And why take ye thought for raiment? Consider the lilies of the field, how they grow; they toil not, neither do they spin: Wherefore, if God so clothe the grass of the field, which to day is, and to morrow is cast into the oven, shall he not much more clothe you, O ye of little faith?

(Now intercede for those facing crisis and emotional turmoil associated with a lack of trust in the living God.)

PRAYER OF PERSONAL REQUEST

FATHER—INSTRUCT: Matthew 14:16-19
But Jesus said unto them, They need not depart; give ye them to eat. And they say unto him, We have here but five loaves, and two fishes. He said, Bring them hither to me. And he commanded the multitude to sit down on the grass, and took the five loaves, and the two fishes, and looking up to heaven, he blessed, and brake, and gave the loaves to his disciples, and the disciples to the multitude.

MOTHER—TEACH: Psalm 28:6-9
Blessed be the LORD, because he hath heard the voice of my supplications. The LORD is my strength and my shield; my heart trusted in him, and I am helped: therefore my heart greatly rejoiceth; and with my song will I praise him. The LORD is their strength, and he is the saving strength of his anointed. Save thy people, and bless thine inheritance: feed them also, and lift them up for ever.

SON(S)—LISTEN: Psalm 30:7-8
LORD, by thy favour thou hast made my mountain to stand strong: thou didst hide thy face, and I was troubled. I cried to thee, O LORD; and unto the LORD I made supplication.

DAUGHTER(S)—RESPOND: Psalm 31:21-22
Blessed be the LORD: for he hath shown me his marvellous kindness in a strong city. For I said in my haste, I am cut off from before thine eyes: nevertheless thou heardest the voice of my supplications when I cried unto thee.

(In prayer for your personal needs today, remember that it is God's desire to feed you with His knowledge from on high.)

PRAYER OF GUIDANCE

FATHER—INSTRUCT: Matthew 13:11-13
He answered and said unto them, Because it is given unto you to know the mysteries of the kingdom of heaven, but to them it is not given. For whosoever hath, to him shall be given, and he shall have more abundance: but whosoever hath not, from him shall be taken away even that he hath. Therefore speak I to them in parables: because they seeing see not; and hearing they hear not, neither do they understand.

MOTHER—TEACH: Psalm 78:65, 72
Then the Lord awaked as one out of sleep, [and] like a mighty man that shouteth by reason of wine. So he fed them according to the integrity of his heart; and guided them by the skilfulness of his hands.

SON(S)—LISTEN: John 16:13-14
Howbeit when he, the Spirit of truth, is come, he will guide you into all truth: for he shall not speak of himself; but whatsoever he shall hear, that shall he speak: and he will show you things to come. He shall glorify me: for he shall receive of mine, and shall show it unto you.

DAUGHTER(S)—RESPOND: Psalm 25:9-10
The meek will he guide in judgment: and the meek will he teach his way. All the paths of the LORD are mercy and truth unto such as keep his covenant and his testimonies.

(Now allow the Word of God to permeate your mind and spirit; seeking only a perfect knowledge of God's way, pray for guidance.)

DEDICATION AND CONSECRATION

FATHER—INSTRUCT: Psalm 31:7-8
I will be glad and rejoice in thy mercy: for thou hast considered my trouble; thou hast known my soul in adversities; And hast not shut me up into the hand of the enemy: thou hast set my feet in a large room.

MOTHER—TEACH: 1 Thessalonians 3:7-9
Therefore, brethren, we were comforted over you in all our affliction and distress by your faith: For now we live, if ye stand fast in the Lord. For what thanks can we render to God again for you, for all the joy wherewith we joy for your sakes before our God.

SON(S)—LISTEN: Philippians 4:10-11
But I rejoiced in the Lord greatly, that now at the last your care of me hath flourished again; wherein ye were also careful, but ye lacked opportunity. Not that I speak in respect of want: for I have learned, in whatsoever state I am, therewith to be content.

DAUGHTER(S)—RESPOND: Ephesians 4:7-8
But unto every one of us is given grace according to the measure of the gift of Christ. Wherefore he saith, When he ascended up on high, he led captivity captive, and gave gifts unto men.

(Our dedication to the Word allows us to be entrenched from within; therein lies our contentment. Now God's blessing will overtake you today.)

DAY 13
PRAYER OF PREPAREDNESS

FATHER—INSTRUCT: Isaiah 52:6-8
Therefore my people shall know my name: therefore they shall know in that day that I am he that doth speak: behold, it is I. How beautiful upon the mountains are the feet of him that bringeth good tidings, that publisheth peace; that bringeth good tidings of good, that publisheth salvation; that saith unto Zion, Thy God reigneth! Thy watchmen shall lift up the voice; with the voice together shall they sing: for they shall see eye to eye, when the LORD shall bring again Zion.

MOTHER—TEACH: Psalm 31:23-24
O love the LORD, all ye his saints: for the LORD preserveth the faithful, and plentifully rewardeth the proud doer. Be of good courage, and he shall strengthen your heart, all ye that hope in the LORD.

SON(S)—LISTEN: Mark 9:41-42, 50
For whosoever shall give you a cup of water to drink in my name, because ye belong to Christ, verily I say unto you, he shall not lose his reward. And whosoever shall offend one of these little ones that believe in me, it is better for him that a millstone were hanged about his neck, and he were cast into the sea. Salt is good: but if the salt have lost his saltness, wherewith will ye season it? Have salt in yourselves, and have peace one with another.

DAUGHTER(S)—RESPOND: John 14:27-29
Peace I leave with you, my peace I give unto you: not as the world giveth, give I unto you. Let not your heart be troubled, neither let it be afraid. Ye have heard how I said unto you, I go away, and come again unto you. If ye loved me, ye would rejoice, because I said, I go unto the Father: for my Father is greater than I. And now I have told you before it come to pass, that, when it is come to pass, ye might believe.

(Our function and purpose is to publish God's peace and his salvation. Now pray that He will prepare you to share His promises.)

WORSHIP AND PRAISE

FATHER—INSTRUCT: Luke 1:76-79
And thou, child, shalt be called the prophet of the Highest: for thou shalt go before the face of the Lord to prepare his ways; To give knowledge of salvation unto his people by the remission of their sins, Through the tender mercy of our God; whereby the dayspring from on high hath visited us, To give light to them that sit in darkness and in the shadow of death, to guide our feet into the way of peace.

MOTHER—TEACH: Malachi 2:5-7
My covenant was with him of life and peace; and I gave them to him for the fear wherewith he feared me, and was afraid before my name. The law of truth was in his mouth, and iniquity was not found in his lips: he walked with me in peace and equity, and did turn many away from iniquity. For the priest's lips should keep knowledge, and they should seek the law at his mouth: for he is the messenger of the LORD of hosts.

SON(S)—LISTEN: Psalm 34:1-3
I will bless the LORD at all times: his praise shall continually be in my mouth. My soul shall make her boast in the LORD: the humble shall hear thereof, and be glad. O magnify the LORD with me, and let us exalt his name together.

DAUGHTER(S)—RESPOND: Acts 10:34-36
Then Peter opened his mouth, and said, Of a truth I perceive that God is no respecter of persons: But in every nation he that feareth him, and worketh righteousness, is accepted with him. The word which God sent unto the children of Israel, preaching peace by Jesus Christ: (he is Lord of all.)

(Jesus is our pattern of perfection. Now praise God for His channel as our acceptable expressions toward Him.)

PRAYER OF CONFESSION

FATHER—INSTRUCT: Hebrews 6:4-6
For it is impossible for those who were once enlightened, and have tasted of the heavenly gift, and were made partakers of the Holy Ghost, And have tasted the good word of God, and the powers of the world to come, If they shall fall away, to renew them again unto repentance; seeing they crucify to themselves the Son of God afresh, and put him to an open shame.

MOTHER—TEACH: Acts 28:26-27
Saying, Go unto this people, and say, Hearing ye shall hear, and shall not understand; and seeing ye shall see, and not perceive: For the heart of this people is waxed gross, and their ears are dull of hearing, and their eyes have they closed; lest they should see with their eyes, and hear with their ears, and understand with their heart, and should be converted, and I should heal them.

SON(S)—LISTEN: 2 Peter 2:20-21
For if after they have escaped the pollutions of the world through the knowledge of the Lord and Saviour Jesus Christ, they are again entangled therein, and overcome, the latter end is worse with them than the beginning. For it had been better for them not to have known the way of righteousness, than, after they have known it, to turn from the holy commandment delivered unto them.

DAUGHTER(S)—RESPOND: Colossians 1:3, 13-14
We give thanks to God the Father of our Lord Jesus Christ, praying always for you, Who hath delivered us from the power of darkness, and hath translated us into the kingdom of his dear Son: In whom we have redemption through his blood, even the forgiveness of sins:

(Now confess any destructive influences or hindrances that prevent you from receiving the heavenly gift, the blood of God's Lamb.)

PRAYER OF GRATITUDE

FATHER—INSTRUCT: Matthew 12:18-20
Behold my servant, whom I have chosen; my beloved, in whom my soul is well pleased: I will put my spirit upon him, and he shall show judgment to the Gentiles. He shall not strive, nor cry; neither shall any man hear his voice in the streets. A bruised reed shall he not break, and smoking flax shall he not quench, till he send forth judgment unto victory.

MOTHER—TEACH: Psalm 92:1-2
It is a good thing to give thanks unto the LORD, and to sing praises unto thy name, O most High: To show forth thy lovingkindness in the morning, and thy faithfulness every night.

SON(S)—LISTEN: 1 Peter 5:10, 14
But the God of all grace, who hath called us unto his eternal glory by Christ Jesus, after that ye have suffered a while, make you perfect, stablish, strengthen, settle you. Greet ye one another with a kiss of charity. Peace be with you all that are in Christ Jesus.

DAUGHTER(S)—RESPOND: Psalm 126:3-6
The LORD hath done great things for us; whereof we are glad. Turn again our captivity, O LORD, as the streams in the south. They that sow in tears shall reap in joy. He that goeth forth and weepeth, bearing precious seed, shall doubtless come again with rejoicing, bringing his sheaves with him.

(Now express your gratitude for the little suffering that we endure for the crown of glory.)

WISDOM AND UNDERSTANDING

FATHER—INSTRUCT: Philippians 4:12-13
I know both how to be abased, and I know how to abound: every where and in all things I am instructed both to be full and to be hungry, both to abound and to suffer need. I can do all things through Christ which strengtheneth me.

MOTHER—TEACH: Ephesians 3:11-12
According to the eternal purpose which he purposed in Christ Jesus our Lord: In whom we have boldness and access with confidence by the faith of him.

SON(S)—LISTEN: Ephesians 2:18-20
For through him we both have access by one Spirit unto the Father. Now therefore ye are no more strangers and foreigners, but fellowcitizens with the saints, and of the household of God; And are built upon the foundation of the apostles and prophets, Jesus Christ himself being the chief corner stone.

DAUGHTER(S)—RESPOND: Ephesians 3:5-6, 16
Which in other ages was not made known unto the sons of men, as it is now revealed unto his holy apostles and prophets by the Spirit; That the Gentiles should be fellowheirs, and of the same body, and partakers of his promise in Christ by the gospel: That he would grant you, according to the riches of his glory, to be strengthened with might by his Spirit in the inner man.

(Our wisdom teaches us that God's eternal purpose has a sure foundation, Jesus Christ the chief corner stone. Now pray for this enlightenment.)

PRAYER OF SERENITY

FATHER—INSTRUCT: Matthew 11:4-6
Jesus answered and said unto them, Go and show John again those things which ye do hear and see: The blind receive their sight, and the lame walk, the lepers are cleansed, and the deaf hear, the dead are raised up, and the poor have the gospel preached to them. And blessed is he, whosoever shall not be offended in me.

MOTHER—TEACH: Matthew 10:37-39
He that loveth father or mother more than me is not worthy of me: and he that loveth son or daughter more than me is not worthy of me. And he that taketh not his cross, and followeth after me, is not worthy of me. He that findeth his life shall lose it: and he that loseth his life for my sake shall find it.

SON(S)—LISTEN: Psalm 34:12-14
What man is he that desireth life, and loveth many days, that he may see good? Keep thy tongue from evil, and thy lips from speaking guile. Depart from evil, and do good; seek peace, and pursue it.

DAUGHTER(S)—RESPOND: Hebrew 6:10-12
For God is not unrighteous to forget your work and labour of love, which ye have shown toward his name, in that ye have ministered to the saints, and do minister. And we desire that every one of you do show the same diligence to the full assurance of hope unto the end: That ye be not slothful, but followers of them who through faith and patience inherit the promises.

(Now pray that all your work and labors of love will be done in sincerity and earnest.)

PRAYER OF INTERCESSION

FATHER—INSTRUCT: Colossians 1:19-21
For it pleased the Father that in him should all fulness dwell; And, having made peace through the blood of his cross, by him to reconcile all things unto himself; by him, I say, whether they be things in earth, or things in heaven. And you, that were sometime alienated and enemies in your mind by wicked works, yet now hath he reconciled.

MOTHER—TEACH: Psalm 34:18-19
The LORD is nigh unto them that are of a broken heart; and saveth such as be of a contrite spirit. Many are the afflictions of the righteous: but the LORD delivereth him out of them all.

SON(S)—LISTEN: James 3:16-18
For where envying and strife is, there is confusion and every evil work. But the wisdom that is from above is first pure, then peaceable, gentle, and easy to be intreated, full of mercy and good fruits, without partiality, and without hypocrisy. And the fruit of righteousness is sown in peace of them that make peace.

DAUGHTER(S)—RESPOND: 1 John 4:20-21
If a man say, I love God, and hateth his brother, he is a liar: for he that loveth not his brother whom he hath seen, how can he love God whom he hath not seen? And this commandment have we from him, That he who loveth God love his brother also.

(Now intercede for those who are yet alienated and are enemies in their minds by wicked works.)

PRAYER OF PERSONAL REQUEST

FATHER—INSTRUCT: Zechariah 8:20-22
Thus saith the LORD of hosts; It shall yet come to pass, that there shall come people, and the inhabitants of many cities: And the inhabitants of one city shall go to another, saying, Let us go speedily to pray before the LORD, and to seek the LORD of hosts: I will go also. Yea, many people and strong nations shall come to seek the LORD of hosts in Jerusalem, and to pray before the LORD.

MOTHER—TEACH: Psalm 34:15-17
The eyes of the LORD are upon the righteous, and his ears are open unto their cry. The face of the LORD is against them that do evil, to cut off the remembrance of them from the earth. The righteous cry, and the LORD heareth, and delivereth them out of all their troubles.

SON(S)—LISTEN: James 1:2-4
My brethren, count it all joy when ye fall into divers temptations; knowing this, that the trying of your faith worketh patience. But let patience have her perfect work, that ye may be perfect and entire, wanting nothing.

DAUGHTER(S)—RESPOND: Hebrews 13:20-21
Now the God of peace, that brought again from the dead our Lord Jesus, that great shepherd of the sheep, through the blood of the everlasting covenant, make you perfect in every good work to do his will, working in you that which is wellpleasing in his sight, through Jesus Christ; to whom be glory for ever and ever.

(Now pray that your experience with the Father and His Son produces genuine fellowship in the everlasting covenant.)

PRAYER OF GUIDANCE

FATHER—INSTRUCT: Hebrews 12:14-15
Follow peace with all men, and holiness, without which no man shall see the Lord: Looking diligently lest any man fail of the grace of God; lest any root of bitterness springing up trouble you, and thereby many be defiled.

MOTHER—TEACH: Romans 12:16-18
Be of the same mind one toward another. Mind not high things, but condescend to men of low estate. Be not wise in your own conceits. Recompense to no man evil for evil. Provide things honest in the sight of all men. If it be possible, as much as lieth in you, live peaceably with all men.

SON(S)—LISTEN: 1 Thessalonians 5:12-13
And we beseech you, brethren, to know them which labour among you, and are over you in the Lord, and admonish you; And to esteem them very highly in love for their work's sake. And be at peace among yourselves.

DAUGHTER(S)—RESPOND: Colossians 3:13-15
Forbearing one another, and forgiving one another, if any man have a quarrel against any: even as Christ forgave you, so also do ye. And above all these things put on charity, which is the bond of perfectness. And let the peace of God rule in your hearts, to the which also ye are called in one body; and be ye thankful.

(Suffering does not contradict God's desire for peace; it establishes it. Now allow the Lord to guide all your decisions today.)

DEDICATION AND CONSECRATION

FATHER—INSTRUCT: Ephesians 6:11-15
Put on the whole armour of God, that ye may be able to stand against the wiles of the devil. For we wrestle not against flesh and blood, but against principalities, against powers, against the rulers of the darkness of this world, against spiritual wickedness in high places. Wherefore take unto you the whole armour of God, that ye may be able to withstand in the evil day, and having done all, to stand. Stand therefore, having your loins girt about with truth, and having on the breastplate of righteousness; And your feet shod with the preparation of the gospel of peace.

MOTHER—TEACH: Romans 10:13-15
For whosoever shall call upon the name of the Lord shall be saved. How then shall they call on him in whom they have not believed? and how shall they believe in him of whom they have not heard? and how shall they hear without a preacher? And how shall they preach, except they be sent? as it is written, How beautiful are the feet of them that preach the gospel of peace, and bring glad tidings of good things!

SON(S)—LISTEN: Galatians 5:22-25
But the fruit of the Spirit is love, joy, peace, longsuffering, gentleness, goodness, faith, Meekness, temperance: against such there is no law. And they that are Christ's have crucified the flesh with the affections and lusts. If we live in the Spirit, let us also walk in the Spirit.

DAUGHTER(S)—RESPOND: 2 Corinthians 13:11-14
Finally, brethren, farewell. Be perfect, be of good comfort, be of one mind, live in peace; and the God of love and peace shall be with you. Greet one another with an holy kiss. All the saints salute you. The grace of the Lord Jesus Christ, and the love of God, and the communion of the Holy Ghost, be with you all.

(It is the gospel of peace that requires our dedication and consecration. Now praise the risen Lord. This is going to be a day of peace.)

DAY 14
PRAYER OF PREPAREDNESS

FATHER—INSTRUCT: 1 Peter 2:3-6
If so be ye have tasted that the Lord is gracious. To whom coming, as unto a living stone, disallowed indeed of men, but chosen of God, and precious, Ye also, as lively stones, are built up a spiritual house, an holy priesthood, to offer up spiritual sacrifices, acceptable to God by Jesus Christ. Wherefore also it is contained in the scripture, Behold, I lay in Sion a chief corner stone, elect, precious: and he that believeth on him shall not be confounded.

MOTHER—TEACH: Isaiah 43:10-12
Ye are my witnesses, saith the LORD, and my servant whom I have chosen: that ye may know and believe me, and understand that I am he: before me there was no God formed, neither shall there be after me. I, even I, am the LORD; and beside me there is no saviour. I have declared, and have saved, and I have shown, when there was no strange god among you: therefore ye are my witnesses, saith the LORD, that I am God.

SON(S)—LISTEN: Matthew 12:15-18
But when Jesus knew it, he withdrew himself from thence: and great multitudes followed him, and he healed them all; And charged them that they should not make him known: That it might be fulfilled which was spoken by Esaias the prophet, saying, Behold my servant, whom I have chosen; my beloved, in whom my soul is well pleased: I will put my spirit upon him, and he shall show judgment to the Gentiles.

DAUGHTER(S)—RESPOND: John 15:16-19
Ye have not chosen me, but I have chosen you, and ordained you, that ye should go and bring forth fruit, and that your fruit should remain: that whatsoever ye shall ask of the Father in my name, he may give it you. These things I command you, that ye love one another. If the world hate you, ye know that it hated me before it hated you. If ye were of the world, the world would love his own: but because ye are not of the world, but I have chosen you out of the world, therefore the world hateth you.

(God doesn't have an option; Jesus is His choice. Now pray that He will prepare you to be a true witness.)

WORSHIP AND PRAISE

FATHER—INSTRUCT: Psalm 90:1-2
Lord, thou hast been our dwelling place in all generations. Before the mountains were brought forth, or ever thou hadst formed the earth and the world, even from everlasting to everlasting, thou art God.

MOTHER—TEACH: Psalm 89:3-7
I have made a covenant with my chosen, I have sworn unto David my servant, Thy seed will I establish for ever, and build up thy throne to all generations. And the heavens shall praise thy wonders, O LORD: thy faithfulness also in the congregation of the saints. For who in the heaven can be compared unto the LORD? who among the sons of the mighty can be likened unto the LORD? God is greatly to be feared in the assembly of the saints, and to be had in reverence of all them that are about him.

SON(S)—LISTEN: Psalm 105:43-45
And he brought forth his people with joy, and his chosen with gladness: And gave them the lands of the heathen: and they inherited the labour of the people; That they might observe his statutes, and keep his laws. Praise ye the LORD.

DAUGHTER(S)—RESPOND: Isaiah 43:19-21
Behold, I will do a new thing; now it shall spring forth; shall ye not know it? I will even make a way in the wilderness, and rivers in the desert. The beast of the field shall honour me, the dragons and the owls: because I give waters in the wilderness, and rivers in the desert, to give drink to my people, my chosen. This people have I formed for myself; they shall show forth my praise.

(Praise the supremacy of the Father for His chosen.)

PRAYER OF CONFESSION

FATHER—INSTRUCT: Titus 3:3-5
For we ourselves also were sometimes foolish, disobedient, deceived, serving divers lusts and pleasures, living in malice and envy, hateful, and hating one another. But after that the kindness and love of God our Saviour toward man appeared, Not by works of righteousness which we have done, but according to his mercy he saved us, by the washing of regeneration, and renewing of the Holy Ghost.

MOTHER—TEACH: Psalm 119:132-133
Look thou upon me, and be merciful unto me, as thou usest to do unto those that love thy name. Order my steps in thy word: and let not any iniquity have dominion over me.

SON(S)—LISTEN: Psalm 130:4-6
But there is forgiveness with thee, that thou mayest be feared. I wait for the LORD, my soul doth wait, and in his word do I hope. My soul waiteth for the Lord more than they that watch for the morning: I say, more than they that watch for the morning.

DAUGHTER(S)—RESPOND: Psalm 119:2-3
Blessed are they that keep his testimonies, and that seek him with the whole heart. They also do no iniquity: they walk in his ways.

(Now confess any dereliction of duty toward others that you may have neglected and claim His assurance of forgiveness.)

PRAYER OF GRATITUDE

FATHER—INSTRUCT: 1 Peter 1:18-20
Forasmuch as ye know that ye were not redeemed with corruptible things, as silver and gold, from your vain conversation received by tradition from your fathers; But with the precious blood of Christ, as of a lamb without blemish and without spot: Who verily was foreordained before the foundation of the world, but was manifest in these last times for you.

MOTHER—TEACH: 1 Peter 2:9-10
But ye are a chosen generation, a royal priesthood, an holy nation, a peculiar people; that ye should show forth the praises of him who hath called you out of darkness into his marvelous light: Which in time past were not a people, but are now the people of God: which had not obtained mercy, but now have obtained mercy.

SON(S)—LISTEN: Colossians 1:12-14
Giving thanks unto the Father, which hath made us meet to be partakers of the inheritance of the saints in light. Who hath delivered us from the power of darkness, and hath translated [us] into the kingdom of his dear Son: In whom we have redemption through his blood, [even] the forgiveness of sins.

DAUGHTER(S)—RESPOND: Psalm 118:21-24
I will praise thee: for thou hast heard me, and art become my salvation. The stone which the builders refused is become the head stone of the corner. This is the LORD'S doing; it is marvelous in our eyes. This is the day which the LORD hath made; we will rejoice and be glad in it.

(Express your gratitude for the precious blood of Christ, the Lamb of God.)

WISDOM AND UNDERSTANDING

FATHER—INSTRUCT: Psalm 33:11-12
The counsel of the LORD standeth for ever, the thoughts of his heart to all generations. Blessed is the nation whose God is the LORD; and the people whom he hath chosen for his own inheritance.

MOTHER—TEACH: 1 Corinthians 1:27-29
But God hath chosen the foolish things of the world to confound the wise; and God hath chosen the weak things of the world to confound the things which are mighty; And base things of the world, and things which are despised, hath God chosen, yea, and things which are not, to bring to nought things that are: That no flesh should glory in his presence.

SON(S)—LISTEN: 1 Corinthians 1:30-31
But of him are ye in Christ Jesus, who of God is made unto us wisdom, and righteousness, and sanctification, and redemption: That, according as it is written, He that glorieth, let him glory in the Lord.

DAUGHTER(S)—RESPOND: 2 Thessalonians 2:13-15
But we are bound to give thanks alway to God for you, brethren beloved of the Lord, because God hath from the beginning chosen you to salvation through sanctification of the Spirit and belief of the truth: Whereunto he called you by our gospel, to the obtaining of the glory of our Lord Jesus Christ. Therefore, brethren, stand fast, and hold the traditions which ye have been taught, whether by word, or our epistle.

(Stand firm in the Lord's counsel in spite of any unpleasant experiences. This is the wisdom from above for which you should pray.)

PRAYER OF SERENITY

FATHER—INSTRUCT: Ephesians 1:3-5
Blessed be the God and Father of our Lord Jesus Christ, who hath blessed us with all spiritual blessings in heavenly places in Christ: According as he hath chosen us in him before the foundation of the world, that we should be holy and without blame before him in love: Having predestinated us unto the adoption of children by Jesus Christ to himself, according to the good pleasure of his will.

MOTHER—TEACH: Psalm 65:4-5
Blessed is the man whom thou choosest, and causest to approach unto thee, that he may dwell in thy courts: we shall be satisfied with the goodness of thy house, even of thy holy temple. By terrible things in righteousness wilt thou answer us, O God of our salvation; who art the confidence of all the ends of the earth, and of them that are afar off upon the sea.

SON(S)—LISTEN: 2 Timothy 2:3-5
Thou therefore endure hardness, as a good soldier of Jesus Christ. No man that warreth entangleth himself with the affairs of this life; that he may please him who hath chosen him to be a soldier. And if a man also strive for masteries, yet is he not crowned, except he strive lawfully.

DAUGHTER(S)—RESPOND: Acts 9:17-19
And Ananias went his way, and entered into the house; and putting his hands on him said, Brother Saul, the Lord, even Jesus, that appeared unto thee in the way as thou camest, hath sent me, that thou mightest receive thy sight, and be filled with the Holy Ghost. And immediately there fell from his eyes as it had been scales: and he received sight forthwith, and arose, and was baptized. And when he had received meat, he was strengthened. Then was Saul certain days with the disciples which were at Damascus.

(You were chosen to dwell in the courts of our God. Now praise God in the integrity of your heart.)

PRAYER OF INTERCESSION

FATHER—INSTRUCT: Joshua 24:14-15
Now therefore fear the LORD, and serve him in sincerity and in truth: and put away the gods which your fathers served on the other side of the flood, and in Egypt; and serve ye the LORD. And if it seem evil unto you to serve the LORD, choose you this day whom ye will serve; whether the gods which your fathers served that were on the other side of the flood, or the gods of the Amorites, in whose land ye dwell: but as for me and my house, we will serve the LORD.

MOTHER—TEACH: John 16:12-14
I have yet many things to say unto you, but ye cannot bear them now. Howbeit when he, the Spirit of truth, is come, he will guide you into all truth: for he shall not speak of himself; but whatsoever he shall hear, that shall he speak: and he will show you things to come. He shall glorify me: for he shall receive of mine, and shall show it unto you.

SON(S)—LISTEN: 1 Corinthians 15:57-58
But thanks be to God, which giveth us the victory through our Lord Jesus Christ. Therefore, my beloved brethren, be ye stedfast, unmoveable, always abounding in the work of the Lord, forasmuch as ye know that your labour is not in vain in the Lord.

DAUGHTER(S)—RESPOND: 2 Thessalonians 3:4-6
And we have confidence in the Lord touching you, that ye both do and will do the things which we command you. And the Lord direct your hearts into the love of God, and into the patient waiting for Christ. Now we command you, brethren, in the name of our Lord Jesus Christ, that ye withdraw yourselves from every brother that walketh disorderly, and not after the tradition which he received of us.

(The Spirit makes intercession for us. Now intercede for others, even those with differences of opinion, of thought and interpretation. Pray for unity.)

PRAYER OF PERSONAL REQUEST

FATHER—INSTRUCT: Acts 9:15-16
But the Lord said unto him, Go thy way: for he is a chosen vessel unto me, to bear my name before the Gentiles, and kings, and the children of Israel: For I will show him how great things he must suffer for my name's sake.

MOTHER—TEACH: 1 Thessalonians 4:1-2
Furthermore then we beseech you, brethren, and exhort you by the Lord Jesus, that as ye have received of us how ye ought to walk and to please God, so ye would abound more and more. For ye know what commandments we gave you by the Lord Jesus.

SON(S)—LISTEN: 2 Timothy 2:21-22
If a man therefore purge himself from these, he shall be a vessel unto honour, sanctified, and meet for the master's use, and prepared unto every good work. Flee also youthful lusts: but follow righteousness, faith, charity, peace, with them that call on the Lord out of a pure heart.

DAUGHTER(S)—RESPOND: Romans 9:22-24
What if God, willing to show his wrath, and to make his power known, endured with much longsuffering the vessels of wrath fitted to destruction: And that he might make known the riches of his glory on the vessels of mercy, which he had afore prepared unto glory, Even us, whom he hath called, not of the Jews only, but also of the Gentiles?

(If God chose Paul to be a vessel of mercy and honor, there is hope for all. Now pray for a special spiritual gift from the Lord.)

PRAYER OF GUIDANCE

FATHER—INSTRUCT: 2 Corinthians 4:7-11
But we have this treasure in earthen vessels, that the excellency of the power may be of God, and not of us. We are troubled on every side, yet not distressed; we are perplexed, but not in despair; Persecuted, but not forsaken; cast down, but not destroyed; Always bearing about in the body the dying of the Lord Jesus, that the life also of Jesus might be made manifest in our body. For we which live are alway delivered unto death for Jesus' sake, that the life also of Jesus might be made manifest in our mortal flesh.

MOTHER—TEACH: Psalm 68:9-11
Thou, O God, didst send a plentiful rain, whereby thou didst confirm thine inheritance, when it was weary. Thy congregation hath dwelt therein: thou, O God, hast prepared of thy goodness for the poor. The Lord gave the word: great was the company of those that published it.

SON(S)—LISTEN: Psalm 32:7-8, 11
Thou art my hiding place; thou shalt preserve me from trouble; thou shalt compass me about with songs of deliverance. I will instruct thee and teach thee in the way which thou shalt go: I will guide thee with mine eye. Be glad in the LORD, and rejoice, ye righteous: and shout for joy, all ye that are upright in heart.

DAUGHTER(S)—RESPOND: Proverbs 11:1-3
A false balance is abomination to the LORD: but a just weight is his delight. When pride cometh, then cometh shame: but with the lowly is wisdom. The integrity of the upright shall guide them: but the perverseness of transgressors shall destroy them.

(We have become the vessels holding the map to God's precious treasure. Ask the Lord to guide you in all His ways.)

DEDICATION AND CONSECRATION

FATHER—INSTRUCT: John 4:40-42
So when the Samaritans were come unto him, they besought him that he would tarry with them: and he abode there two days. And many more believed because of his own word; And said unto the woman, Now we believe, not because of thy saying: for we have heard him ourselves, and know that this is indeed the Christ, the Saviour of the world.

MOTHER—TEACH: Matthew 16:24-25
Then said Jesus unto his disciples, If any man will come after me, let him deny himself, and take up his cross, and follow me. For whosoever will save his life shall lose it: and whosoever will lose his life for my sake shall find it.

SON(S)—LISTEN: 1 John 4:14-15
And we have seen and do testify that the Father sent the Son to be the Saviour of the world. Whosoever shall confess that Jesus is the Son of God, God dwelleth in him, and he in God.

DAUGHTER(S)—RESPOND: Jude 24-25
Now unto him that is able to keep you from falling, and to present you faultless before the presence of his glory with exceeding joy, To the only wise God our Saviour, be glory and majesty, dominion and power, both now and ever. Amen.

(We are dedicated to the purposes of Christ, the Savior of the world. Now pray to be filled with the Holy Ghost.)

DAY 15
PRAYER OF PREPAREDNESS

FATHER—INSTRUCT: John 14:21, 23-24
He that hath my commandments, and keepeth them, he it is that loveth me: and he that loveth me shall be loved of my Father, and I will love him, and will manifest myself to him. Jesus answered and said unto him, If a man love me, he will keep my words: and my Father will love him, and we will come unto him, and make our abode with him. He that loveth me not keepeth not my sayings: and the word which ye hear is not mine, but the Father's which sent me.

MOTHER—TEACH: Acts 2:42-43
And they continued stedfastly in the apostles' doctrine and fellowship, and in breaking of bread, and in prayers. And fear came upon every soul: and many wonders and signs were done by the apostles.

SON(S)—LISTEN: Psalm 119:129-131
Thy testimonies are wonderful: therefore doth my soul keep them. The entrance of thy words giveth light; it giveth understanding unto the simple. I opened my mouth, and panted: for I longed for thy commandments.

DAUGHTER(S)—RESPOND: Psalm 92:4-5
For thou, LORD, hast made me glad through thy work: I will triumph in the works of thy hands. O LORD, how great are thy works! and thy thoughts are very deep.

(Now pray that His love, fellowship, and works prepare your hearts to serve Him today.)

WORSHIP AND PRAISE

FATHER—INSTRUCT: John 4:23-24
But the hour cometh, and now is, when the true worshippers shall worship the Father in spirit and in truth: for the Father seeketh such to worship him. God is a Spirit: and they that worship him must worship him in spirit and in truth.

MOTHER—TEACH: Philippians 2:16-18
Holding forth the word of life; that I may rejoice in the day of Christ, that I have not run in vain, neither laboured in vain. Yea, and if I be offered upon the sacrifice and service of your faith, I joy, and rejoice with you all. For the same cause also do ye joy, and rejoice with me.

SON(S)—LISTEN: Psalm 12:6-7
The words of the LORD are pure words: as silver tried in a furnace of earth, purified seven times. Thou shalt keep them, O LORD, thou shalt preserve them from this generation for ever.

DAUGHTER(S)—RESPOND: Psalm 16:7-9
I will bless the LORD, who hath given me counsel: my reins also instruct me in the night seasons. I have set the LORD always before me: because he is at my right hand, I shall not be moved. Therefore my heart is glad, and my glory rejoiceth: my flesh also shall rest in hope.

(Now rejoice in the Spirit of His Word.)

PRAYER OF CONFESSION

FATHER—INSTRUCT: <u>1 Peter</u> 4:17-18
For the time is come that judgment must begin at the house of God: and if it first begin at us, what shall the end be of them that obey not the gospel of God? And if the righteous scarcely be saved, where shall the ungodly and the sinner appear?

MOTHER—TEACH: <u>Acts</u> 26:19-20, 22
Whereupon, O king Agrippa, I was not disobedient unto the heavenly vision: But showed first unto them of Damascus, and at Jerusalem, and throughout all the coasts of Judaea, and then to the Gentiles, that they should repent and turn to God, and do works meet for repentance. Having therefore obtained help of God, I continue unto this day, witnessing both to small and great, saying none other things than those which the prophets and Moses did say should come.

SON(S)—LISTEN: <u>1 Corinthians</u> 3:18-20
Let no man deceive himself. If any man among you seemeth to be wise in this world, let him become a fool, that he may be wise. For the wisdom of this world is foolishness with God. For it is written, He taketh the wise in their own craftiness. And again, The Lord knoweth the thoughts of the wise, that they are vain.

DAUGHTER(S)—RESPOND: <u>Hebrews</u> 3:6-8, 10
But Christ as a son over his own house; whose house are we, if we hold fast the confidence and the rejoicing of the hope firm unto the end. Wherefore (as the Holy Ghost saith, To day if ye will hear his voice, Harden not your hearts, as in the provocation, in the day of temptation in the wilderness: Wherefore I was grieved with that generation, and said, They do always err in their heart; and they have not known my ways.

(We can err in our hearts as true believers. Now confess any errors or omissions. Then, thank God for His pardon.)

PRAYER OF GRATITUDE

FATHER—INSTRUCT: Romans 8:1-2
There is therefore now no condemnation to them which are in Christ Jesus, who walk not after the flesh, but after the Spirit. For the law of the Spirit of life in Christ Jesus hath made me free from the law of sin and death.

MOTHER—TEACH: 1 Corinthians 1:4-7
I thank my God always on your behalf, for the grace of God which is given you by Jesus Christ; That in every thing ye are enriched by him, in all utterance, and in all knowledge; Even as the testimony of Christ was confirmed in you: So that ye come behind in no gift; waiting for the coming of our Lord Jesus Christ.

SON(S)—LISTEN: John 3:16-17
For God so loved the world, that he gave his only begotten Son, that whosoever believeth in him should not perish, but have everlasting life. For God sent not his Son into the world to condemn the world; but that the world through him might be saved.

DAUGHTER(S)—RESPOND: Romans 8:28-29
And we know that all things work together for good to them that love God, to them who are the called according to his purpose. For whom he did foreknow, he also did predestinate to be conformed to the image of his Son, that he might be the firstborn among many brethren.

(Now offer gratitude to God for including you as a newborn in His family of faith.)

WISDOM AND UNDERSTANDING

FATHER—INSTRUCT: Luke 14:10-11
But when thou art bidden, go and sit down in the lowest room; that when he that bade thee cometh, he may say unto thee, Friend, go up higher: then shalt thou have worship in the presence of them that sit at meat with thee. For whosoever exalteth himself shall be abased; and he that humbleth himself shall be exalted.

MOTHER—TEACH: Proverbs 1:5-7
A wise man will hear, and will increase learning; and a man of understanding shall attain unto wise counsels: To understand a proverb, and the interpretation; the words of the wise, and their dark sayings. The fear of the LORD is the beginning of knowledge: but fools despise wisdom and instruction.

SON(S)—LISTEN: Proverbs 3:12-13
For whom the LORD loveth he correcteth; even as a father the son in whom he delighteth. Happy is the man that findeth wisdom, and the man that getteth understanding.

DAUGHTER(S)—RESPOND: Proverbs 6:6-8
Go to the ant, thou sluggard; consider her ways, and be wise: Which having no guide, overseer, or ruler, provideth her meat in the summer, and gathereth her food in the harvest.

(Obtaining wisdom and humility requires patience. Now ask the Lord to give you both in His timing.)

PRAYER OF SERENITY

FATHER—INSTRUCT: 1 Peter 4:12-14
Beloved, think it not strange concerning the fiery trial which is to try you, as though some strange thing happened unto you: But rejoice, inasmuch as ye are partakers of Christ's sufferings; that, when his glory shall be revealed, ye may be glad also with exceeding joy. If ye be reproached for the name of Christ, happy are ye; for the spirit of glory and of God resteth upon you: on their part he is evil spoken of, but on your part he is glorified.

MOTHER—TEACH: 1 Corinthians 5:7-8, 13
Purge out therefore the old leaven, that ye may be a new lump, as ye are unleavened. For even Christ our passover is sacrificed for us: Therefore let us keep the feast, not with old leaven, neither with the leaven of malice and wickedness; but with the unleavened bread of sincerity and truth. But them that are without God judgeth. Therefore put away from among yourselves that wicked person.

SON(S)—LISTEN: Romans 8:35-37
Who shall separate us from the love of Christ? shall tribulation, or distress, or persecution, or famine, or nakedness, or peril, or sword? As it is written, For thy sake we are killed all the day long; we are accounted as sheep for the slaughter. Nay, in all these things we are more than conquerors through him that loved us.

DAUGHTER(S)—RESPOND: Mark 14:67-68, 72
And when she saw Peter warming himself, she looked upon him, and said, And thou also wast with Jesus of Nazareth. But he denied, saying, I know not, neither understand I what thou sayest. And he went out into the porch; and the cock crowed. And the second time the cock crowed. And Peter called to mind the word that Jesus said unto him, Before the cock crow twice, thou shalt deny me thrice. And when he thought thereon, he wept.

(Don't allow unpleasant experiences or severe tests and trials to change your motives to be faithful. Now express your love to the Lord.)

PRAYER OF INTERCESSION

FATHER—INSTRUCT: 2 Corinthians 1:3-5
Blessed be God, even the Father of our Lord Jesus Christ, the Father of mercies, and the God of all comfort; Who comforteth us in all our tribulation, that we may be able to comfort them which are in any trouble, by the comfort wherewith we ourselves are comforted of God. For as the sufferings of Christ abound in us, so our consolation also aboundeth by Christ.

MOTHER—TEACH: Romans 8:26-27
Likewise the Spirit also helpeth our infirmities: for we know not what we should pray for as we ought: but the Spirit itself maketh intercession for us with groanings which cannot be uttered. And he that searcheth the hearts knoweth what is the mind of the Spirit, because he maketh intercession for the saints according to the will of God.

SON(S)—LISTEN: Proverbs 8:22-25
The LORD possessed me in the beginning of his way, before his works of old. I was set up from everlasting, from the beginning, or ever the earth was. When there were no depths, I was brought forth; when there were no fountains abounding with water. Before the mountains were settled, before the hills was I brought forth.

DAUGHTER(S)—RESPOND: John 17:11-13
And now I am no more in the world, but these are in the world, and I come to thee. Holy Father, keep through thine own name those whom thou hast given me, that they may be one, as we are. While I was with them in the world, I kept them in thy name: those that thou gavest me I have kept, and none of them is lost, but the son of perdition; that the scripture might be fulfilled. And now come I to thee; and these things I speak in the world, that they might have my joy fulfilled in themselves.

(The Helper of our infirmities is Christ. Now intercede for those loved ones who need Christ.)

PRAYER OF PERSONAL REQUEST

FATHER—INSTRUCT: <u>1 Corinthians</u> 3:8-10
Now he that planteth and he that watereth are one: and every man shall receive his own reward according to his own labour. For we are labourers together with God: ye are God's husbandry, ye are God's building. According to the grace of God which is given unto me, as a wise masterbuilder, I have laid the foundation, and another buildeth thereon. But let every man take heed how he buildeth thereupon.

MOTHER—TEACH: <u>Romans</u> 4:16-17
Therefore it is of faith, that it might be by grace; to the end the promise might be sure to all the seed; not to that only which is of the law, but to that also which is of the faith of Abraham; who is the father of us all, (As it is written, I have made thee a father of many nations,) before him whom he believed, even God, who quickeneth the dead, and calleth those things which be not as though they were.

SON(S)—LISTEN: <u>Isaiah</u> 41:9-11
Thou whom I have taken from the ends of the earth, and called thee from the chief men thereof, and said unto thee, Thou art my servant; I have chosen thee, and not cast thee away. Fear thou not; for I am with thee: be not dismayed; for I am thy God: I will strengthen thee; yea, I will help thee; yea, I will uphold thee with the right hand of my righteousness. Behold, all they that were incensed against thee shall be ashamed and confounded: they shall be as nothing; and they that strive with thee shall perish.

DAUGHTER(S)—RESPOND: <u>Hebrews</u> 4:11-12
Let us labour therefore to enter into that rest, lest any man fall after the same example of unbelief. For the word of God is quick, and powerful, and sharper than any twoedged sword, piercing even to the dividing asunder of soul and spirit, and of the joints and marrow, and is a discerner of the thoughts and intents of the heart.

(As a laborer with God, tell Him what you need to complete the work assigned to your hands.)

PRAYER OF GUIDANCE

FATHER—INSTRUCT: Mark 16:14-16
Afterward he appeared unto the eleven as they sat at meat, and upbraided them with their unbelief and hardness of heart, because they believed not them which had seen him after he was risen. And he said unto them, Go ye into all the world, and preach the gospel to every creature. He that believeth and is baptized shall be saved; but he that believeth not shall be damned.

MOTHER—TEACH: 1 Corinthians 6:1-4
Dare any of you, having a matter against another, go to law before the unjust, and not before the saints? Do ye not know that the saints shall judge the world? and if the world shall be judged by you, are ye unworthy to judge the smallest matters? Know ye not that we shall judge angels? how much more things that pertain to this life? If then ye have judgments of things pertaining to this life, set them to judge who are least esteemed in the church.

SON(S)—LISTEN: Luke 22:29-32
And I appoint unto you a kingdom, as my Father hath appointed unto me; That ye may eat and drink at my table in my kingdom, and sit on thrones judging the twelve tribes of Israel. And the Lord said, Simon, Simon, behold, Satan hath desired to have you, that he may sift you as wheat: But I have prayed for thee, that thy faith fail not: and when thou art converted, strengthen thy brethren.

DAUGHTER(S)—RESPOND: Proverbs 4:7-9
Wisdom is the principal thing; therefore get wisdom: and with all thy getting get understanding. Exalt her, and she shall promote thee: she shall bring thee to honour, when thou dost embrace her. She shall give to thine head an ornament of grace: a crown of glory shall she deliver to thee.

(Our path of life is paved with foreknowledge. Now pray to God for His guidance in decisions you must make today.)

DEDICATION AND CONSECRATION

FATHER—INSTRUCT: Romans 16:25-27
Now to him that is of power to stablish you according to my gospel, and the preaching of Jesus Christ, according to the revelation of the mystery, which was kept secret since the world began, But now is made manifest, and by the scriptures of the prophets, according to the commandment of the everlasting God, made known to all nations for the obedience of faith: To God only
wise, be glory through Jesus Christ for ever. Amen.

MOTHER—TEACH: John 13:34-35
A new commandment I give unto you, That ye love one another; as I have loved you, that ye also love one another. By this shall all men know that ye are my disciples, if ye have love one to another.

SON(S)—LISTEN: Proverbs 8:12-15
I wisdom dwell with prudence, and find out knowledge of witty inventions. The fear of the LORD is to hate evil: pride, and arrogancy, and the evil way, and the froward mouth, do I hate. Counsel is mine, and sound wisdom: I am understanding; I have strength. By me kings reign, and princes decree justice.

DAUGHTER(S)—RESPOND: Romans 5:1-5
Therefore being justified by faith, we have peace with God through our Lord Jesus Christ: By whom also we have access by faith into this grace wherein we stand, and rejoice in hope of the glory of God. And not only so, but we glory in tribulations also: knowing that tribulation worketh patience; And patience, experience; and experience, hope: And hope maketh not ashamed; because the love of God is shed abroad in our hearts by the Holy Ghost which is given unto us.

(The thought for tomorrow is the same as that of today. Jesus Christ is the same forever more. Now dedicate your life to Christ.)

DAY 16
PRAYER OF PREPAREDNESS

FATHER—INSTRUCT: Luke 9:23-25
And he said to them all, If any man will come after me, let him deny himself, and take up his cross daily, and follow me. For whosoever will save his life shall lose it: but whosoever will lose his life for my sake, the same shall save it. For what is a man advantaged, if he gain the whole world, and lose himself, or be cast away?

MOTHER—TEACH: Luke 16:27-30
Then he said, I pray thee therefore, father, that thou wouldest send him to my father's house: For I have five brethren; that he may testify unto them, lest they also come into this place of torment. Abraham saith unto him, They have Moses and the prophets; let them hear them. And he said, Nay, father Abraham: but if one went unto them from the dead, they will repent.

SON(S)—LISTEN: John 19:16-18
Then delivered he him therefore unto them to be crucified. And they took Jesus, and led him away. And he bearing his cross went forth into a place called the place of a skull, which is called in the Hebrew Golgotha: Where they crucified him, and two other with him, on either side one, and Jesus in the midst.

DAUGHTER(S)—RESPOND: Colossians 2:13-15
And you, being dead in your sins and the uncircumcision of your flesh, hath he quickened together with him, having forgiven you all trespasses; Blotting out the handwriting of ordinances that was against us, which was contrary to us, and took it out of the way, nailing it to his cross; And having spoiled principalities and powers, he made a show of them openly, triumphing over them in it.

(Now yield to God's call in preparation today to bear your cross in the comfort of His words. Glorify the Lord.)

WORSHIP AND PRAISE

FATHER—INSTRUCT: Psalm 96:7-9
Give unto the LORD, O ye kindreds of the people, give unto the LORD glory and strength. Give unto the LORD the glory due unto his name: bring an offering, and come into his courts. O worship the LORD in the beauty of holiness: fear before him, all the earth.

MOTHER—TEACH: Psalm 108:4-5
For thy mercy is great above the heavens: and thy truth reacheth unto the clouds. Be thou exalted, O God, above the heavens: and thy glory above all the earth.

SON(S)—LISTEN: Psalm 149:5-6
Let the saints be joyful in glory: let them sing aloud upon their beds. Let the high praises of God be in their mouth, and a twoedged sword in their hand.

DAUGHTER(S)—RESPOND: Psalm 45:3-4
Gird thy sword upon thy thigh, O most mighty, with thy glory and thy majesty. And in thy majesty ride prosperously because of truth and meekness and righteousness; and thy right hand shall teach thee terrible things.

(Our redemption was completed in Christ's finished work on the cross. Now worship the Lord.)

PRAYER OF CONFESSION

FATHER—INSTRUCT: Matthew 8:24-26
And, behold, there arose a great tempest in the sea, insomuch that the ship was covered with the waves: but he was asleep. And his disciples came to him, and awoke him, saying, Lord, save us: we perish. And he saith unto them, Why are ye fearful, O ye of little faith? Then he arose, and rebuked the winds and the sea; and there was a great calm.

MOTHER—TEACH: John 6:60-63
Many therefore of his disciples, when they had heard this, said, This is an hard saying; who can hear it? When Jesus knew in himself that his disciples murmured at it, he said unto them, Doth this offend you? What and if ye shall see the Son of man ascend up where he was before? It is the spirit that quickeneth; the flesh profiteth nothing: the words that I speak unto you, they are spirit, and they are life.

SON(S)—LISTEN: Romans 11:8-10
(According as it is written, God hath given them the spirit of slumber, eyes that they should not see, and ears that they should not hear;) unto this day. And David saith, Let their table be made a snare, and a trap, and a stumblingblock, and a recompence unto them: Let their eyes be darkened, that they may not see, and bow down their back always.

DAUGHTER(S)—RESPOND: Acts 5:30-32
The God of our fathers raised up Jesus, whom ye slew and hanged on a tree. Him hath God exalted with his right hand to be a Prince and a Saviour, for to give repentance to Israel, and forgiveness of sins. And we are his witnesses of these things; and so is also the Holy Ghost, whom God hath given to them that obey him.

(Every experience in trials comes to help us fulfill our destiny. Claim forgiveness for any doubts or fears you may have encountered.)

PRAYER OF GRATITUDE

FATHER—INSTRUCT: 1 Peter 1:22-23
Seeing ye have purified your souls in obeying the truth through the Spirit unto unfeigned love of the brethren, see that ye love one another with a pure heart fervently: Being born again, not of corruptible seed, but of incorruptible, by the word of God, which liveth and abideth for ever.

MOTHER—TEACH: Luke 10:17-20
And the seventy returned again with joy, saying, Lord, even the devils are subject unto us through thy name. And he said unto them, I beheld Satan as lightning fall from heaven. Behold, I give unto you power to tread on serpents and scorpions, and over all the power of the enemy: and nothing shall by any means hurt you. Notwithstanding in this rejoice not, that the spirits are subject unto you; but rather rejoice, because your names are written in heaven.

SON(S)—LISTEN: 1 John 3:2-3
Beloved, now are we the sons of God, and it doth not yet appear what we shall be: but we know that, when he shall appear, we shall be like him; for we shall see him as he is. And every man that hath this hope in him purifieth himself, even as he is pure.

DAUGHTER(S)—RESPOND: Titus 1:1-3
Paul, a servant of God, and an apostle of Jesus Christ, according to the faith of God's elect, and the acknowledging of the truth which is after godliness; In hope of eternal life, which God, that cannot lie, promised before the world began; But hath in due times manifested his word through preaching, which is committed unto me according to the commandment of God our Saviour.

(Just as with Paul and the seventy, God gives us golden opportunities to witness. Be grateful for your sonship status.)

WISDOM AND UNDERSTANDING

FATHER—INSTRUCT: 1 Corinthians 12:27-29
Now ye are the body of Christ, and members in particular. And God hath set some in the church, first apostles, secondarily prophets, thirdly teachers, after that miracles, then gifts of healings, helps, governments, diversities of tongues. Are all apostles? are all prophets? are all teachers? are all workers of miracles?

MOTHER—TEACH: Acts 4:32-33
And the multitude of them that believed were of one heart and of one soul: neither said any of them that aught of the things which he possessed was his own; but they had all things common. And with great power gave the apostles witness of the resurrection of the Lord Jesus: and great grace was upon them all.

SON(S)—LISTEN: Malachi 2:6-7
The law of truth was in his mouth, and iniquity was not found in his lips: he walked with me in peace and equity, and did turn many away from iniquity. For the priest's lips should keep knowledge, and they should seek the law at his mouth: for he is the messenger of the LORD of hosts.

DAUGHTER(S)—RESPOND: Ephesians 4:11-13
And he gave some, apostles; and some, prophets; and some, evangelists; and some, pastors and teachers; For the perfecting of the saints, for the work of the ministry, for the edifying of the body of Christ: Till we all come in the unity of the faith, and of the knowledge of the Son of God, unto a perfect man, unto the measure of the stature of the fulness of Christ.

(Our responsibility to the Father and the Son is perfected when we serve others. Now pray for spiritual growth.)

PRAYER OF SERENITY

FATHER—INSTRUCT: Acts 5:39-42
But if it be of God, ye cannot overthrow it; lest haply ye be found even to fight against God. And to him they agreed: and when they had called the apostles, and beaten them, they commanded that they should not speak in the name of Jesus, and let them go. And they departed from the presence of the council, rejoicing that they were counted worthy to suffer shame for his name. And daily in the temple, and in every house, they ceased not to teach and preach Jesus Christ.

MOTHER—TEACH: 1 Peter 1:3-4
Blessed be the God and Father of our Lord Jesus Christ, which according to his abundant mercy hath begotten us again unto a lively hope by the resurrection of Jesus Christ from the dead, To an inheritance incorruptible, and undefiled, and that fadeth not away, reserved in heaven for you.

SON(S)—LISTEN: 1 Timothy 6:3-4
If any man teach otherwise, and consent not to wholesome words, even the words of our Lord Jesus Christ, and to the doctrine which is according to godliness; He is proud, knowing nothing, but doting about questions and strifes of words, whereof cometh envy, strife, railings, evil surmisings,

DAUGHTER(S)—RESPOND: 1 Timothy 6:11-12
But thou, O man of God, flee these things; and follow after righteousness, godliness, faith, love, patience, meekness. Fight the good fight of faith, lay hold on eternal life, whereunto thou art also called, and hast professed a good profession before many witnesses.

(Our faith becomes stronger by seizing the opportunities to witness. Now pray for boldness.)

PRAYER OF INTERCESSION

FATHER—INSTRUCT: Matthew 16:13-16
When Jesus came into the coasts of Caesarea Philippi, he asked his disciples, saying, Whom do men say that I the Son of man am? And they said, Some say that thou art John the Baptist: some, Elias; and others, Jeremias, or one of the prophets. He saith unto them, But whom say ye that I am? And Simon Peter answered and said, Thou art the Christ, the Son of the living God.

MOTHER—TEACH: John 16:22-24
And ye now therefore have sorrow: but I will see you again, and your heart shall rejoice, and your joy no man taketh from you. And in that day ye shall ask me nothing. Verily, verily, I say unto you, Whatsoever ye shall ask the Father in my name, he will give it you. Hitherto have ye asked nothing in my name: ask, and ye shall receive, that your joy may be full.

SON(S)—LISTEN: 1 John 5:14-15
And this is the confidence that we have in him, that, if we ask any thing according to his will, he heareth us: And if we know that he hear us, whatsoever we ask, we know that we have the petitions that we desired of him.

DAUGHTER(S)—RESPOND: Luke 8:9-10
And his disciples asked him, saying, What might this parable be? And he said, Unto you it is given to know the mysteries of the kingdom of God: but to others in parables; that seeing they might not see, and hearing they might not understand.

(When there was no man, God's own arm brought salvation to us. Now intercede for family, friends, your church family, and the sick.)

PRAYER OF PERSONAL REQUEST

FATHER—INSTRUCT: James 5:17-18
Elias was a man subject to like passions as we are, and he prayed earnestly that it might not rain: and it rained not on the earth by the space of three years and six months. And he prayed again, and the heaven gave rain, and the earth brought forth her fruit.

MOTHER—TEACH: Acts 10:3-4
He saw in a vision evidently about the ninth hour of the day an angel of God coming in to him, and saying unto him, Cornelius. And when he looked on him, he was afraid, and said, What is it, Lord? And he said unto him, Thy prayers and thine alms are come up for a memorial before God.

SON(S)—LISTEN: Daniel 9:3-4
And I set my face unto the Lord God, to seek by prayer and supplications, with fasting, and sackcloth, and ashes: And I prayed unto the LORD my God, and made my confession, and said, O Lord, the great and dreadful God, keeping the covenant and mercy to them that love him, and to them that keep his commandments.

DAUGHTER(S)—RESPOND: Colossians 4:2-3
Continue in prayer, and watch in the same with thanksgiving; Withal praying also for us, that God would open unto us a door of utterance, to speak the mystery of Christ, for which I am also in bonds.

(Elijah, Cornelius, and Daniel were men who had prayers answered; so will you today if your prayers are according to God's will.)

PRAYER OF GUIDANCE

FATHER—INSTRUCT: Micah 4:1-2
But in the last days it shall come to pass, that the mountain of the house of the LORD shall be established in the top of the mountains, and it shall be exalted above the hills; and people shall flow unto it. And many nations shall come, and say, Come, and let us go up to the mountain of the LORD, and to the house of the God of Jacob; and he will teach us of his ways, and we will walk in his paths: for the law shall go forth of Zion, and the word of the LORD from Jerusalem.

MOTHER—TEACH: Isaiah 42:8-10
I am the LORD: that is my name: and my glory will I not give to another, neither my praise to graven images. Behold, the former things are come to pass, and new things do I declare: before they spring forth I tell you of them. Sing unto the LORD a new song, and his praise from the end of the earth, ye that go down to the sea, and all that is therein; the isles, and the inhabitants thereof.

SON(S)—LISTEN: Psalm 18:35-36
Thou hast also given me the shield of thy salvation: and thy right hand hath holden me up, and thy gentleness hath made me great. Thou hast enlarged my steps under me, that my feet did not slip.

DAUGHTER(S)—RESPOND: Psalm 119:57-60
Thou art my portion, O LORD: I have said that I would keep thy words. I intreated thy favour with my whole heart: be merciful unto me according to thy word. I thought on my ways, and turned my feet unto thy testimonies. I made haste, and delayed not to keep thy commandments.

(When we learn God's ways and walk in His paths, we will discover unlimited possibilities. Now pray for His guidance.)

DEDICATION AND CONSECRATION

FATHER—INSTRUCT: Ephesians 3:14-19
For this cause I bow my knees unto the Father of our Lord Jesus Christ, Of whom the whole family in heaven and earth is named, That he would grant you, according to the riches of his glory, to be strengthened with might by his Spirit in the inner man; That Christ may dwell in your hearts by faith; that ye, being rooted and grounded in love, May be able to comprehend with all saints what is the breadth, and length, and depth, and height; And to know the love of Christ, which passeth knowledge, that ye might be filled with all the fulness of God.

MOTHER—TEACH: 1 John 1:5-7
This then is the message which we have heard of him, and declare unto you, that God is light, and in him is no darkness at all. If we say that we have fellowship with him, and walk in darkness, we lie, and do not the truth: But if we walk in the light, as he is in the light, we have fellowship one with another, and the blood of Jesus Christ his Son cleanseth us from all sin.

SON(S)—LISTEN: Jude 21-23
Keep yourselves in the love of God, looking for the mercy of our Lord Jesus Christ unto eternal life. And of some have compassion, making a difference: And others save with fear, pulling them out of the fire; hating even the garment spotted by the flesh.

DAUGHTER(S)—RESPOND: 2 Peter 3:17-18
Ye therefore, beloved, seeing ye know these things before, beware lest ye also, being led away with the error of the wicked, fall from your own stedfastness. But grow in grace, and in the knowledge of our Lord and Saviour Jesus Christ. To him be glory both now and for ever. Amen.

(The pattern in our daily activity shows forth the Light we are walking in. Now pray for steadfastness in His love. This is going to be a wonderful day.)

DAY 17
PRAYER OF PREPAREDNESS

FATHER—INSTRUCT: 1 Corinthians 15:12-14
Now if Christ be preached that he rose from the dead, how say some among you that there is no resurrection of the dead? But if there be no resurrection of the dead, then is Christ not risen: And if Christ be not risen, then is our preaching vain, and your faith is also vain.

MOTHER—TEACH: Philippians 3:8-10
Yea doubtless, and I count all things but loss for the excellency of the knowledge of Christ Jesus my Lord: for whom I have suffered the loss of all things, and do count them but dung, that I may win Christ, And be found in him, not having mine own righteousness, which is of the law, but that which is through the faith of Christ, the righteousness which is of God by faith: That I may know him, and the power of his resurrection, and the fellowship of his sufferings, being made conformable unto his death.

SON(S)—LISTEN: Romans 6:4-6
Therefore we are buried with him by baptism into death: that like as Christ was raised up from the dead by the glory of the Father, even so we also should walk in newness of life. For if we have been planted together in the likeness of his death, we shall be also in the likeness of his resurrection: Knowing this, that our old man is crucified with him, that the body of sin might be destroyed, that henceforth we should not serve sin.

DAUGHTER(S)—RESPOND: Colossians 1:18-20
And he is the head of the body, the church: who is the beginning, the firstborn from the dead; that in all things he might have the preeminence. For it pleased the Father that in him should all fulness dwell; And, having made peace through the blood of his cross, by him to reconcile all things unto himself; by him, I say, whether they be things in earth, or things in heaven.

(The excellent knowledge of Christ, the power of His resurrection, and the fellowship of His suffering prepares us for eternity. Praise the risen Lord.)

WORSHIP AND PRAISE

FATHER—INSTRUCT: Job 19:25-27
For I know that my redeemer liveth, and that he shall stand at the latter day upon the earth: And though after my skin worms destroy this body, yet in my flesh shall I see God: Whom I shall see for myself, and mine eyes shall behold, and not another; though my reins be consumed within me.

MOTHER—TEACH: Luke 24:37-39
But they were terrified and affrighted, and supposed that they had seen a spirit. And he said unto them, Why are ye troubled? and why do thoughts arise in your hearts? Behold my hands and my feet, that it is I myself: handle me, and see; for a spirit hath not flesh and bones, as ye see me have.

SON(S)—LISTEN: Revelation 5:11-12
And I beheld, and I heard the voice of many angels round about the throne and the beasts and the elders: and the number of them was ten thousand times ten thousand, and thousands of thousands; Saying with a loud voice, Worthy is the Lamb that was slain to receive power, and riches, and wisdom, and strength, and honour, and glory, and blessing.

DAUGHTER(S)—RESPOND: Mark 16:9-12
Now when Jesus was risen early the first day of the week, he appeared first to Mary Magdalene, out of whom he had cast seven devils. And she went and told them that had been with him, as they mourned and wept. And they, when they had heard that he was alive, and had been seen of her, believed not. After that he appeared in another form unto two of them, as they walked, and went into the country.

(Now continue to sing and praise Him with the angels. He is risen indeed.)

PRAYER OF CONFESSION

FATHER—INSTRUCT: Zephaniah 1:14-15
The great day of the LORD is near, it is near, and hasteth greatly, even the voice of the day of the LORD: the mighty man shall cry there bitterly. That day is a day of wrath, a day of trouble and distress, a day of wasteness and desolation, a day of darkness and gloominess, a day of clouds and thick darkness.

MOTHER—TEACH: Luke 23:42-44
And he said unto Jesus, Lord, remember me when thou comest into thy kingdom. And Jesus said unto him, Verily I say unto thee, Today shalt thou be with me in paradise. And it was about the sixth hour, and there was a darkness over all the earth until the ninth hour.

SON(S)—LISTEN: 1 Peter 3:10-12
For he that will love life, and see good days, let him refrain his tongue from evil, and his lips that they speak no guile: Let him eschew evil, and do good; let him seek peace, and ensue it. For the eyes of the Lord are over the righteous, and his ears are open unto their prayers: but the face of the Lord is against them that do evil.

DAUGHTER(S)—RESPOND: Psalm 79:8-9
O remember not against us former iniquities: let thy tender mercies speedily prevent us: for we are brought very low. Help us, O God of our salvation, for the glory of thy name: and deliver us, and purge away our sins, for thy name's sake.

(Make your confession the same as that of the thief: "Lord, remember me." Now ask the Lord to show you any errors that need His forgiveness.)

PRAYER OF GRATITUDE

FATHER—INSTRUCT: 1 Corinthians 15:23-26
But every man in his own order: Christ the firstfruits; afterward they that are Christ's at his coming. Then cometh the end, when he shall have delivered up the kingdom to God, even the Father; when he shall have put down all rule and all authority and power. For he must reign, till he hath put all enemies under his feet. The last enemy that shall be destroyed is death.

MOTHER—TEACH: 1 Peter 1:3-4
Blessed be the God and Father of our Lord Jesus Christ, which according to his abundant mercy hath begotten us again unto a lively hope by the resurrection of Jesus Christ from the dead, To an inheritance incorruptible, and undefiled, and that fadeth not away, reserved in heaven for you.

SON(S)—LISTEN: 1 Peter 2:1-2
Wherefore laying aside all malice, and all guile, and hypocrisies, and envies, and all evil speakings, As newborn babes, desire the sincere milk of the word, that ye may grow thereby.

DAUGHTER(S)—RESPOND: James 5:7-8
Be patient therefore, brethren, unto the coming of the Lord. Behold, the husbandman waiteth for the precious fruit of the earth, and hath long patience for it, until he receive the early and latter rain. Be ye also patient; stablish your hearts: for the coming of the Lord draweth nigh.

(Now express your gratitude to the Lord for destroying the last enemy, death.)

WISDOM AND UNDERSTANDING

FATHER—INSTRUCT: Matthew 22:28-30
Therefore in the resurrection whose wife shall she be of the seven? for they all had her. Jesus answered and said unto them, Ye do err, not knowing the scriptures, nor the power of God. For in the resurrection they neither marry, nor are given in marriage, but are as the angels of God in heaven.

MOTHER—TEACH: John 11:23-26
Jesus saith unto her, Thy brother shall rise again. Martha saith unto him, I know that he shall rise again in the resurrection at the last day. Jesus said unto her, I am the resurrection, and the life: he that believeth in me, though he were dead, yet shall he live: And whosoever liveth and believeth in me shall never die. Believest thou this?

SON(S)—LISTEN: Acts 1:21-22
Wherefore of these men which have companied with us all the time that the Lord Jesus went in and out among us, Beginning from the baptism of John, unto that same day that he was taken up from us, must one be ordained to be a witness with us of his resurrection.

DAUGHTER(S)—RESPOND: Matthew 27:50-53
Jesus, when he had cried again with a loud voice, yielded up the ghost. And, behold, the veil of the temple was rent in twain from the top to the bottom; and the earth did quake, and the rocks rent; And the graves were opened; and many bodies of the saints which slept arose, And came out of the graves after his resurrection, and went into the holy city, and appeared unto many.

(Webster defines resurrection as "rising from the dead." Jesus defines it as Himself for He is the revival of His creation. Now praise Him in your own words.)

PRAYER OF SERENITY

FATHER—INSTRUCT: Luke 24:25-27
Then he said unto them, O fools, and slow of heart to believe all that the prophets have spoken: Ought not Christ to have suffered these things, and to enter into his glory? And beginning at Moses and all the prophets, he expounded unto them in all the scriptures the things concerning himself.

MOTHER—TEACH: 1 Corinthians 15:42-44
So also is the resurrection of the dead. It is sown in corruption; it is raised in incorruption: It is sown in dishonour; it is raised in glory: it is sown in weakness; it is raised in power: It is sown a natural body; it is raised a spiritual body. There is a natural body, and there is a spiritual body.

SON(S)—LISTEN: 1 Thessalonians 4:14-15
For if we believe that Jesus died and rose again, even so them also which sleep in Jesus will God bring with him. For this we say unto you by the word of the Lord, that we which are alive and remain unto the coming of the Lord shall not prevent them which are asleep.

DAUGHTER(S)—RESPOND: 1 Thessalonians 4:16-18
For the Lord himself shall descend from heaven with a shout, with the voice of the archangel, and with the trump of God: and the dead in Christ shall rise first: Then we which are alive and remain shall be caught up together with them in the clouds, to meet the Lord in the air: and so shall we ever be with the Lord. Wherefore comfort one another with these words.

(Christ would not allow suffering to rob Him of His glory. Now pray for a sincere heart to serve the Lord.)

PRAYER OF INTERCESSION

FATHER—INSTRUCT: Isaiah 59:16-17
And he saw that there was no man, and wondered that there was no intercessor: therefore his arm brought salvation unto him; and his righteousness, it sustained him. For he put on righteousness as a breastplate, and an helmet of salvation upon his head; and he put on the garments of vengeance for clothing, and was clad with zeal as a cloak.

MOTHER—TEACH: Hebrews 7:22-25
By so much was Jesus made a surety of a better testament. And they truly were many priests, because they were not suffered to continue by reason of death: But this man, because he continueth ever, hath an unchangeable priesthood. Wherefore he is able also to save them to the uttermost that come unto God by him, seeing he ever liveth to make intercession for them.

SON(S)—LISTEN: Ezekiel 22:30-31
And I sought for a man among them, that should make up the hedge, and stand in the gap before me for the land, that I should not destroy it: but I found none. Therefore have I poured out mine indignation upon them; I have consumed them with the fire of my wrath: their own way have I recompensed upon their heads, saith the Lord GOD.

DAUGHTER(S)—RESPOND: 1 Corinthians 9:13-14, 16
Do ye not know that they which minister about holy things live of the things of the temple? and they which wait at the altar are partakers with the altar? Even so hath the Lord ordained that they which preach the gospel should live of the gospel. For though I preach the gospel, I have nothing to glory of: for necessity is laid upon me; yea, woe is unto me, if I preach not the gospel!

(Now intercede for pastors, missionaries, those who are ministers of the gospel of our Lord, and the sick.)

PRAYER OF PERSONAL REQUEST

FATHER—INSTRUCT: Matthew 11:2-6
Now when John had heard in the prison the works of Christ, he sent two of his disciples, And said unto him, Art thou he that should come, or do we look for another? Jesus answered and said unto them, Go and show John again those things which ye do hear and see: The blind receive their sight, and the lame walk, the lepers are cleansed, and the deaf hear, the dead are raised up, and the poor have the gospel preached to them. And blessed is he, whosoever shall not be offended in me.

MOTHER—TEACH: Acts 2:30-32
Therefore being a prophet, and knowing that God had sworn with an oath to him, that of the fruit of his loins, according to the flesh, he would raise up Christ to sit on his throne; He seeing this before spake of the resurrection of Christ, that his soul was not left in hell, neither his flesh did see corruption. This Jesus hath God raised up, whereof we all are witnesses.

SON(S)—LISTEN: Romans 10:8-10
But what saith it? The word is nigh thee, even in thy mouth, and in thy heart: that is, the word of faith, which we preach; That if thou shalt confess with thy mouth the Lord Jesus, and shalt believe in thine heart that God hath raised him from the dead, thou shalt be saved. For with the heart man believeth unto righteousness; and with the mouth confession is made unto salvation.

DAUGHTER(S)—RESPOND: Romans 8:10-11, 14
And if Christ be in you, the body is dead because of sin; but the Spirit is life because of righteousness. But if the Spirit of him that raised up Jesus from the dead dwell in you, he that raised up Christ from the dead shall also quicken your mortal bodies by his Spirit that dwelleth in you. For as many as are led by the Spirit of God, they are the sons of God.

(Neither John nor Christ was fearful of death, but that the will of God be done in each life. Now pray that God's will be done in yours.)

PRAYER OF GUIDANCE

FATHER—INSTRUCT: Ephesians 2:4-7
But God, who is rich in mercy, for his great love wherewith he loved us, Even when we were dead in sins, hath quickened us together with Christ, (by grace ye are saved;) And hath raised us up together, and made us sit together in heavenly places in Christ Jesus: That in the ages to come he might show the exceeding riches of his grace in his kindness toward us through Christ Jesus.

MOTHER—TEACH: Psalm 119:33-35
Teach me, O LORD, the way of thy statutes; and I shall keep it unto the end. Give me understanding, and I shall keep thy law; yea, I shall observe it with my whole heart. Make me to go in the path of thy commandments; for therein do I delight.

SON(S)—LISTEN: 1 Timothy 2:3-6
For this is good and acceptable in the sight of God our Saviour; Who will have all men to be saved, and to come unto the knowledge of the truth. For there is one God, and one mediator between God and men, the man Christ Jesus; Who gave himself a ransom for all, to be testified in due time.

DAUGHTER(S)—RESPOND: 1 Peter 3:18, 21
For Christ also hath once suffered for sins, the just for the unjust, that he might bring us to God, being put to death in the flesh, but quickened by the Spirit: The like figure whereunto even baptism doth also now save us (not the putting away of the filth of the flesh, but the answer of a good conscience toward God,) by the resurrection of Jesus Christ.

(God's rich mercy, His kindness, His desire to have all men saved points to Jesus His Son. Now pray for His guidance.)

DEDICATION AND CONSECRATION

FATHER—INSTRUCT: Revelation 21:1-3
And I saw a new heaven and a new earth: for the first heaven and the first earth were passed away; and there was no more sea. And I John saw the holy city, new Jerusalem, coming down from God out of heaven, prepared as a bride adorned for her husband. And I heard a great voice out of heaven saying, Behold, the tabernacle of God is with men, and he will dwell with them, and they shall be his people, and God himself shall be with them, and be their God.

MOTHER—TEACH: Revelation 21:4-6
And God shall wipe away all tears from their eyes; and there shall be no more death, neither sorrow, nor crying, neither shall there be any more pain: for the former things are passed away. And he that sat upon the throne said, Behold, I make all things new. And he said unto me, Write: for these words are true and faithful. And he said unto me, It is done. I am Alpha and Omega, the beginning and the end. I will give unto him that is athirst of the fountain of the water of life freely.

SON(S)—LISTEN: Revelation 21:7-8
He that overcometh shall inherit all things; and I will be his God, and he shall be my son. But the fearful, and unbelieving, and the abominable, and murderers, and whoremongers, and sorcerers, and idolaters, and all liars, shall have their part in the lake which burneth with fire and brimstone: which is the second death.

DAUGHTER(S)—RESPOND: 1 Peter 3:21-22
The like figure whereunto even baptism doth also now save us (not the putting away of the filth of the flesh, but the answer of a good conscience toward God,) by the resurrection of Jesus Christ: Who is gone into heaven, and is on the right hand of God; angels and authorities and powers being made subject unto him.

(Today is the day to walk in the Spirit of Him that raised Christ from the dead. This is a great day to serve the Lord.)

DAY 18
PRAYER OF PREPAREDNESS

FATHER—INSTRUCT: 1 Corinthians 2:12-13
Now we have received, not the spirit of the world, but the spirit which is of God; that we might know the things that are freely given to us of God. Which things also we speak, not in the words which man's wisdom teacheth, but which the Holy Ghost teacheth; comparing spiritual things with spiritual.

MOTHER—TEACH: 1 Corinthians 2:14-16
But the natural man receiveth not the things of the Spirit of God: for they are foolishness unto him: neither can he know them, because they are spiritually discerned. But he that is spiritual judgeth all things, yet he himself is judged of no man. For who hath known the mind of the Lord, that he may instruct him? But we have the mind of Christ.

SON(S)—LISTEN: James 1:17-18
Every good gift and every perfect gift is from above, and cometh down from the Father of lights, with whom is no variableness, neither shadow of turning. Of his own will begat he us with the word of truth, that we should be a kind of firstfruits of his creatures.

DAUGHTER(S)—RESPOND: Hebrews 13:17-18
Obey them that have the rule over you, and submit yourselves: for they watch for your souls, as they that must give account, that they may do it with joy, and not with grief: for that is unprofitable for you. Pray for us: for we trust we have a good conscience, in all things willing to live honestly.

(In preparation today, allow the Holy Ghost to teach you the things of God that are spiritually discerned. Pray now for this precious gift.)

WORSHIP AND PRAISE

FATHER—INSTRUCT: Psalm 59:16-17
But I will sing of thy power; yea, I will sing aloud of thy mercy in the morning: for thou hast been my defence and refuge in the day of my trouble. Unto thee, O my strength, will I sing: for God is my defence, and the God of my mercy.

MOTHER—TEACH: 1 Peter 3:15-16
But sanctify the Lord God in your hearts: and be ready always to give an answer to every man that asketh you a reason of the hope that is in you with meekness and fear: Having a good conscience; that, whereas they speak evil of you, as of evildoers, they may be ashamed that falsely accuse your good conversation in Christ.

SON(S)—LISTEN: Psalm 62:1-2, 12
Truly my soul waiteth upon God: from him cometh my salvation. He only is my rock and my salvation; he is my defence; I shall not be greatly moved. Also unto thee, O Lord, belongeth mercy: for thou renderest to every man according to his work.

DAUGHTER(S)—RESPOND: Hebrews 13:15-16
By him therefore let us offer the sacrifice of praise to God continually, that is, the fruit of our lips giving thanks to his name. But to do good and to communicate forget not: for with such sacrifices God is well pleased.

(Now begin to worship God from your heart within your understanding of His awesome power.)

PRAYER OF CONFESSION

FATHER—INSTRUCT: Romans 16:19-20
For your obedience is come abroad unto all men. I am glad therefore on your behalf: but yet I would have you wise unto that which is good, and simple concerning evil. And the God of peace shall bruise Satan under your feet shortly. The grace of our Lord Jesus Christ be with you. Amen.

MOTHER—TEACH: Isaiah 1:18-19
Come now, and let us reason together, saith the LORD: though your sins be as scarlet, they shall be as white as snow; though they be red like crimson, they shall be as wool. If ye be willing and obedient, ye shall eat the good of the land.

SON(S)—LISTEN: James 1:4-5
But let patience have her perfect work, that ye may be perfect and entire, wanting nothing. If any of you lack wisdom, let him ask of God, that giveth to all men liberally, and upbraideth not; and it shall be given him.

DAUGHTER(S)—RESPOND: Romans 6:12-14
Let not sin therefore reign in your mortal body, that ye should obey it in the lusts thereof. Neither yield ye your members as instruments of unrighteousness unto sin: but yield yourselves unto God, as those that are alive from the dead, and your members as instruments of righteousness unto God. For sin shall not have dominion over you: for ye are not under the law, but under grace.

(We make voluntary confessions to keep sin off the throne of our members. Now confess any acts of disobedience and claim assurance of forgiveness.)

PRAYER OF GRATITUDE

FATHER—INSTRUCT: Ecclesiastes 5:19-20
Every man also to whom God hath given riches and wealth, and hath given him power to eat thereof, and to take his portion, and to rejoice in his labour; this is the gift of God. For he shall not much remember the days of his life; because God answereth him in the joy of his heart.

MOTHER—TEACH: Romans 6:17-18
But God be thanked, that ye were the servants of sin, but ye have obeyed from the heart that form of doctrine which was delivered you. Being then made free from sin, ye became the servants of righteousness.

SON(S)—LISTEN: Acts 2:38-39
Then Peter said unto them, Repent, and be baptized every one of you in the name of Jesus Christ for the remission of sins, and ye shall receive the gift of the Holy Ghost. For the promise is unto you, and to your children, and to all that are afar off, even as many as the Lord our God shall call.

DAUGHTER(S)—RESPOND: Romans 1:11-12
For I long to see you, that I may impart unto you some spiritual gift, to the end ye may be established; That is, that I may be comforted together with you by the mutual faith both of you and me.

(The spiritual gifts are eternal and more precious than gold. Now thank God for His personal best: Jesus and the Holy Ghost.)

WISDOM AND UNDERSTANDING

FATHER—INSTRUCT: Ecclesiastes 8:8-9
There is no man that hath power over the spirit to retain the spirit; neither hath he power in the day of death: and there is no discharge in that war; neither shall wickedness deliver those that are given to it. All this have I seen, and applied my heart unto every work that is done under the sun: there is a time wherein one man ruleth over another to his own hurt.

MOTHER—TEACH: Proverbs 21:13-15
Whoso stoppeth his ears at the cry of the poor, he also shall cry himself, but shall not be heard. A gift in secret pacifieth anger: and a reward in the bosom strong wrath. It is joy to the just to do judgment: but destruction shall be to the workers of iniquity.

SON(S)—LISTEN: Acts 10:44-45
While Peter yet spake these words, the Holy Ghost fell on all them which heard the word. And they of the circumcision which believed were astonished, as many as came with Peter, because that on the Gentiles also was poured out the gift of the Holy Ghost.

DAUGHTER(S)—RESPOND: Romans 5:15-16
But not as the offence, so also is the free gift. For if through the offence of one many be dead, much more the grace of God, and the gift by grace, which is by one man, Jesus Christ, hath abounded unto many. And not as it was by one that sinned, so is the gift: for the judgment was by one to condemnation, but the free gift is of many offences unto justification.

(All that we receive from God is His free gift. Therefore, we should freely give. Now pray for this wisdom.)

PRAYER OF SERENITY

FATHER—INSTRUCT: Isaiah 58:5-6
Is it such a fast that I have chosen? a day for a man to afflict his soul? is it to bow down his head as a bulrush, and to spread sackcloth and ashes under him? wilt thou call this a fast, and an acceptable day to the LORD? Is not this the fast that I have chosen? to loose the bands of wickedness, to undo the heavy burdens, and to let the oppressed go free, and that ye break every yoke?

MOTHER—TEACH: Luke 4:18-19
The Spirit of the Lord is upon me, because he hath anointed me to preach the gospel to the poor; he hath sent me to heal the brokenhearted, to preach deliverance to the captives, and recovering of sight to the blind, to set at liberty them that are bruised, To preach the acceptable year of the Lord.

SON(S)—LISTEN: Psalm 62:5-6
My soul, wait thou only upon God; for my expectation is from him. He only is my rock and my salvation: he is my defence; I shall not be moved.

DAUGHTER(S)—RESPOND: Hebrews 12:28-29
Wherefore we receiving a kingdom which cannot be moved, let us have grace, whereby we may serve God acceptably with reverence and godly fear: For our God is a consuming fire.

(Now pray for God's anointing today to help someone in need.)

PRAYER OF INTERCESSION

FATHER—INSTRUCT: Isaiah 58:1-3
Cry aloud, spare not, lift up thy voice like a trumpet, and show my people their transgression, and the house of Jacob their sins. Yet they seek me daily, and delight to know my ways, as a nation that did righteousness, and forsook not the ordinance of their God: they ask of me the ordinances of justice; they take delight in approaching to God. Wherefore have we fasted, say they, and thou seest not? wherefore have we afflicted our soul, and thou takest no knowledge?
Behold, in the day of your fast ye find pleasure, and exact all your labours.

MOTHER—TEACH: John 11:43-45
And when he thus had spoken, he cried with a loud voice, Lazarus, come forth. And he that was dead came forth, bound hand and foot with graveclothes: and his face was bound about with a napkin. Jesus saith unto them, Loose him, and let him go. Then many of the Jews which came to Mary, and had seen the things which Jesus did, believed on him.

SON(S)—LISTEN: John 16:27-29
For the Father himself loveth you, because ye have loved me, and have believed that I came out from God. I came forth from the Father, and am come into the world: again, I leave the world, and go to the Father. His disciples said unto him, Lo, now speakest thou plainly, and speakest no proverb.

DAUGHTER(S)—RESPOND: Luke 10:2-3
Therefore said he unto them, The harvest truly is great, but the labourers are few: pray ye therefore the Lord of the harvest, that he would send forth labourers into his harvest. Go your ways: behold, I send you forth as lambs among wolves.

(Now intercede for those who have taken for granted this precious gift of God. Jesus said that you have the power to loose them.)

PRAYER OF PERSONAL REQUEST

FATHER—INSTRUCT: Psalm 55:1-2, 6
Give ear to my prayer, O God; and hide not thyself from my supplication. Attend unto me, and hear me: I mourn in my complaint, and make a noise.

MOTHER—TEACH: 1 Corinthians 14:1-3
Follow after charity, and desire spiritual gifts, but rather that ye may prophesy. For he that speaketh in an unknown tongue speaketh not unto men, but unto God: for no man understandeth him; howbeit in the spirit he speaketh mysteries. But he that prophesieth speaketh unto men to edification, and exhortation, and comfort.

SON(S)—LISTEN: Psalm 55:12-14
For it was not an enemy that reproached me; then I could have borne it: neither was it he that hated me that did magnify himself against me; then I would have hid myself from him: But it was thou, a man mine equal, my guide, and mine acquaintance. We took sweet counsel together, and walked unto the house of God in company.

DAUGHTER(S)—RESPOND: John 13:18-20
I speak not of you all: I know whom I have chosen: but that the scripture may be fulfilled, He that eateth bread with me hath lifted up his heel against me. Now I tell you before it come, that, when it is come to pass, ye may believe that I am he. Verily, verily, I say unto you, He that receiveth whomsoever I send receiveth me; and he that receiveth me receiveth him that sent me.

(Now pray that God grants you his favor to speak his mysteries to comfort others.)

PRAYER OF GUIDANCE

FATHER—INSTRUCT: Isaiah 33:5-6, 8, 10
The LORD is exalted; for he dwelleth on high: he hath filled Zion with judgment and righteousness. And wisdom and knowledge shall be the stability of thy times, and strength of salvation: the fear of the LORD is his treasure. The highways lie waste, the wayfaring man ceaseth: he hath broken the covenant, he hath despised the cities, he regardeth no man. Now will I rise, saith the LORD; now will I be exalted; now will I lift up myself.

MOTHER—TEACH: Isaiah 40:2-5
Speak ye comfortably to Jerusalem, and cry unto her, that her warfare is accomplished, that her iniquity is pardoned: for she hath received of the LORD'S hand double for all her sins. The voice of him that crieth in the wilderness, Prepare ye the way of the LORD, make straight in the desert a highway for our God. Every valley shall be exalted, and every mountain and hill shall be made low: and the crooked shall be made straight, and the rough places plain: And the glory of the LORD shall be revealed, and all flesh shall see it together: for the mouth of the LORD hath spoken it.

SON(S)—LISTEN: Proverbs 4:10-12
Hear, O my son, and receive my sayings; and the years of thy life shall be many. I have taught thee in the way of wisdom; I have led thee in right paths. When thou goest, thy steps shall not be straitened; and when thou runnest, thou shalt not stumble.

DAUGHTER(S)—RESPOND: Hebrews 12:11-13
Now no chastening for the present seemeth to be joyous, but grievous: nevertheless afterward it yieldeth the peaceable fruit of righteousness unto them which are exercised thereby. Wherefore lift up the hands which hang down, and the feeble knees; And make straight paths for your feet, lest that which is lame be turned out of the way; but let it rather be healed.

(Now ask the Lord for guidance for any healing you need today.)

DEDICATION AND CONSECRATION

FATHER—INSTRUCT: Galatians 5:16-18
This I say then, Walk in the Spirit, and ye shall not fulfil the lust of the flesh. For the flesh lusteth against the Spirit, and the Spirit against the flesh: and these are contrary the one to the other: so that ye cannot do the things that ye would. But if ye be led of the Spirit, ye are not under the law.

MOTHER—TEACH: 1 Timothy 4:7-8
But refuse profane and old wives' fables, and exercise thyself rather unto godliness. For bodily exercise profiteth little: but godliness is profitable unto all things, having promise of the life that now is, and of that which is to come.

SON(S)—LISTEN: Hebrews 8:1-3
Now of the things which we have spoken this is the sum: We have such an high priest, who is set on the right hand of the throne of the Majesty in the heavens; A minister of the sanctuary, and of the true tabernacle, which the Lord pitched, and not man. For every high priest is ordained to offer gifts and sacrifices: wherefore it is of necessity that this man have somewhat also to offer.

DAUGHTER(S)—RESPOND: Hebrews 9:13-15
For if the blood of bulls and of goats, and the ashes of an heifer sprinkling the unclean, sanctifieth to the purifying of the flesh: How much more shall the blood of Christ, who through the eternal Spirit offered himself without spot to God, purge your conscience from dead works to serve the living God? And for this cause he is the mediator of the new testament, that by means of death, for the redemption of the transgressions that were under the first testament, they which are called might receive the promise of eternal inheritance.

It is clear; today, if we honor the Spirit of God, we shall reap eternal rewards. Now devote your life in service to God.)

DAY 19
PRAYER OF PREPAREDNESS

FATHER – INSTRUCT: Psalm 62:7-8, 11
In God *is* my salvation and my glory: the rock of my strength, *and* my refuge, *is* in God. Trust in him at all times; ye people, pour out your heart before him: God *is* a refuge for us. God hath spoken once; twice have I heard this; that power *belongeth* unto God.

MOTHER – TEACH: Nehemiah 1:10-11
Now these *are* thy servants and thy people, whom thou hast redeemed by thy great power, and by thy strong hand. O Lord, I beseech thee, let now thine ear be attentive to the prayer of thy servant, and to the prayer of thy servants, who desire to fear thy name: and prosper, I pray thee, thy servant this day, and grant him mercy in the sight of this man. For I was the king's cupbearer.

SON(S) – LISTEN: Matthew 4:16-19
The people which sat in darkness saw great light; and to them which sat in the region and shadow of death light is sprung up. From that time Jesus began to preach, and to say, Repent: for the kingdom of heaven is at hand. And Jesus, walking by the sea of Galilee, saw two brethren, Simon called Peter, and Andrew his brother, casting a net into the sea: for they were fishers. And he saith unto them, Follow me, and I will make you fishers of men.

DAUGHTER(S) – RESPOND: 1 Chronicles 29:11-13
Thine, O LORD, *is* the greatness, and the power, and the glory, and the victory, and the majesty: for all *that is* in the heaven and in the earth *is thine;* thine *is* the kingdom, O LORD, and thou art exalted as head above all. Both riches and honour *come* of thee, and thou reignest over all; and in thine hand *is* power and might; and in thine hand *it is* to make great, and to give strength unto all. Now therefore, our God, we thank thee, and praise thy glorious name.

(God has chosen us for His purpose to walk in the power of His Word in preparation, today. Only believe.)

WORSHIP AND PRAISE

FATHER – INSTRUCT: Psalm 49:15-17
But God will redeem my soul from the power of the grave: for he shall receive me. Selah. Be not thou afraid when one is made rich, when the glory of his house is increased; For when he dieth he shall carry nothing away: his glory shall not descend after him.

MOTHER – TEACH: Hebrews 10:24-25
And let us consider one another to provoke unto love and to good works: Not forsaking the assembling of ourselves together, as the manner of some *is;* but exhorting *one another:* and so much the more, as ye see the day approaching.

SON(S) – LISTEN: Psalm 21:3-4, 13
For thou preventest him with the blessings of goodness: thou settest a crown of pure gold on his head. He asked life of thee, *and* thou gavest *it* him, *even* length of days for ever and ever. Be thou exalted, LORD, in thine own strength: *so* will we sing and praise thy power.

DAUGHTER(S) – RESPOND: Psalm 63:2-5
To see thy power and thy glory, so *as* I have seen thee in the sanctuary. Because thy lovingkindness *is* better than life, my lips shall praise thee. Thus will I bless thee while I live: I will lift up my hands in thy name. My soul shall be satisfied as *with* marrow and fatness; and my mouth shall praise *thee* with joyful lips.

(Now delight in the Lord's loving-kindness and worship Him that is exalted above all creatures.)

PRAYER OF CONFESSION

FATHER – INSTRUCT: Hebrews 10:15-17
Whereof the Holy Ghost also is a witness to us: for after that he had said before, This *is* the covenant that I will make with them after those days, saith the Lord, I will put my laws into their hearts, and in their minds will I write them; And their sins and iniquities will I remember no more.

MOTHER – TEACH: James 1:19-20
Wherefore, my beloved brethren, let every man be swift to hear, slow to speak, slow to wrath. For the wrath of man worketh not the righteousness of God.

SON(S) – LISTEN: Hebrews 11:23-25
By faith Moses, when he was born, was hid three months of his parents, because they saw *he was* a proper child; and they were not afraid of the king's commandment. By faith Moses, when he was come to years, refused to be called the son of Pharaoh's daughter; Choosing rather to suffer affliction with the people of God, than to enjoy the pleasures of sin for a season.

DAUGHTER(S) – RESPOND: Matthew 5:36-37
Neither shalt thou swear by thy head, because thou canst not make one hair white or black. But let your communication be, Yea, yea; Nay, nay: for whatsoever is more than these cometh of evil.

(Remember, any sin that is confessed today is remembered no more. Now confess any fear or doubt that is in your pathway today.)

PRAYER OF GRATITUDE

FATHER – INSTRUCT: <u>1 Corinthians</u> 10:1-4
Moreover, brethren, I would not that ye should be ignorant, how that all our fathers were under the cloud, and all passed through the sea; And were all baptized unto Moses in the cloud and in the sea; And did all eat the same spiritual meat; And did all drink the same spiritual drink: for they drank of that spiritual Rock that followed them: and that Rock was Christ.

MOTHER – TEACH: <u>Matthew</u> 14:30-31, 33
But when he saw the wind boisterous, he was afraid; and beginning to sink, he cried, saying, Lord, save me. And immediately Jesus stretched forth *his* hand, and caught him, and said unto him, O thou of little faith, wherefore didst thou doubt? Then they that were in the ship came and worshipped him, saying, Of a truth thou art the Son of God.

SON(S) – LISTEN: <u>Psalm</u> 149:4-6
For the LORD taketh pleasure in his people: he will beautify the meek with salvation. Let the saints be joyful in glory: let them sing aloud upon their beds. *Let* the high *praises* of God *be* in their mouth, and a twoedged sword in their hand.

DAUGHTER(S) – RESPOND: <u>1 Peter</u> 1:3-5
Blessed *be* the God and Father of our Lord Jesus Christ, which according to his abundant mercy hath begotten us again unto a lively hope by the resurrection of Jesus Christ from the dead, To an inheritance incorruptible, and undefiled, and that fadeth not away, reserved in heaven for you, Who are kept by the power of God through faith unto salvation ready to be revealed in the last time.

(Now begin to thank God for His love, His Son, and His keeping power.)

WISDOM AND UNDERSTANDING

FATHER – INSTRUCT: 1 Corinthians 1:17-18
For Christ sent me not to baptize, but to preach the gospel: not with wisdom of words, lest the cross of Christ should be made of none effect. For the preaching of the cross is to them that perish foolishness; but unto us which are saved it is the power of God.

MOTHER – TEACH: 1 Corinthians 1:19-21
For it is written, I will destroy the wisdom of the wise, and will bring to nothing the understanding of the prudent. Where *is* the wise? where *is* the scribe? where *is* the disputer of this world? hath not God made foolish the wisdom of this world? For after that in the wisdom of God the world by wisdom knew not God, it pleased God by the foolishness of preaching to save them that believe.

SON(S) – LISTEN: Ecclesiastes 9:13-15
This wisdom have I seen also under the sun, and it *seemed* great unto me: *There was* a little city, and few men within it; and there came a great king against it, and besieged it, and built great bulwarks against it: Now there was found in it a poor wise man, and he by his wisdom delivered the city; yet no man remembered that same poor man.

DAUGHTER(S) – RESPOND: 1 Corinthians 2:2-5
For I determined not to know any thing among you, save Jesus Christ, and him crucified. And I was with you in weakness, and in fear, and in much trembling. And my speech and my preaching *was* not with enticing words of man's wisdom, but in demonstration of the Spirit and of power: That your faith should not stand in the wisdom of men, but in the power of God.

(The cross of Christ marked a crime scene, transformed into a crowning scene in three hours. Now pray asking God to help you stand in His wisdom.)

PRAYER OF SERENITY

FATHER – INSTRUCT: Psalm 22:1-2
My God, my God, why hast thou forsaken me? *why art thou so* far from helping me, *and from* the words of my roaring? O my God, I cry in the daytime, but thou hearest not; and in the night season, and am not silent.

MOTHER – TEACH: Ecclesiastes 9:4-7
For to him that is joined to all the living there is hope: for a living dog is better than a dead lion. For the living know that they shall die: but the dead know not any thing, neither have they any more a reward; for the memory of them is forgotten. Also their love, and their hatred, and their envy, is now perished; neither have they any more a portion for ever in any *thing* that is done under the sun. Go thy way, eat thy bread with joy, and drink thy wine with a merry heart; for God now accepteth thy works.

SON(S) – LISTEN: Matthew 23:37-39
O Jerusalem, Jerusalem, *thou* that killest the prophets, and stonest them which are sent unto thee, how often would I have gathered thy children together, even as a hen gathereth her chickens under *her* wings, and ye would not! Behold, your house is left unto you desolate. For I say unto you, Ye shall not see me henceforth, till ye shall say, Blessed *is* he that cometh in the name of the Lord.

DAUGHTER(S) – RESPOND: John 21:15-17
So when they had dined, Jesus saith to Simon Peter, Simon, *son* of Jonas, lovest thou me more than these? He saith unto him, Yea, Lord; thou knowest that I love thee. He saith unto him, Feed my lambs. He saith to him again the second time, Simon, *son* of Jonas, lovest thou me? He saith unto him, Yea, Lord; thou knowest that I love thee. He saith unto him, Feed my sheep. He saith unto him the third time, Simon, *son* of Jonas, lovest thou me? Peter was grieved because he said unto him the third time, Lovest thou me? And he said unto him, Lord, thou knowest all
things; thou knowest that I love thee. Jesus saith unto him, Feed my sheep.

(With an attitude of sincerity, God wants us to use all of our power to help others. Now pray that your love will never have to be questioned by the Lord.)

PRAYER OF INTERCESSION

FATHER – INSTRUCT: Hebrews 1:3-5
Who being the brightness of *his* glory, and the express image of his person, and upholding all things by the word of his power, when he had by himself purged our sins, sat down on the right hand of the Majesty on high; Being made so much better than the angels, as he hath by inheritance obtained a more excellent name than they. For unto which of the angels said he at any time, Thou art my Son, this day have I begotten thee? And again, I will be to him a Father, and he shall be to me a Son?

MOTHER – TEACH: 2 Corinthians 12:9-10
And he said unto me, My grace is sufficient for thee: for my strength is made perfect in weakness. Most gladly therefore will I rather glory in my infirmities, that the power of Christ may rest upon me. Therefore I take pleasure in infirmities, in reproaches, in necessities, in persecutions, in distresses for Christ's sake: for when I am weak, then am I strong.

SON(S) – LISTEN: Romans 13:1-3
Let every soul be subject unto the higher powers. For there is no power but of God: the powers that be are ordained of God. Whosoever therefore resisteth the power, resisteth the ordinance of God: and they that resist shall receive to themselves damnation. For rulers are not a terror to good works, but to the evil. Wilt thou then not be afraid of the power? do that which is good, and thou shalt have praise of the same.

DAUGHTER(S) – RESPOND: Psalm 37:29-31
The righteous shall inherit the land, and dwell therein for ever. The mouth of the righteous speaketh wisdom, and his tongue talketh of judgment. The law of his God is in his heart; none of his steps shall slide.

(As the righteous, we have become a channel of expression for God's love to win others. Now intercede for church leaders, those in government, and the President.)

PRAYER OF PERSONAL REQUEST

FATHER – INSTRUCT: 2 Corinthians 13:4-5
For though he was crucified through weakness, yet he liveth by the power of God. For we also are weak in him, but we shall live with him by the power of God toward you. Examine yourselves, whether ye be in the faith; prove your own selves. Know ye not your own selves, how that Jesus Christ is in you, except ye be reprobates?

MOTHER – TEACH: Psalm 29:2-4
Give unto the LORD the glory due unto his name; worship the LORD in the beauty of holiness. The voice of the LORD is upon the waters: the God of glory thundereth: the LORD is upon many waters. The voice of the LORD is powerful; the voice of the LORD is full of majesty.

SON(S) – LISTEN: Psalm 30:7-9
LORD, by thy favour thou hast made my mountain to stand strong: thou didst hide thy face, and I was troubled. I cried to thee, O LORD; and unto the LORD I made supplication. What profit is there in my blood, when I go down to the pit? Shall the dust praise thee? shall it declare thy truth?

DAUGHTER(S) – RESPOND: Psalm 30:2-3
O LORD my God, I cried unto thee, and thou hast healed me. O LORD, thou hast brought up my soul from the grave: thou hast kept me alive, that I should not go down to the pit.

(When we examine ourselves and give ourselves, we find the favor of the Lord. Now pray for your physical and spiritual healing today.)

PRAYER OF GUIDANCE

FATHER – INSTRUCT: Psalm 31:14-15
But I trusted in thee, O LORD: I said, Thou art my God. My times are in thy hand: deliver me from the hand of mine enemies, and from them that persecute me.

MOTHER – TEACH: Psalm 29:10-11
The LORD sitteth upon the flood; yea, the LORD sitteth King for ever. The LORD will give strength unto his people; the LORD will bless his people with peace.

SON(S) – LISTEN: Psalm 37:37-39
Mark the perfect man, and behold the upright: for the end of that man is peace. But the transgressors shall be destroyed together: the end of the wicked shall be cut off. But the salvation of the righteous is of the LORD: he is their strength in the time of trouble.

DAUGHTER(S) – RESPOND: 2 Corinthians 13:11-14
Finally, brethren, farewell. Be perfect, be of good comfort, be of one mind, live in peace; and the God of love and peace shall be with you. Greet one another with an holy kiss. All the saints salute you. The grace of the Lord Jesus Christ, and the love of God, and the communion of the Holy Ghost, be with you all. Amen.

(Perfection, comfort, harmony, and peace are the four lanes to God's highway. Now ask him to direct your steps today.)

DEDICATION AND CONSECRATION

FATHER – INSTRUCT: Psalm 61:5, 8
For thou, O God, hast heard my vows: thou hast given *me* the heritage of those that fear thy name. So will I sing praise unto thy name for ever, that I may daily perform my vows.

MOTHER – TEACH: Romans 6:4-7
Therefore we are buried with him by baptism into death: that like as Christ was raised up from the dead by the glory of the Father, even so we also should walk in newness of life. For if we have been planted together in the likeness of his death, we shall be also *in the likeness* of *his* resurrection: Knowing this, that our old man is crucified with *him,* that the body of sin might be destroyed, that henceforth we should not serve sin. For he that is dead is freed from sin.

SON(S) – LISTEN: Matthew 10:30-32
But the very hairs of your head are all numbered. Fear ye not therefore, ye are of more value than many sparrows. Whosoever therefore shall confess me before men, him will I confess also before my Father which is in heaven.

DAUGHTER(S) – RESPOND: James 1:22-25
But be ye doers of the word, and not hearers only, deceiving your own selves. For if any be a hearer of the word, and not a doer, he is like unto a man beholding his natural face in a glass: For he beholdeth himself, and goeth his way, and straightway forgetteth what manner of man he was. But whoso looketh into the perfect law of liberty, and continueth *therein,* he being not a forgetful hearer, but a doer of the work, this man shall be blessed in his deed.

(To live a consecrated life is self-sacrifice, not self-gratification. Now renew your commitment to work for the Lord today.)

DAY 20
PRAYER OF PREPAREDNESS

FATHER – INSTRUCT: Exodus 18:19-20
Hearken now unto my voice, I will give thee counsel, and God shall be with thee: Be thou for the people to God-ward, that thou mayest bring the causes unto God: And thou shalt teach them ordinances and laws, and shalt show them the way wherein they must walk, and the work that they must do.

MOTHER – TEACH: Hebrews 13:20-21
Now the God of peace, that brought again from the dead our Lord Jesus, that great shepherd of the sheep, through the blood of the everlasting covenant, Make you perfect in every good work to do his will, working in you that which is well-pleasing in his sight, through Jesus Christ; to whom *be* glory for ever and ever. Amen.

SON(S) – LISTEN: Ephesians 2:10, 13, 18
For we are his workmanship, created in Christ Jesus unto good works, which God hath before ordained that we should walk in them. But now in Christ Jesus ye who sometimes were far off are made nigh by the blood of Christ. For through him we both have access by one Spirit unto the Father.

DAUGHTER(S) – RESPOND: Matthew 5:14-16
Ye are the light of the world. A city that is set on an hill cannot be hid. Neither do men light a candle, and put it under a bushel, but on a candlestick; and it giveth light unto all that are in the house. Let your light so shine before men, that they may see your good works, and glorify your Father which is in heaven.

(Good works were ordained by God. Now prepare your heart to the attunement of God's will.)

WORSHIP AND PRAISE

FATHER – INSTRUCT: Psalm 111:6-8
He hath shown his people the power of his works, that he may give them the heritage of the heathen. The works of his hands *are* verity and judgment; all his commandments *are* sure. They stand fast for ever and ever, *and are* done in truth and uprightness.

MOTHER – TEACH: Lamentations 3:22-23
It is of the LORD'S mercies that we are not consumed, because his compassions fail not. *They are* new every morning: great *is* thy faithfulness.

SON(S) – LISTEN: Psalm 93:1-2, 5
The LORD reigneth, he is clothed with majesty; the LORD is clothed with strength, *wherewith* he hath girded himself: the world also is stablished, that it cannot be moved. Thy throne *is* established of old: thou *art* from everlasting. Thy testimonies are very sure: holiness becometh thine house, O LORD, for ever.

DAUGHTER(S) – RESPOND: Psalm 96:1-2
O sing unto the LORD a new song: sing unto the LORD, all the earth. Sing unto the LORD, bless his name; show forth his salvation from day to day.

(Now worship the Lord. You are the works of His hands; He is worthy of all praises.)

PRAYER OF CONFESSION

FATHER – INSTRUCT: 1 Peter 4:17-19
For the time *is come* that judgment must begin at the house of God: and if *it* first *begin* at us, what shall the end *be* of them that obey not the gospel of God? And if the righteous scarcely be saved, where shall the ungodly and the sinner appear? Wherefore let them that suffer according to the will of God commit the keeping of their souls *to him* in well doing, as unto a faithful Creator.

MOTHER – TEACH: 2 Chronicles 7:14
If my people, which are called by my name, shall humble themselves, and pray, and seek my face, and turn from their wicked ways; then will I hear from heaven, and will forgive their sin, and will heal their land.

SON(S) – LISTEN: Psalm 19:13-14
Keep back thy servant also from presumptuous *sins;* let them not have dominion over me: then shall I be upright, and I shall be innocent from the great transgression. Let the words of my mouth, and the meditation of my heart, be acceptable in thy sight, O LORD, my strength, and my redeemer.

DAUGHTER(S) – RESPOND: Psalm 60:1, 11-12
O God, thou hast cast us off, thou hast scattered us, thou hast been displeased; O turn thyself to us again. Give us help from trouble: for vain *is* the help of man. Through God we shall do valiantly: for he *it is that* shall tread down our enemies.

(The Bible tells us to cleanse ourselves of all filthiness of the flesh and spirit. Now confess any spiritual rebellion in your life today and claim your forgiveness.)

PRAYER OF GRATITUDE

FATHER – INSTRUCT: Psalm 100:1-5
Make a joyful noise unto the LORD, all ye lands. Serve the LORD with gladness: come before his presence with singing. Know ye that the LORD he *is* God: *it is* he *that* hath made us, and not we ourselves; *we are* his people, and the sheep of his pasture. Enter into his gates with thanksgiving, *and* into his courts with praise: be thankful unto him, *and* bless his name. For the LORD *is* good; his mercy *is* everlasting; and his truth *endureth* to all generations.

MOTHER – TEACH: John 14:10-12
Believest thou not that I am in the Father, and the Father in me? the words that I speak unto you I speak not of myself: but the Father that dwelleth in me, he doeth the works. Believe me that I *am* in the Father, and the Father in me: or else believe me for the very works' sake. Verily, verily, I say unto you, He that believeth on me, the works that I do shall he do also; and greater *works* than these shall he do; because I go unto my Father.

SON(S) – LISTEN: Psalm 30:4-5, 12
Sing unto the LORD, O ye saints of his, and give thanks at the remembrance of his holiness. For his anger *endureth but* a moment; in his favour *is* life: weeping may endure for a night, but joy *cometh* in the morning. To the end that *my* glory may sing praise to thee, and not be silent. O LORD my God, I will give thanks unto thee for ever.

DAUGHTER(S) – RESPOND: Mark 14:6-8
And Jesus said, Let her alone; why trouble ye her? she hath wrought a good work on me. For ye have the poor with you always, and whensoever ye will ye may do them good: but me ye have not always. She hath done what she could: she is come aforehand to anoint my body to the burying.

(Give thanks within and without the gates because Jesus is worthy. Now thank God with a grateful heart.)

WISDOM AND UNDERSTANDING

FATHER – INSTRUCT: Ecclesiastes 9:9-10
Live joyfully with the wife whom thou lovest all the days of the life of thy vanity, which he hath given thee under the sun, all the days of thy vanity: for that *is* thy portion in *this* life, and in thy labour which thou takest under the sun. Whatsoever thy hand findeth to do, do *it* with thy might; for *there is* no work, nor device, nor knowledge, nor wisdom, in the grave, whither thou goest.

MOTHER – TEACH: Psalm 111:1-4
Praise ye the LORD. I will praise the LORD with my whole heart, in the assembly of the upright, and in the congregation. The works of the LORD are great, sought out of all them that have pleasure therein. His work is honourable and glorious: and his righteousness endureth for ever. He hath made his wonderful works to be remembered: the LORD is gracious and full of compassion.

SON(S) – LISTEN: Proverbs 3:19-21
The LORD by wisdom hath founded the earth; by understanding hath he established the heavens. By his knowledge the depths are broken up, and the clouds drop down the dew. My son, let not them depart from thine eyes: keep sound wisdom and discretion.

DAUGHTER(S) – RESPOND: Luke 14:27-30
And whosoever doth not bear his cross, and come after me, cannot be my disciple. For which of you, intending to build a tower, sitteth not down first, and counteth the cost, whether he have sufficient to finish it? Lest haply, after he hath laid the foundation, and is not able to finish it, all that behold it begin to mock him, saying, This man began to build, and was not able to finish.

(The Father's sacrifice was His only begotten Son. Now ask the Father to prepare you for His feast properly dressed.)

PRAYER OF SERENITY

FATHER – INSTRUCT: Lamentations 3:24-26
The LORD is my portion, saith my soul; therefore will I hope in him. The LORD is good unto them that wait for him, to the soul that seeketh him. It is good that a man should both hope and quietly wait for the salvation of the LORD.

MOTHER – TEACH: Zephaniah 1:7-8
Hold thy peace at the presence of the Lord GOD: for the day of the LORD is at hand: for the LORD hath prepared a sacrifice, he hath bid his guests. And it shall come to pass in the day of the LORD'S sacrifice, that I will punish the princes, and the king's children, and all such as are clothed with strange apparel.

SON(S) – LISTEN: Luke 14:21-23
So that servant came, and showed his lord these things. Then the master of the house being angry said to his servant, Go out quickly into the streets and lanes of the city, and bring in hither the poor, and the maimed, and the halt, and the blind. And the servant said, Lord, it is done as thou hast commanded, and yet there is room. And the lord said unto the servant, Go out into the highways and hedges, and compel them to come in, that my house may be filled.

DAUGHTER(S) – RESPOND: Colossians 3:16-17
Let the word of Christ dwell in you richly in all wisdom; teaching and admonishing one another in psalms and hymns and spiritual songs, singing with grace in your hearts to the Lord. And whatsoever ye do in word or deed, do all in the name of the Lord Jesus, giving thanks to God and the Father by him.

(The words of Christ are rich! Taste and see that He is good.)

PRAYER OF INTERCESSION

FATHER – INSTRUCT: 2 Corinthians 12:14-16
Behold, the third time I am ready to come to you; and I will not be burdensome to you: for I seek not yours, but you: for the children ought not to lay up for the parents, but the parents for the children. And I will very gladly spend and be spent for you, though the more abundantly I love you, the less I be loved. But be it so, I did not burden you: nevertheless, being crafty, I caught you with guile.

MOTHER – TEACH: Proverbs 3:27-28
Withhold not good from them to whom it is due, when it is in the power of thine hand to do *it*. Say not unto thy neighbour, Go, and come again, and tomorrow I will give; when thou hast it by thee.

SON(S) – LISTEN: Hebrews 2:14-16
Forasmuch then as the children are partakers of flesh and blood, he also himself likewise took part of the same; that through death he might destroy him that had the power of death, that is, the devil; And deliver them who through fear of death were all their lifetime subject to bondage. For verily he took not on *him the nature of* angels; but he took on *him* the seed of Abraham.

DAUGHTER(S) – RESPOND: James 2:14-16
What *doth it* profit, my brethren, though a man say he hath faith, and have not works? can faith save him? If a brother or sister be naked, and destitute of daily food, And one of you say unto them, Depart in peace, be *ye* warmed and filled; notwithstanding ye give them not those things which are needful to the body; what *doth it* profit?

(True intercession requires that we are actively involved with winning souls from the power of death. Now ask God for His wisdom.)

PRAYER OF PERSONAL REQUEST

FATHER – INSTRUCT: Jeremiah 24:6-7
For I will set mine eyes upon them for good, and I will bring them again to this land: and I will build them, and not pull *them* down; and I will plant them, and not pluck *them* up. And I will give them an heart to know me, that I *am* the LORD: and they shall be my people, and I will be their God: for they shall return unto me with their whole heart.

MOTHER – TEACH: Luke 12:31-32
But rather seek ye the kingdom of God; and all these things shall be added unto you. Fear not, little flock; for it is your Father's good pleasure to give you the kingdom.

SON(S) – LISTEN: 2 Corinthians 9:8-9
And God *is* able to make all grace abound toward you; that ye, always having all sufficiency in all *things,* may abound to every good work: (As it is written, He hath dispersed abroad; he hath given to the poor: his righteousness remaineth for ever.)

DAUGHTER(S) – RESPOND: Ezekiel 14:4-5
Therefore speak unto them, and say unto them, Thus saith the Lord GOD; Every man of the house of Israel that setteth up his idols in his heart, and putteth the stumblingblock of his iniquity before his face, and cometh to the prophet; I the LORD will answer him that cometh according to the multitude of his idols; That I may take the house of Israel in their own heart, because they are all estranged from me through their idols.

(Now ask the Lord to establish you in every good work that you may be an example of His righteousness.)

PRAYER OF GUIDANCE

FATHER – INSTRUCT: Psalm 37:23-25
The steps of a *good* man are ordered by the LORD: and he delighteth in his way. Though he fall, he shall not be utterly cast down: for the LORD upholdeth *him with* his hand. I have been young, and *now* am old; yet have I not seen the righteous forsaken, nor his seed begging bread.

MOTHER – TEACH: Isaiah 1:19-20
If ye be willing and obedient, ye shall eat the good of the land: But if ye refuse and rebel, ye shall be devoured with the sword: for the mouth of the LORD hath spoken *it*.

SON(S) – LISTEN: Proverbs 2:10-12
When wisdom entereth into thine heart, and knowledge is pleasant unto thy soul; Discretion shall preserve thee, understanding shall keep thee: To deliver thee from the way of the evil *man,* from the man that speaketh froward things.

DAUGHTER(S) – RESPOND: Proverbs 14:33-34
Wisdom resteth in the heart of him that hath understanding: but *that which is* in the midst of fools is made known. Righteousness exalteth a nation: but sin *is* a reproach to any people.

(The straight and narrow way is the path of His assurance. Now ask the Lord to surround you with His presence today.)

DEDICATION AND CONSECRATION

FATHER – INSTRUCT: Matthew 10:37-39
He that loveth father or mother more than me is not worthy of me: and he that loveth son or daughter more than me is not worthy of me. And he that taketh not his cross, and followeth after me, is not worthy of me. He that findeth his life shall lose it: and he that loseth his life for my sake shall find it.

MOTHER – TEACH: James 3:13-16
Who *is* a wise man and endued with knowledge among you? let him show out of a good conversation his works with meekness of wisdom. But if ye have bitter envying and strife in your hearts, glory not, and lie not against the truth. This wisdom descendeth not from above, but *is* earthly, sensual, devilish. For where envying and strife *is*, there *is* confusion and every evil work.

SON(S) – LISTEN: Colossians 3:12-14
Put on therefore, as the elect of God, holy and beloved, bowels of mercies, kindness, humbleness of mind, meekness, longsuffering; Forbearing one another, and forgiving one another, if any man have a quarrel against any: even as Christ forgave you, so also *do* ye. And above all these things *put on* charity, which is the bond of perfectness.

DAUGHTER(S) – RESPOND: Matthew 10:32-33
Whosoever therefore shall confess me before men, him will I confess also before my Father which is in heaven. But whosoever shall deny me before men, him will I also deny before my Father which is in heaven.

(Remember when we give all to God, He gives us His all and there is nothing that can compare. Now consecrate this day to the Savior.)

DAY 21
PRAYER OF PREPAREDNESS

FATHER – INSTRUCT: 1 Timothy 4:10-11
For therefore we both labour and suffer reproach, because we trust in the living God, who is the Saviour of all men, specially of those that believe. These things command and teach.

MOTHER – TEACH: Nahum 1:2-3, 7
God *is* jealous, and the LORD revengeth; the LORD revengeth, and *is* furious; the LORD will take vengeance on his adversaries, and he reserveth *wrath* for his enemies. The LORD *is* slow to anger, and great in power, and will not at all acquit *the wicked:* the LORD *hath* his way in the whirlwind and in the storm, and the clouds *are* the dust of his feet. The LORD *is* good, a strong hold in the day of trouble; and he knoweth them that trust in him.

SON(S) – LISTEN: Psalm 112:5-7
A good man showeth favour, and lendeth: he will guide his affairs with discretion. Surely he shall not be moved for ever: the righteous shall be in everlasting remembrance. He shall not be afraid of evil tidings: his heart is fixed, trusting in the LORD.

DAUGHTER(S) – RESPOND: Isaiah 26:3-4
Thou wilt keep *him* in perfect peace, *whose* mind *is* stayed *on thee:* because he trusteth in thee. Trust ye in the LORD for ever: for in the LORD JEHOVAH *is* everlasting strength.

(Through many challenges we are prepared for life with God's purpose and Christ's provisions. Now trust the Lord today.)

WORSHIP AND PRAISE

FATHER – INSTRUCT: Colossians 3:1-4
If ye then be risen with Christ, seek those things which are above, where Christ sitteth on the right hand of God. Set your affection on things above, not on things on the earth. For ye are dead, and your life is hid with Christ in God. When Christ, *who is* our life, shall appear, then shall ye also appear with him in glory.

MOTHER – TEACH: Psalm 4:5-6
Offer the sacrifices of righteousness, and put your trust in the LORD. *There be* many that say, Who will show us *any* good? LORD, lift thou up the light of thy countenance upon us.

SON(S) – LISTEN: 1 Peter 2:9-10
But ye *are* a chosen generation, a royal priesthood, an holy nation, a peculiar people; that ye should show forth the praises of him who hath called you out of darkness into his marvelous light: Which in time past *were* not a people, but *are* now the people of God: which had not obtained mercy, but now have obtained mercy.

DAUGHTER(S) – RESPOND: Isaiah 49:11-13
And I will make all my mountains a way, and my highways shall be exalted. Behold, these shall come from far: and, lo, these from the north and from the west; and these from the land of Sinim. Sing, O heavens; and be joyful, O earth; and break forth into singing, O mountains: for the LORD hath comforted his people, and will have mercy upon his afflicted.

(There is a Man in heaven who made possible our royal status. Now worship God for His eternal counsel.)

PRAYER OF CONFESSION

FATHER – INSTRUCT: Matthew 24:12-14
And because iniquity shall abound, the love of many shall wax cold. But he that shall endure unto the end, the same shall be saved. And this gospel of the kingdom shall be preached in all the world for a witness unto all nations; and then shall the end come.

MOTHER – TEACH: Lamentations 3:31-33
For the Lord will not cast off for ever: But though he cause grief, yet will he have compassion according to the multitude of his mercies. For he doth not afflict willingly nor grieve the children of men.

SON(S) – LISTEN: Luke 11:34-35
The light of the body is the eye: therefore when thine eye is single, thy whole body also is full of light; but when *thine eye* is evil, thy body also *is* full of darkness. Take heed therefore that the light which is in thee be not darkness.

DAUGHTER(S) – RESPOND: Amos 5:14-15
Seek good, and not evil, that ye may live: and so the LORD, the God of hosts, shall be with you, as ye have spoken. Hate the evil, and love the good, and establish judgment in the gate: it may be that the LORD God of hosts will be gracious unto the remnant of Joseph.

(Hidden agendas define iniquity; Jesus was bruised for our iniquities. Now repent of anything that dilutes the purpose of God that is to be fulfilled in your life.)

PRAYER OF GRATITUDE

FATHER – INSTRUCT: 2 Thessalonians 2:13-15
But we are bound to give thanks always to God for you, brethren beloved of the Lord, because God hath from the beginning chosen you to salvation through sanctification of the Spirit and belief of the truth: Whereunto he called you by our gospel, to the obtaining of the glory of our Lord Jesus Christ. Therefore, brethren, stand fast, and hold the traditions which ye have been taught, whether by word, or our epistle.

MOTHER – TEACH: Luke 13:11-13
And, behold, there was a woman which had a spirit of infirmity eighteen years, and was bowed together, and could in no wise lift up *herself*. And when Jesus saw her, he called *her to him*, and said unto her, Woman, thou art loosed from thine infirmity. And he laid *his* hands on her: and immediately she was made straight, and glorified God.

SON(S) – LISTEN: Psalm 119:105-106
Thy word *is* a lamp unto my feet, and a light unto my path. I have sworn, and I will perform *it*, that I will keep thy righteous judgments.

DAUGHTER(S) – RESPOND: Romans 15:9-12
And that the Gentiles might glorify God for *his* mercy; as it is written, For this cause I will confess to thee among the Gentiles, and sing unto thy name. And again he saith, Rejoice, ye Gentiles, with his people. And again, Praise the Lord, all ye Gentiles; and laud him all ye people. And again, Esaias saith, There shall be a root of Jesse, and he that shall rise to reign over the Gentiles; in him shall the Gentiles trust.

(Now thank God for His Word which points us to truth and His compassion forevermore.)

WISDOM AND UNDERSTANDING

FATHER – INSTRUCT: Isaiah 50:9-10
Behold, the Lord GOD will help me; who *is* he *that* shall condemn me? lo, they all shall wax old as a garment; the moth shall eat them up. Who *is* among you that feareth the LORD, that obeyeth the voice of his servant, that walketh *in* darkness, and hath no light? let him trust in the name of the LORD, and stay upon his God.

MOTHER – TEACH: Psalm 118:8-9
It is better to trust in the LORD than to put confidence in man. *It is* better to trust in the LORD than to put confidence in princes.

SON(S) – LISTEN: 1 Timothy 4:12-13
Let no man despise thy youth; but be thou an example of the believers, in word, in conversation, in charity, in spirit, in faith, in purity. Till I come, give attendance to reading, to exhortation, to doctrine.

DAUGHTER(S) – RESPOND: 1 Timothy 4:15-16
Meditate upon these things; give thyself wholly to them; that thy profiting may appear to all. Take heed unto thyself, and unto the doctrine; continue in them: for in doing this thou shalt both save thyself, and them that hear thee.

(Continued study in God's Word adds more blessings because His knowledge frees the soul. Now pray asking God for a diligent heart.)

PRAYER OF SERENITY

FATHER – INSTRUCT: Romans 15:13-14
Now the God of hope fill you with all joy and peace in believing, that ye may abound in hope, through the power of the Holy Ghost. And I myself also am persuaded of you, my brethren, that ye also are full of goodness, filled with all knowledge, able also to admonish one another.

MOTHER – TEACH: 1 Timothy 4:9-10
This *is* a faithful saying and worthy of all acceptation. For therefore we both labour and suffer reproach, because we trust in the living God, who is the Saviour of all men, specially of those that believe.

SON(S) – LISTEN: Isaiah 61:1-2
The Spirit of the Lord GOD *is* upon me; because the LORD hath anointed me to preach good tidings unto the meek; he hath sent me to bind up the brokenhearted, to proclaim liberty to the captives, and the opening of the prison to *them that are* bound; To proclaim the acceptable year of the LORD, and the day of vengeance of our God; to comfort all that mourn.

DAUGHTER(S) – RESPOND: Psalm 119:88-89
Quicken me after thy loving-kindness; so shall I keep the testimony of thy mouth. For ever, O LORD, thy word is settled in heaven.

(God-given faith with temperance anoints and equips us for the work of the Lord. Now ask the Lord to give you a spirit of endurance.)

PRAYER OF INTERCESSION

FATHER – INSTRUCT: John 5:43-45
I am come in my Father's name, and ye receive me not: if another shall come in his name, him ye will receive. How can ye believe, which receive honour one of another, and seek not the honour that *cometh* from God only? Do not think that I will accuse you to the Father: there is *one* that accuseth you, *even* Moses, in whom ye trust.

MOTHER – TEACH: Ruth 2:12-13
The LORD recompense thy work, and a full reward be given thee of the LORD God of Israel, under whose wings thou art come to trust. Then she said, Let me find favour in thy sight, my lord; for that thou hast comforted me, and for that thou hast spoken friendly unto thine handmaid, though I be not like unto one of thine handmaidens.

SON(S) – LISTEN: Psalm 94:11-14
The LORD knoweth the thoughts of man, that they *are* vanity. Blessed *is* the man whom thou chastenest, O LORD, and teachest him out of thy law; That thou mayest give him rest from the days of adversity, until the pit be digged for the wicked. For the LORD will not cast off his people, neither will he forsake his inheritance.

DAUGHTER(S) – RESPOND: Philippians 2:19-21
But I trust in the Lord Jesus to send Timotheus shortly unto you, that I also may be of good comfort, when I know your state. For I have no man likeminded, who will naturally care for your state. For all seek their own, not the things which are Jesus Christ's.

(Now pray for those whom you know are under the judgment of the Lord. Ask for mercy and comfort.)

PRAYER OF PERSONAL REQUEST

FATHER – INSTRUCT: Psalm 20:1, 7-8
The LORD hear thee in the day of trouble; the name of the God of Jacob defend thee; Some *trust* in chariots, and some in horses: but we will remember the name of the LORD our God. They are brought down and fallen: but we are risen, and stand upright.

MOTHER – TEACH: Ephesians 1:11-13
In whom also we have obtained an inheritance, being predestinated according to the purpose of him who worketh all things after the counsel of his own will: That we should be to the praise of his glory, who first trusted in Christ. In whom ye also *trusted,* after that ye heard the word of truth, the gospel of your salvation: in whom also after that ye believed, ye were sealed with that holy Spirit of promise.

SON(S) – LISTEN: 1 Thessalonians 2:19-20
For what *is* our hope, or joy, or crown of rejoicing? *Are* not even ye in the presence of our Lord Jesus Christ at his coming? For ye are our glory and joy.

DAUGHTER(S) – RESPOND: 1 Timothy 5:3-5
Honour widows that are widows indeed. But if any widow have children or nephews, let them learn first to show piety at home, and to requite their parents: for that is good and acceptable before God. Now she that is a widow indeed, and desolate, trusteth in God, and continueth in supplications and prayers night and day.

(All of our personal experiences are for our personal spiritual development that we may learn to trust God completely. Now pray that you can emulate the widow indeed.)

PRAYER OF GUIDANCE

FATHER – INSTRUCT: Matthew 14:13-16
When Jesus heard *of it,* he departed thence by ship into a desert place apart: and when the people had heard *thereof,* they followed him on foot out of the cities. And Jesus went forth, and saw a great multitude, and was moved with compassion toward them, and he healed their sick. And when it was evening, his disciples came to him, saying, This is a desert place, and the time is now past; send the multitude away, that they may go into the villages, and buy themselves victuals. But Jesus said unto them, They need not depart; give ye them to eat.

MOTHER – TEACH: Galatians 5:24-26
And they that are Christ's have crucified the flesh with the affections and lusts. If we live in the Spirit, let us also walk in the Spirit. Let us not be desirous of vain glory, provoking one another, envying one another.

SON(S) – LISTEN: Galatians 6:4-8
But let every man prove his own work, and then shall he have rejoicing in himself alone, and not in another. For every man shall bear his own burden. Let him that is taught in the word communicate unto him that teacheth in all good things. Be not deceived; God is not mocked: for whatsoever a man soweth, that shall he also reap. For he that soweth to his flesh shall of the flesh reap corruption; but he that soweth to the Spirit shall of the Spirit reap life everlasting.

DAUGHTER(S) – RESPOND: Psalm 94:14-15
For the LORD will not cast off his people, neither will he forsake his inheritance. But judgment shall return unto righteousness: and all the upright in heart shall follow it.

(A personal compassionate Savior is our leader. Now pray that God gives you the ability to follow His pattern.)

DEDICATION AND CONSECRATION

FATHER – INSTRUCT: Galatians 6:1-3
Brethren, if a man be overtaken in a fault, ye which are spiritual, restore such an one in the spirit of meekness; considering thyself, lest thou also be tempted. Bear ye one another's burdens, and so fulfil the law of Christ. For if a man think himself to be something, when he is nothing, he deceiveth himself.

MOTHER – TEACH: John 10:17-18
Therefore doth my Father love me, because I lay down my life, that I might take it again. No man taketh it from me, but I lay it down of myself. I have power to lay it down, and I have power to take it again. This commandment have I received of my Father.

SON(S) – LISTEN: Ephesians 3:7-9
Whereof I was made a minister, according to the gift of the grace of God given unto me by the effectual working of his power. Unto me, who am less than the least of all saints, is this grace given, that I should preach among the Gentiles the unsearchable riches of Christ; And to make all men see what is the fellowship of the mystery, which from the beginning of the world hath been hid in God, who created all things by Jesus Christ.

DAUGHTER(S) – RESPOND: 2 Corinthians 5:9-10
Wherefore we labour, that, whether present or absent, we may be accepted of him. For we must all appear before the judgment seat of Christ; that every one may receive the things done in his body, according to that he hath done, whether it be good or bad.

(The love relationship between our Father and His Son figured each of us into the equation. Now dedicate your life to Christ anew.)

DAY 22
PRAYER OF PREPAREDNESS

FATHER – INSTRUCT: Ephesians 1:17-19
That the God of our Lord Jesus Christ, the Father of glory, may give unto you the spirit of wisdom and revelation in the knowledge of him: The eyes of your understanding being enlightened; that ye may know what is the hope of his calling, and what the riches of the glory of his inheritance in the saints, And what *is* the exceeding greatness of his power to us-ward who believe, according to the working of his mighty power.

MOTHER – TEACH: Ephesians 6:17-19
And take the helmet of salvation, and the sword of the Spirit, which is the word of God: Praying always with all prayer and supplication in the Spirit, and watching thereunto with all perseverance and supplication for all saints; And for me, that utterance may be given unto me, that I may open my mouth boldly, to make known the mystery of the gospel.

SON(S) – LISTEN: John 6:45-46
It is written in the prophets, And they shall be all taught of God. Every man therefore that hath heard, and hath learned of the Father, cometh unto me. Not that any man hath seen the Father, save he which is of God, he hath seen the Father.

DAUGHTER(S) – RESPOND: Deuteronomy 8:3-4
And he humbled thee, and suffered thee to hunger, and fed thee with manna, which thou knewest not, neither did thy fathers know; that he might make thee know that man doth not live by bread only, but by every *word* that proceedeth out of the mouth of the LORD doth man live. Thy raiment waxed not old upon thee, neither did thy foot swell, these forty years.

(God has prepared us in this transition to have the spirit of wisdom and revelation in the knowledge of Christ. Now thank Him today for His mighty power in your life.)

WORSHIP AND PRAISE

FATHER – INSTRUCT: Psalm 33:1-4
Rejoice in the LORD, O ye righteous: *for* praise is comely for the upright. Praise the LORD with harp: sing unto him with the psaltery *and* an instrument of ten strings. Sing unto him a new song; play skilfully with a loud noise. For the word of the LORD *is* right; and all his works *are done* in truth.

MOTHER – TEACH: Matthew 5:3, 7
Blessed *are* the poor in spirit: for theirs is the kingdom of heaven. Blessed *are* the merciful: for they shall obtain mercy.

SON(S) – LISTEN: John 1:14, 17
And the Word was made flesh, and dwelt among us, (and we beheld his glory, the glory as of the only begotten of the Father,) full of grace and truth. For the law was given by Moses, *but* grace and truth came by Jesus Christ.

DAUGHTER(S) – RESPOND: Psalm 13:5-6
But I have trusted in thy mercy; my heart shall rejoice in thy salvation. I will sing unto the LORD, because he hath dealt bountifully with me.

(When the kingdom of Heaven has its influence in our lives, we worship spontaneously. Now, begin to worship the King of glory.)

PRAYER OF CONFESSION

FATHER – INSTRUCT: Hebrews 7:25-26
Wherefore he is able also to save them to the uttermost that come unto God by him, seeing he ever liveth to make intercession for them. For such an high priest became us, *who is* holy, harmless, undefiled, separate from sinners, and made higher than the heavens.

MOTHER – TEACH: 2 Corinthians 13:7-9
Now I pray to God that ye do no evil; not that we should appear approved, but that ye should do that which is honest, though we be as reprobates. For we can do nothing against the truth, but for the truth. For we are glad, when we are weak, and ye are strong: and this also we wish, *even* your perfection.

SON(S) – LISTEN: Luke 12:2-3
For there is nothing covered, that shall not be revealed; neither hid, that shall not be known. Therefore whatsoever ye have spoken in darkness shall be heard in the light; and that which ye have spoken in the ear in closets shall be proclaimed upon the housetops.

DAUGHTER(S) – RESPOND: 1 John 1:8-10
If we say that we have no sin, we deceive ourselves, and the truth is not in us. If we confess our sins, he is faithful and just to forgive us *our* sins, and to cleanse us from all unrighteousness. If we say that we have not sinned, we make him a liar, and his word is not in us.

(Jesus, as high priest forever, suffered and overcame every temptation. Now, confess any ungodly influences that have overtaken you today.)

PRAYER OF GRATITUDE

FATHER – INSTRUCT: John 14:1-3
Let not your heart be troubled: ye believe in God, believe also in me. In my Father's house are many mansions: if *it were* not *so,* I would have told you. I go to prepare a place for you. And if I go and prepare a place for you, I will come again, and receive you unto myself; that where I am, *there* ye may be also.

MOTHER – TEACH: John 6:47-48
Verily, verily, I say unto you, He that believeth on me hath everlasting life. I am that bread of life.

SON(S) – LISTEN: 2 Thessalonians 1:3-5
We are bound to thank God always for you, brethren, as it is meet, because that your faith groweth exceedingly, and the charity of every one of you all toward each other aboundeth; So that we ourselves glory in you in the churches of God for your patience and faith in all your persecutions and tribulations that ye endure: *Which is* a manifest token of the righteous judgment of God, that ye may be counted worthy of the kingdom of God, for which ye also suffer.

DAUGHTER(S) – RESPOND: Revelation 21:1-3
And I saw a new heaven and a new earth: for the first heaven and the first earth were passed away; and there was no more sea. And I John saw the holy city, new Jerusalem, coming down from God out of heaven, prepared as a bride adorned for her husband. And I heard a great voice out of heaven saying, Behold, the tabernacle of God *is* with men, and he will dwell with them, and they shall be his people, and God himself shall be with them, *and be* their God.

(Jesus is the Son that made the Father glad. Our faith in Him is considered our contributing factor. Now be thankful to be children of God.)

WISDOM AND UNDERSTANDING

FATHER – INSTRUCT: 1 John 2:15-17
Love not the world, neither the things that are in the world. If any man love the world, the love of the Father is not in him. For all that is in the world, the lust of the flesh, and the lust of the eyes, and the pride of life, is not of the Father, but is of the world. And the world passeth away, and the lust thereof: but he that doeth the will of God abideth for ever.

MOTHER – TEACH: John 6:61-63
When Jesus knew in himself that his disciples murmured at it, he said unto them, Doth this offend you? What and if ye shall see the Son of man ascend up where he was before? It is the spirit that quickeneth; the flesh profiteth nothing: the words that I speak unto you, they are spirit, and they are life.

SON(S) – LISTEN: 1 Thessalonians 4:16-18
For the Lord himself shall descend from heaven with a shout, with the voice of the archangel, and with the trump of God: and the dead in Christ shall rise first: Then we which are alive and remain shall be caught up together with them in the clouds, to meet the Lord in the air: and so shall we ever be with the Lord. Wherefore comfort one another with these words.

DAUGHTER(S) – RESPOND: James 1: 21-22
Wherefore lay apart all filthiness and superfluity of naughtiness, and receive with meekness the engrafted word, which is able to save your souls. But be ye doers of the word, and not hearers only, deceiving your own selves.

(Allow the love of the Father which was expressed through the engrafted word, Jesus, to save your soul. Now pray in the comfort of these words.)

PRAYER OF SERENITY

FATHER – INSTRUCT: Luke 21:32-34
Heaven and earth shall pass away: but my words shall not pass away. Heaven and earth shall pass away: but my words shall not pass away. And take heed to yourselves, lest at any time your hearts be overcharged with surfeiting, and drunkenness, and cares of this life, and so that day come upon you unawares.

MOTHER – TEACH: 1 Thessalonians 2:8-10
So being affectionately desirous of you, we were willing to have imparted unto you, not the gospel of God only, but also our own souls, because ye were dear unto us. For ye remember, brethren, our labour and travail: for labouring night and day, because we would not be chargeable unto any of you, we preached unto you the gospel of God. Ye are witnesses, and God also, how holily and justly and unblameably we behaved ourselves among you that believe.

SON(S) – LISTEN: 2 Thessalonians 2:3-4
Let no man deceive you by any means: for that day shall not come, except there come a falling away first, and that man of sin be revealed, the son of perdition; Who opposeth and exalteth himself above all that is called God, or that is worshipped; so that he as God sitteth in the temple of God, showing himself that he is God.

DAUGHTER(S) – RESPOND: Colossians 4:5-6
Walk in wisdom toward them that are without, redeeming the time. Let your speech be always with grace, seasoned with salt, that ye may know how ye ought to answer every man.

(When we watch and pray while laboring, it assures us of deliverance. Now pray that you will never be caught unaware.)

PRAYER OF INTERCESSION

FATHER – INSTRUCT: Romans 8:26-27
Likewise the Spirit also helpeth our infirmities: for we know not what we should pray for as we ought: but the Spirit itself maketh intercession for us with groanings which cannot be uttered. And he that searcheth the hearts knoweth what *is* the mind of the Spirit, because he maketh intercession for the saints according to *the will of* God.

MOTHER – TEACH: Romans 10:16-18
But they have not all obeyed the gospel. For Esaias saith, Lord, who hath believed our report? So then faith cometh by hearing, and hearing by the word of God. But I say, Have they not heard? Yes verily, their sound went into all the earth, and their words unto the ends of the world.

SON(S) – LISTEN: Matthew 4:3-4
And when the tempter came to him, he said, If thou be the Son of God, command that these stones be made bread. But he answered and said, It is written, Man shall not live by bread alone, but by every word that proceedeth out of the mouth of God.

DAUGHTER(S) – RESPOND: Mark 4:8, 13-14
And other fell on good ground, and did yield fruit that sprang up and increased; and brought forth, some thirty, and some sixty, and some an hundred. And he said unto them, Know ye not this parable? and how then will ye know all parables? The sower soweth the word.

(When we sow the word of life, others reap the blessings of God. Now intercede for loved ones, friends, and those in authority.)

PRAYER OF PERSONAL REQUEST

FATHER – INSTRUCT: 1 Peter 1:13-14
Wherefore gird up the loins of your mind, be sober, and hope to the end for the grace that is to be brought unto you at the revelation of Jesus Christ; As obedient children, not fashioning yourselves according to the former lusts in your ignorance.

MOTHER – TEACH: James 4:13-17
Go to now, ye that say, Today or tomorrow we will go into such a city, and continue there a year, and buy and sell, and get gain: Whereas ye know not what shall be on the morrow. For what is your life? It is even a vapour, that appeareth for a little time, and then vanisheth away. For that ye ought to say, If the Lord will, we shall live, and do this, or that. But now ye rejoice in your boastings: all such rejoicing is evil. Therefore to him that knoweth to do good, and doeth it not, to him it is sin.

SON(S) – LISTEN: 1 Timothy 1:11-12
According to the glorious gospel of the blessed God, which was committed to my trust. And I thank Christ Jesus our Lord, who hath enabled me, for that he counted me faithful, putting me into the ministry.

DAUGHTER(S) – RESPOND: 1 Thessalonians 2:1-2
For yourselves, brethren, know our entrance in unto you, that it was not in vain: But even after that we had suffered before, and were shamefully entreated, as ye know, at Philippi, we were bold in our God to speak unto you the gospel of God with much contention.

(It is the glorious Gospel that creates our greatest opportunities to labor in the ministry of our Lord. Now pray that He can count you faithful.)

PRAYER OF GUIDANCE

FATHER – INSTRUCT: Jude 17-20
But, beloved, remember ye the words which were spoken before of the apostles of our Lord Jesus Christ; How that they told you there should be mockers in the last time, who should walk after their own ungodly lusts. These be they who separate themselves, sensual, having not the Spirit. But ye, beloved, building up yourselves on your most holy faith, praying in the Holy Ghost.

MOTHER – TEACH: Philippians 2:5-8
Let this mind be in you, which was also in Christ Jesus: Who, being in the form of God, thought it not robbery to be equal with God: But made himself of no reputation, and took upon him the form of a servant, and was made in the likeness of men: And being found in fashion as a man, he humbled himself, and became obedient unto death, even the death of the cross.

SON(S) – LISTEN: Ephesians 6:1-3
Children, obey your parents in the Lord: for this is right. Honour thy father and mother; which is the first commandment with promise; That it may be well with thee, and thou mayest live long on the earth.

DAUGHTER(S) – RESPOND: Psalm 90:12-14
So teach us to number our days, that we may apply our hearts unto wisdom. Return, O LORD, how long? and let it repent thee concerning thy servants. O satisfy us early with thy mercy; that we may rejoice and be glad all our days.

(Our source and example of humility came through Christ who became obedient unto death. Now ask the Lord to lead you by His Spirit via the obedient trail.)

WORSHIP AND PRAISE

FATHER – INSTRUCT: Colossians 3:1-4
If ye then be risen with Christ, seek those things which are above, where Christ sitteth on the right hand of God. Set your affection on things above, not on things on the earth. For ye are dead, and your life is hid with Christ in God. When Christ, *who is* our life, shall appear, then shall ye also appear with him in glory.

MOTHER – TEACH: Psalm 4:5-6
Offer the sacrifices of righteousness, and put your trust in the LORD. *There be* many that say, Who will show us *any* good? LORD, lift thou up the light of thy countenance upon us.

SON(S) – LISTEN: 1 Peter 2:9-10
But ye *are* a chosen generation, a royal priesthood, an holy nation, a peculiar people; that ye should show forth the praises of him who hath called you out of darkness into his marvelous light: Which in time past *were* not a people, but *are* now the people of God: which had not obtained mercy, but now have obtained mercy.

DAUGHTER(S) – RESPOND: Isaiah 49:11-13
And I will make all my mountains a way, and my highways shall be exalted. Behold, these shall come from far: and, lo, these from the north and from the west; and these from the land of Sinim. Sing, O heavens; and be joyful, O earth; and break forth into singing, O mountains: for the LORD hath comforted his people, and will have mercy upon his afflicted.

(There is a Man in heaven who made possible our royal status. Now worship God for His eternal counsel.)

DAY 23
PRAYER OF PREPAREDNESS

FATHER – INSTRUCT: 1 John 3:23-24
And this is his commandment, That we should believe on the name of his Son Jesus Christ, and love one another, as he gave us commandment. And he that keepeth his commandments dwelleth in him, and he in him. And hereby we know that he abideth in us, by the Spirit which he hath given us.

MOTHER – TEACH: 2 John 3-4
Grace be with you, mercy, and peace, from God the Father, and from the Lord Jesus Christ, the Son of the Father, in truth and love. I rejoiced greatly that I found of thy children walking in truth, as we have received a commandment from the Father.

SON(S) – LISTEN: Psalm 18:1-2
I will love thee, O LORD, my strength. The LORD is my rock, and my fortress, and my deliverer; my God, my strength, in whom I will trust; my buckler, and the horn of my salvation, and my high tower.

DAUGHTER(S) – RESPOND: John 16:25-27
These things have I spoken unto you in proverbs: but the time cometh, when I shall no more speak unto you in proverbs, but I shall show you plainly of the Father. At that day ye shall ask in my name: and I say not unto you, that I will pray the Father for you: For the Father himself loveth you, because ye have loved me, and have believed that I came out from God.

(God's love for His Son and for us prepares us for the manifestations of the Father. Now ask God to increase your faith by His Word.)

WORSHIP AND PRAISE

FATHER – INSTRUCT: 3 John 2-4
Beloved, I wish above all things that thou mayest prosper and be in health, even as thy soul prospereth. For I rejoiced greatly, when the brethren came and testified of the truth that is in thee, even as thou walkest in the truth. I have no greater joy than to hear that my children walk in truth.

MOTHER – TEACH: Psalm 100:1-3
Make a joyful noise unto the LORD, all ye lands. Serve the LORD with gladness: come before his presence with singing. Know ye that the LORD he is God: it is he that hath made us, and not we ourselves; we are his people, and the sheep of his pasture.

SON(S) – LISTEN: 1 John 4:7-8
Beloved, let us love one another: for love is of God; and every one that loveth is born of God, and knoweth God. He that loveth not knoweth not God; for God is love.

DAUGHTER(S) – RESPOND: 1 John 4:9-11
In this was manifested the love of God toward us, because that God sent his only begotten Son into the world, that we might live through him. Herein is love, not that we loved God, but that he loved us, and sent his Son to be the propitiation for our sins. Beloved, if God so loved us, we ought also to love one another.

(Now worship the Father who meets all of our needs by His great love for us.)

PRAYER OF CONFESSION

FATHER – INSTRUCT: Psalm 69:13-15
But as for me, my prayer is unto thee, O LORD, in an acceptable time: O God, in the multitude of thy mercy hear me, in the truth of thy salvation. Deliver me out of the mire, and let me not sink: let me be delivered from them that hate me, and out of the deep waters. Let not the waterflood overflow me, neither let the deep swallow me up, and let not the pit shut her mouth upon me.

MOTHER – TEACH: Lamentations 3:39-41
Wherefore doth a living man complain, a man for the punishment of his sins? Let us search and try our ways, and turn again to the LORD. Let us lift up our heart with our hands unto God in the heavens.

SON(S) – LISTEN: Jeremiah 6:16-17
Thus saith the LORD, Stand ye in the ways, and see, and ask for the old paths, where is the good way, and walk therein, and ye shall find rest for your souls. But they said, We will not walk therein. Also I set watchmen over you, saying, Hearken to the sound of the trumpet. But they said, We will not hearken.

DAUGHTER(S) – RESPOND: James 5:14-16
Is any sick among you? let him call for the elders of the church; and let them pray over him, anointing him with oil in the name of the Lord: And the prayer of faith shall save the sick, and the Lord shall raise him up; and if he have committed sins, they shall be forgiven him. Confess your faults one to another, and pray one for another, that ye may be healed. The effectual fervent prayer of a righteous man availeth much.

(Confessions purify the desires of the heart that we may be conformed to His image. Now ask the Lord to search your heart today.)

PRAYER OF GRATITUDE

FATHER – INSTRUCT: Philippians 4:6-7
Be careful for nothing; but in every thing by prayer and supplication with thanksgiving let your requests be made known unto God. And the peace of God, which passeth all understanding, shall keep your hearts and minds through Christ Jesus.

MOTHER – TEACH: 1 Thessalonians 1:2-4
We give thanks to God always for you all, making mention of you in our prayers; Remembering without ceasing your work of faith, and labour of love, and patience of hope in our Lord Jesus Christ, in the sight of God and our Father; Knowing, brethren beloved, your election of God.

SON(S) – LISTEN: Colossians 4:2-3
Continue in prayer, and watch in the same with thanksgiving; Withal praying also for us, that God would open unto us a door of utterance, to speak the mystery of Christ, for which I am also in bonds.

DAUGHTER(S) – RESPOND: 2 Corinthians 9:10-12, 15
Now he that ministereth seed to the sower both minister bread for your food, and multiply your seed sown, and increase the fruits of your righteousness;) Being enriched in every thing to all bountifulness, which causeth through us thanksgiving to God. For the administration of this service not only supplieth the want of the saints, but is abundant also by many thanksgivings unto God. Thanks be unto God for his unspeakable gift.

(Thanksgiving in our activity and our grateful expressions makes us aware of God's presence. Now thank Him with a grateful heart.)

WISDOM AND UNDERSTANDING

FATHER – INSTRUCT: Psalm 105:1-4
O give thanks unto the LORD; call upon his name: make known his deeds among the people. Sing unto him, sing psalms unto him: talk ye of all his wondrous works. Glory ye in his holy name: let the heart of them rejoice that seek the LORD. Seek the LORD, and his strength: seek his face evermore.

MOTHER – TEACH: Proverbs 2:6-8
For the LORD giveth wisdom: out of his mouth cometh knowledge and understanding. He layeth up sound wisdom for the righteous: he is a buckler to them that walk uprightly. He keepeth the paths of judgment, and preserveth the way of his saints.

SON(S) – LISTEN: Isaiah 50:4-5
The Lord GOD hath given me the tongue of the learned, that I should know how to speak a word in season to him that is weary: he wakeneth morning by morning, he wakeneth mine ear to hear as the learned. The Lord GOD hath opened mine ear, and I was not rebellious, neither turned away back.

DAUGHTER(S) – RESPOND: 2 Corinthians 9:6-8
But this I say, He which soweth sparingly shall reap also sparingly; and he which soweth bountifully shall reap also bountifully. Every man according as he purposeth in his heart, so let him give; not grudgingly, or of necessity: for God loveth a cheerful giver. And God is able to make all grace abound toward you; that ye, always having all sufficiency in all things, may abound to every good work.

(Your study is the Lord's preparation to crystallize God's purpose for your life which is to speak encouraging words to the weary. Now pray that you will complete His assignment.)

PRAYER OF SERENITY

FATHER – INSTRUCT: 2 Corinthians 5:11-12
Knowing therefore the terror of the Lord, we persuade men; but we are made manifest unto God; and I trust also are made manifest in your consciences. For we commend not ourselves again unto you, but give you occasion to glory on our behalf, that ye may have somewhat to answer them which glory in appearance, and not in heart.

MOTHER – TEACH: Jeremiah 31:3-4
The LORD hath appeared of old unto me, saying, Yea, I have loved thee with an everlasting love: therefore with lovingkindness have I drawn thee. Again I will build thee, and thou shalt be built, O virgin of Israel: thou shalt again be adorned with thy tabrets, and shalt go forth in the dances of them that make merry.

SON(S) – LISTEN: Psalm 91:1-2
He that dwelleth in the secret place of the most High shall abide under the shadow of the Almighty. I will say of the LORD, He is my refuge and my fortress: my God; in him will I trust.

DAUGHTER(S) – RESPOND: Psalm 94:17-19
Unless the LORD had been my help, my soul had almost dwelt in silence. When I said, My foot slippeth; thy mercy, O LORD, held me up. In the multitude of my thoughts within me thy comforts delight my soul.

(With his loving-kindness, He drew us to make us a channel of blessing to others. Now express your love toward Him in sincerity.)

PRAYER OF INTERCESSION

FATHER – INSTRUCT: Matthew 5:43-44
Ye have heard that it hath been said, Thou shalt love thy neighbour, and hate thine enemy. But I say unto you, Love your enemies, bless them that curse you, do good to them that hate you, and pray for them which despitefully use you, and persecute you.

MOTHER – TEACH: John 14:21, 23-24
He that hath my commandments, and keepeth them, he it is that loveth me: and he that loveth me shall be loved of my Father, and I will love him, and will manifest myself to him. Jesus answered and said unto him, If a man love me, he will keep my words: and my Father will love him, and we will come unto him, and make our abode with him. He that loveth me not keepeth not my sayings: and the word which ye hear is not mine, but the Father's which sent me.

SON(S) – LISTEN: John 15:12-14
This is my commandment, That ye love one another, as I have loved you. Greater love hath no man than this, that a man lay down his life for his friends. Ye are my friends, if ye do whatsoever I command you.

DAUGHTER(S) – RESPOND: 2 Corinthians 5:17-18
Therefore if any man be in Christ, he is a new creature: old things are passed away; behold, all things are become new. And all things are of God, who hath reconciled us to himself by Jesus Christ, and hath given to us the ministry of reconciliation.

(We intercede for others because the love of God interceded on our behalf. Now pray for those in the ministry, your enemies, and those with special needs.)

PRAYER OF PERSONAL REQUEST

FATHER – INSTRUCT: Mark 12:30-33
And thou shalt love the Lord thy God with all thy heart, and with all thy soul, and with all thy mind, and with all thy strength: this is the first commandment. And the second is like, namely this, Thou shalt love thy neighbour as thyself. There is none other commandment greater than these. And the scribe said unto him, Well, Master, thou hast said the truth: for there is one God; and there is none other but he: And to love him with all the heart, and with all the understanding, and with all the soul, and with all the strength, and to love his neighbour as himself, is more than all whole burnt offerings and sacrifices.

MOTHER – TEACH: Romans 5:8-9
But God commendeth his love toward us, in that, while we were yet sinners, Christ died for us. Much more then, being now justified by his blood, we shall be saved from wrath through him.

SON(S) – LISTEN: John 15:9-10
As the Father hath loved me, so have I loved you: continue ye in my love. If ye keep my commandments, ye shall abide in my love; even as I have kept my Father's commandments, and abide in his love.

DAUGHTER(S) – RESPOND: Acts 2:36-38
Therefore let all the house of Israel know assuredly, that God hath made that same Jesus, whom ye have crucified, both Lord and Christ. Now when they heard this, they were pricked in their heart, and said unto Peter and to the rest of the apostles, Men and brethren, what shall we do? Then Peter said unto them, Repent, and be baptized every one of you in the name of Jesus Christ for the remission of sins, and ye shall receive the gift of the Holy Ghost.

(Now ask the Lord to prioritize your desires to be conformed to the first and second commandments.)

PRAYER OF GUIDANCE

FATHER – INSTRUCT: John 17:3-5
And this is life eternal, that they might know thee the only true God, and Jesus Christ, whom thou hast sent. I have glorified thee on the earth: I have finished the work which thou gavest me to do. And now, O Father, glorify thou me with thine own self with the glory which I had with thee before the world was.

MOTHER – TEACH: Titus 3:3-7
For we ourselves also were sometimes foolish, disobedient, deceived, serving divers lusts and pleasures, living in malice and envy, hateful, and hating one another. But after that the kindness and love of God our Saviour toward man appeared, Not by works of righteousness which we have done, but according to his mercy he saved us, by the washing of regeneration, and renewing of the Holy Ghost; Which he shed on us abundantly through Jesus Christ our Saviour; That being justified by his grace, we should be made heirs according to the hope of eternal life.

SON(S) – LISTEN: John 10:14-15
I am the good shepherd, and know my sheep, and am known of mine. As the Father knoweth me, even so know I the Father: and I lay down my life for the sheep.

DAUGHTER(S) – RESPOND: Hebrews 12:6-7
For whom the Lord loveth he chasteneth, and scourgeth every son whom he receiveth. If ye endure chastening, God dealeth with you as with sons; for what son is he whom the father chasteneth not?

(Jesus the man glorified the eternal Father in the earth. He earned His leadership status. Now pray for God's guidance in your life.)

DEDICATION AND CONSECRATION

FATHER – INSTRUCT: <u>1 John</u> 3:1-3
Behold, what manner of love the Father hath bestowed upon us, that we should be called the sons of God: therefore the world knoweth us not, because it knew him not. Beloved, now are we the sons of God, and it doth not yet appear what we shall be: but we know that, when he shall appear, we shall be like him; for we shall see him as he is. And every man that hath this hope in him purifieth himself, even as he is pure.

MOTHER – TEACH: <u>John</u> 3:16-17
For God so loved the world, that he gave his only begotten Son, that whosoever believeth in him should not perish, but have everlasting life. For God sent not his Son into the world to condemn the world; but that the world through him might be saved.

SON(S) – LISTEN: <u>2 Corinthians</u> 5:14-15
For the love of Christ constraineth us; because we thus judge, that if one died for all, then were all dead: And that he died for all, that they which live should not henceforth live unto themselves, but unto him which died for them, and rose again.

DAUGHTER(S) – RESPOND: <u>1 Corinthians</u> 13:8, 13
Charity never faileth: but whether there be prophecies, they shall fail; whether there be tongues, they shall cease; whether there be knowledge, it shall vanish away. And now abideth faith, hope, charity, these three; but the greatest of these is charity.

(Earth, the terrestrial planet, used to demonstrate the divine love of an eternal Father. What a revelation! Now dedicate your life to His eternal purpose today.)

DAY 24
PRAYER OF PREPAREDNESS

FATHER – INSTRUCT: 2 Corinthians 3:17-18
Now the Lord is that Spirit: and where the Spirit of the Lord is, there is liberty. But we all, with open face beholding as in a glass the glory of the Lord, are changed into the same image from glory to glory, even as by the Spirit of the Lord.

MOTHER – TEACH: James 1:25-27
But whoso looketh into the perfect law of liberty, and continueth therein, he being not a forgetful hearer, but a doer of the work, this man shall be blessed in his deed. If any man among you seem to be religious, and bridleth not his tongue, but deceiveth his own heart, this man's religion is vain. Pure religion and undefiled before God and the Father is this, To visit the fatherless and widows in their affliction, and to keep himself unspotted from the world.

SON(S) – LISTEN: 1 Peter 2:13-16
Submit yourselves to every ordinance of man for the Lord's sake: whether it be to the king, as supreme; Or unto governors, as unto them that are sent by him for the punishment of evildoers, and for the praise of them that do well. For so is the will of God, that with well doing ye may put to silence the ignorance of foolish men: As free, and not using your liberty for a cloak of maliciousness, but as the servants of God.

DAUGHTER(S) – RESPOND: Luke 4:18-19
The Spirit of the Lord is upon me, because he hath anointed me to preach the gospel to the poor; he hath sent me to heal the brokenhearted, to preach deliverance to the captives, and recovering of sight to the blind, to set at liberty them that are bruised, To preach the acceptable year of the Lord.

(The Word, the Spirit prepared us for our liberty in Christ Jesus. Now praise God for the changes in your life.)

WORSHIP AND PRAISE

FATHER – INSTRUCT: Psalm 119:41, 44-45
Let thy mercies come also unto me, O LORD, even thy salvation, according to thy word. So shall I keep thy law continually for ever and ever. And I will walk at liberty: for I seek thy precepts.

MOTHER – TEACH: Proverbs 11:24-25
There is that scattereth, and yet increaseth; and there is that withholdeth more than is meet, but it tendeth to poverty. The liberal soul shall be made fat: and he that watereth shall be watered also himself.

SON(S) – LISTEN: Psalm 112:1-3
Praise ye the LORD. Blessed is the man that feareth the LORD, that delighteth greatly in his commandments. His seed shall be mighty upon earth: the generation of the upright shall be blessed. Wealth and riches shall be in his house: and his righteousness endureth for ever.

DAUGHTER(S) – RESPOND: Psalm 117:1-2
O praise the LORD, all ye nations: praise him, all ye people. For his merciful kindness is great toward us: and the truth of the LORD endureth for ever. Praise ye the LORD.

(Now worship the Lord for His merciful kindness; He is worthy.)

PRAYER OF CONFESSION

FATHER – INSTRUCT: Luke 15:4, 7
What man of you, having an hundred sheep, if he lose one of them, doth not leave the ninety and nine in the wilderness, and go after that which is lost, until he find it? I say unto you, that likewise joy shall be in heaven over one sinner that repenteth, more than over ninety and nine just persons, which need no repentance.

MOTHER – TEACH: 1 John 1:6-7
If we say that we have fellowship with him, and walk in darkness, we lie, and do not the truth: But if we walk in the light, as he is in the light, we have fellowship one with another, and the blood of Jesus Christ his Son cleanseth us from all sin.

SON(S) – LISTEN: Colossians 1:3, 13-14
We give thanks to God and the Father of our Lord Jesus Christ, praying always for you, Who hath delivered us from the power of darkness, and hath translated us into the kingdom of his dear Son: In whom we have redemption through his blood, even the forgiveness of sins.

DAUGHTER(S) – RESPOND: 1 John 1:8-10
If we say that we have no sin, we deceive ourselves, and the truth is not in us. If we confess our sins, he is faithful and just to forgive us our sins, and to cleanse us from all unrighteousness. If we say that we have not sinned, we make him a liar, and his word is not in us.

(Walking in darkness means yielding to our physical desires more than the spiritual. Now confess any unrighteous acts in your life today, and claim assurance of forgiveness.)

PRAYER OF GRATITUDE

FATHER – INSTRUCT: Colossians 3:16-17, 24
Let the word of Christ dwell in you richly in all wisdom; teaching and admonishing one another in psalms and hymns and spiritual songs, singing with grace in your hearts to the Lord. And whatsoever ye do in word or deed, do all in the name of the Lord Jesus, giving thanks to God and the Father by him. Knowing that of the Lord ye shall receive the reward of the inheritance: for ye serve the Lord Christ.

MOTHER – TEACH: Psalm 107:1-2
O give thanks unto the LORD, for he is good: for his mercy endureth for ever. Let the redeemed of the LORD say so, whom he hath redeemed from the hand of the enemy.

SON(S) – LISTEN: Philippians 2:1-3
If there be therefore any consolation in Christ, if any comfort of love, if any fellowship of the Spirit, if any bowels and mercies, Fulfil ye my joy, that ye be likeminded, having the same love, being of one accord, of one mind. Let nothing be done through strife or vainglory; but in lowliness of mind let each esteem other better than themselves.

DAUGHTER(S) – RESPOND: Ephesians 5:19-21
Speaking to yourselves in psalms and hymns and spiritual songs, singing and making melody in your heart to the Lord; Giving thanks always for all things unto God and the Father in the name of our Lord Jesus Christ; Submitting yourselves one to another in the fear of God.

(Now thank God for everlasting mercy and our redemption from the enemy.)

WISDOM AND UNDERSTANDING

FATHER – INSTRUCT: Ephesians 5:28-30, 32
So ought men to love their wives as their own bodies. He that loveth his wife loveth himself. For no man ever yet hated his own flesh; but nourisheth and cherisheth it, even as the Lord the church: For we are members of his body, of his flesh, and of his bones. This is a great mystery: but I speak concerning Christ and the church.

MOTHER – TEACH: Romans 8:21-23
Because the creature itself also shall be delivered from the bondage of corruption into the glorious liberty of the children of God. For we know that the whole creation groaneth and travaileth in pain together until now. And not only they, but ourselves also, which have the firstfruits of the Spirit, even we ourselves groan within ourselves, waiting for the adoption, to wit, the redemption of our body.

SON(S) – LISTEN: Luke 24:38-41
And he said unto them, Why are ye troubled? and why do thoughts arise in your hearts? Behold my hands and my feet, that it is I myself: handle me, and see; for a spirit hath not flesh and bones, as ye see me have. And when he had thus spoken, he showed them his hands and his feet. And while they yet believed not for joy, and wondered, he said unto them, Have ye here any meat?

DAUGHTER(S) – RESPOND: Luke 24:42-45
And they gave him a piece of a broiled fish, and of an honeycomb. And he took it, and did eat before them. And he said unto them, These are the words which I spake unto you, while I was yet with you, that all things must be fulfilled, which were written in the law of Moses, and in the prophets, and in the psalms, concerning me. Then opened he their understanding, that they might understand the scriptures.

(It is God's desire that we have a good understanding in our relationship with Him. Now ask Him to increase your wisdom and give you understanding.)

PRAYER OF SERENITY

FATHER – INSTRUCT: 2 Corinthians 7:1-3
Having therefore these promises, dearly beloved, let us cleanse ourselves from all filthiness of the flesh and spirit, perfecting holiness in the fear of God. Receive us; we have wronged no man, we have corrupted no man, we have defrauded no man. I speak not this to condemn you: for I have said before, that ye are in our hearts to die and live with you.

MOTHER – TEACH: Romans 15:5-6
Now the God of patience and consolation grant you to be likeminded one toward another according to Christ Jesus: That ye may with one mind and one mouth glorify God, even the Father of our Lord Jesus Christ.

SON(S) – LISTEN: Philippians 1:26-27
That your rejoicing may be more abundant in Jesus Christ for me by my coming to you again. Only let your conversation be as it becometh the gospel of Christ: that whether I come and see you, or else be absent, I may hear of your affairs, that ye stand fast in one spirit, with one mind striving together for the faith of the gospel.

DAUGHTER(S) – RESPOND: Galatians 5:13-15
For, brethren, ye have been called unto liberty; only use not liberty for an occasion to the flesh, but by love serve one another. For all the law is fulfilled in one word, even in this; Thou shalt love thy neighbour as thyself. But if ye bite and devour one another, take heed that ye be not consumed one of another.

(Now with one mind and one mouth, glorify the Father from your heart.)

PRAYER OF INTERCESSION

FATHER – INSTRUCT: 2 Corinthians 4:5-6
For we preach not ourselves, but Christ Jesus the Lord; and ourselves your servants for Jesus' sake. For God, who commanded the light to shine out of darkness, hath shined in our hearts, to give the light of the knowledge of the glory of God in the face of Jesus Christ.

MOTHER – TEACH: Romans 1:16-17
For I am not ashamed of the gospel of Christ: for it is the power of God unto salvation to every one that believeth; to the Jew first, and also to the Greek. For therein is the righteousness of God revealed from faith to faith: as it is written, The just shall live by faith.

SON(S) – LISTEN: Luke 6:36, 38
Be ye therefore merciful, as your Father also is merciful. Give, and it shall be given unto you; good measure, pressed down, and shaken together, and running over, shall men give into your bosom. For with the same measure that ye mete withal it shall be measured to you again.

DAUGHTER(S) – RESPOND: Matthew 10:7-8
And as ye go, preach, saying, The kingdom of heaven is at hand. Heal the sick, cleanse the lepers, raise the dead, cast out devils: freely ye have received, freely give.

(Now intercede on behalf of those loved ones who have not experienced the love of God both Jews and Gentiles.)

PRAYER OF PERSONAL REQUEST

FATHER – INSTRUCT: 2 Corinthians 9:8-9
And God is able to make all grace abound toward you; that ye, always having all sufficiency in all things, may abound to every good work: (As it is written, He hath dispersed abroad; he hath given to the poor: his righteousness remaineth for ever.)

MOTHER – TEACH: Acts 10:1-4
There was a certain man in Caesarea called Cornelius, a centurion of the band called the Italian band, A devout man, and one that feared God with all his house, which gave much alms to the people, and prayed to God alway. He saw in a vision evidently about the ninth hour of the day an angel of God coming in to him, and saying unto him, Cornelius. And when he looked on him, he was afraid, and said, What is it, Lord? And he said unto him, Thy prayers and thine alms are come up for a memorial before God.

SON(S) – LISTEN: Ephesians 6:10, 18-19
Finally, my brethren, be strong in the Lord, and in the power of his might. Praying always with all prayer and supplication in the Spirit, and watching thereunto with all perseverance and supplication for all saints; And for me, that utterance may be given unto me, that I may open my mouth boldly, to make known the mystery of the gospel.

DAUGHTER(S) – RESPOND: 2 Corinthians 3:5-6
Not that we are sufficient of ourselves to think any thing as of ourselves; but our sufficiency is of God; Who also hath made us able ministers of the new testament; not of the letter, but of the spirit: for the letter killeth, but the spirit giveth life.

(Now pray for the peace that surpasses all of our understanding for His grace is sufficient.)

PRAYER OF GUIDANCE

FATHER – INSTRUCT: Acts 10:34-36
Then Peter opened his mouth, and said, Of a truth I perceive that God is no respecter of persons: But in every nation he that feareth him, and worketh righteousness, is accepted with him. The word which God sent unto the children of Israel, preaching peace by Jesus Christ: (he is Lord of all.)

MOTHER – TEACH: Isaiah 10:21, 27
The remnant shall return, even the remnant of Jacob, unto the mighty God. And it shall come to pass in that day, that his burden shall be taken away from off thy shoulder, and his yoke from off thy neck, and the yoke shall be destroyed because of the anointing.

SON(S) – LISTEN: 1 John 2:27-29
But the anointing which ye have received of him abideth in you, and ye need not that any man teach you: but as the same anointing teacheth you of all things, and is truth, and is no lie, and even as it hath taught you, ye shall abide in him. And now, little children, abide in him; that, when he shall appear, we may have confidence, and not be ashamed before him at his coming. If ye know that he is righteous, ye know that every one that doeth righteousness is born of him.

DAUGHTER(S) – RESPOND: 2 Corinthians 1:20-22
For all the promises of God in him are yea, and in him Amen, unto the glory of God by us. Now he which stablisheth us with you in Christ, and hath anointed us, is God; Who hath also sealed us, and given the earnest of the Spirit in our hearts.

(Just as Peter discovered our ambitions should be guided by the God who knows every heart. Pray that He will continue to guide all your decisions.)

DEDICATION AND CONSECRATION

FATHER – INSTRUCT: 2 Corinthians 5:20-21
Now then we are ambassadors for Christ, as though God did beseech you by us: we pray you in Christ's stead, be ye reconciled to God. For he hath made him to be sin for us, who knew no sin; that we might be made the righteousness of God in him.

MOTHER – TEACH: 2 Corinthians 4:7-8, 10
But we have this treasure in earthen vessels, that the excellency of the power may be of God, and not of us. We are troubled on every side, yet not distressed; we are perplexed, but not in despair. Always bearing about in the body the dying of the Lord Jesus, that the life also of Jesus might be made manifest in our body.

SON(S) – LISTEN: Luke 23:45-46
And the sun was darkened, and the veil of the temple was rent in the midst. And when Jesus had cried with a loud voice, he said, Father, into thy hands I commend my spirit: and having said thus, he gave up the ghost.

DAUGHTER(S) – RESPOND: Ephesians 4:10-13
He that descended is the same also that ascended up far above all heavens, that he might fill all things. And he gave some, apostles; and some, prophets; and some, evangelists; and some, pastors and teachers; For the perfecting of the saints, for the work of the ministry, for the edifying of the body of Christ: Till we all come in the unity of the faith, and of the knowledge of the Son of God, unto a perfect man, unto the measure of the stature of the fulness of Christ.

(We are ambassadors with the precious treasure, the living Word of God. Now consecrate your life today.)

DAY 25
PRAYER OF PREPAREDNESS

FATHER – INSTRUCT: John 5:24-27
Verily, verily, I say unto you, He that heareth my word, and believeth on him that sent me, hath everlasting life, and shall not come into condemnation; but is passed from death unto life. Verily, verily, I say unto you, The hour is coming, and now is, when the dead shall hear the voice of the Son of God: and they that hear shall live. For as the Father hath life in himself; so hath he given to the Son to have life in himself; And hath given him authority to execute judgment also, because he is the Son of man.

MOTHER – TEACH: Luke 9:56-58
For the Son of man is not come to destroy men's lives, but to save them. And they went to another village. And it came to pass, that, as they went in the way, a certain man said unto him, Lord, I will follow thee whithersoever thou goest. And Jesus said unto him, Foxes have holes, and birds of the air have nests; but the Son of man hath not where to lay his head.

SON(S) – LISTEN: Matthew 21:23-27
And when he was come into the temple, the chief priests and the elders of the people came unto him as he was teaching, and said, By what authority doest thou these things? and who gave thee this authority? And Jesus answered and said unto them, I also will ask you one thing, which if ye tell me, I in like wise will tell you by what authority I do these things. The baptism of John, whence was it? from heaven, or of men? And they reasoned with themselves, saying, If we shall say, From heaven; he will say unto us, Why did ye not then believe him? But if we shall say, Of men; we fear the people; for all hold John as a prophet. And they answered Jesus, and said, We cannot tell. And he said unto them, Neither tell I you by what authority I do these things.

DAUGHTER(S) – RESPOND: Mark 6:4-5
But Jesus, said unto them, A prophet is not without honour, but in his own country, and among his own kin, and in his own house. And he could there do no mighty work, save that he laid his hands upon a few sick folk, and healed them.

(We are prepared for everlasting life, not condemnation. Jesus made it possible. Now express your love for Him.)

WORSHIP AND PRAISE

FATHER – INSTRUCT: Ecclesiastes 3:11-13
He hath made every thing beautiful in his time: also he hath set the world in their heart, so that no man can find out the work that God maketh from the beginning to the end. I know that there is no good in them, but for a man to rejoice, and to do good in his life. And also that every man should eat and drink, and enjoy the good of all his labour, it is the gift of God.

MOTHER – TEACH: Psalm 147:1, 5
Praise ye the LORD: for it is good to sing praises unto our God; for it is pleasant; and praise is comely. Great is our Lord, and of great power: his understanding is infinite.

SON(S) – LISTEN: Psalm 150:4-6
Praise him with the timbrel and dance: praise him with stringed instruments and organs. Praise him upon the loud cymbals: praise him upon the high sounding cymbals. Let every thing that hath breath praise the LORD. Praise ye the LORD.

DAUGHTER(S) – RESPOND: John 7:37-38
In the last day, that great day of the feast, Jesus stood and cried, saying, If any man thirst, let him come unto me, and drink. He that believeth on me, as the scripture hath said, out of his belly shall flow rivers of living water.

(Our beauty originally came from God. Now praise Him in the beauty of holiness.)

PRAYER OF CONFESSION

FATHER – INSTRUCT: Job 42:1-3
Then Job answered the LORD, and said, I know that thou canst do every thing, and that no thought can be withholden from thee. Who is he that hideth counsel without knowledge? therefore have I uttered that I understood not; things too wonderful for me, which I knew not.

MOTHER – TEACH: Hebrews 2:17-18
Wherefore in all things it behoved him to be made like unto his brethren, that he might be a merciful and faithful high priest in things pertaining to God, to make reconciliation for the sins of the people. For in that he himself hath suffered being tempted, he is able to succour them that are tempted.

SON(S) – LISTEN: Hebrews 2:2-3
For if the word spoken by angels was stedfast, and every transgression and disobedience received a just recompence of reward; How shall we escape, if we neglect so great salvation; which at the first began to be spoken by the Lord, and was confirmed unto us by them that heard him.

DAUGHTER(S) – RESPOND: Hebrews 4:1-2
Let us therefore fear, lest, a promise being left us of entering into his rest, any of you should seem to come short of it. For unto us was the gospel preached, as well as unto them: but the word preached did not profit them, not being mixed with faith in them that heard it.

(Without faith, it is impossible to please God. Now confess any doubts that may be a stumbling block in your heart today.)

PRAYER OF GRATITUDE

FATHER – INSTRUCT: Philippians 2:12-13, 16
Wherefore, my beloved, as ye have always obeyed, not as in my presence only, but now much more in my absence, work out your own salvation with fear and trembling. For it is God which worketh in you both to will and to do of his good pleasure. Holding forth the word of life; that I may rejoice in the day of Christ, that I have not run in vain, neither laboured in vain.

MOTHER – TEACH: Ezekiel 33:14-16
Again, when I say unto the wicked, Thou shalt surely die; if he turn from his sin, and do that which is lawful and right; If the wicked restore the pledge, give again that he had robbed, walk in the statutes of life, without committing iniquity; he shall surely live, he shall not die. None of his sins that he hath committed shall be mentioned unto him: he hath done that which is lawful and right; he shall surely live.

SON(S) – LISTEN: Ephesians 4:1-3
I therefore, the prisoner of the Lord, beseech you that ye walk worthy of the vocation wherewith ye are called, With all lowliness and meekness, with longsuffering, forbearing one another in love; endeavoring to keep the unity of the Spirit in the bond of peace.

DAUGHTER(S) – RESPOND: Philippians 1:3-5
I thank my God upon every remembrance of you, Always in every prayer of mine for you all making request with joy, For your fellowship in the gospel from the first day until now.

(Now express your gratitude to a Savior who is merciful and longsuffering to all who will believe the Gospel.)

WISDOM AND UNDERSTANDING

FATHER – INSTRUCT: Ecclesiastes 2:24, 26
There is nothing better for a man, than that he should eat and drink, and that he should make his soul enjoy good in his labour. This also I saw, that it was from the hand of God. For God giveth to a man that is good in his sight wisdom, and knowledge, and joy: but to the sinner he giveth travail, to gather and to heap up, that he may give to him that is good before God. This also is vanity and vexation of spirit.

MOTHER – TEACH: 1 Corinthians 11:31-32
For if we would judge ourselves, we should not be judged. But when we are judged, we are chastened of the Lord, that we should not be condemned with the world.

SON(S) – LISTEN: 2 Chronicles 19:5-7
And he set judges in the land throughout all the fenced cities of Judah, city by city, And said to the judges, Take heed what ye do: for ye judge not for man, but for the LORD, who is with you in the judgment. Wherefore now let the fear of the LORD be upon you; take heed and do it: for there is no iniquity with the LORD our God, nor respect of persons, nor taking of gifts.

DAUGHTER(S) – RESPOND: Proverbs 11:1-3
A false balance is abomination to the LORD: but a just weight is his delight. When pride cometh, then cometh shame: but with the lowly is wisdom. The integrity of the upright shall guide them: but the perverseness of transgressors shall destroy them.

(The Lord is the true Judge. As believers, He allows us to judge ourselves in truth. Now ask the Lord to give you this wisdom.)

PRAYER OF SERENITY

FATHER – INSTRUCT: <u>1 Kings</u> 18:20-22
So Ahab sent unto all the children of Israel, and gathered the prophets together unto mount Carmel. And Elijah came unto all the people, and said, How long halt ye between two opinions? if the LORD be God, follow him: but if Baal, then follow him. And the people answered him not a word. Then said Elijah unto the people, I, even I only, remain a prophet of the LORD; but Baal's prophets are four hundred and fifty men.

MOTHER – TEACH: <u>John</u> 14:6-7, 11
Jesus saith unto him, I am the way, the truth, and the life: no man cometh unto the Father, but by me. If ye had known me, ye should have known my Father also: and from henceforth ye know him, and have seen him. Believe me that I am in the Father, and the Father in me: or else believe me for the very works' sake.

SON(S) – LISTEN: <u>Acts</u> 7:59-60
And they stoned Stephen, calling upon God, and saying, Lord Jesus, receive my spirit. And he kneeled down, and cried with a loud voice, Lord, lay not this sin to their charge. And when he had said this, he fell asleep.

DAUGHTER(S) – RESPOND: <u>Job</u> 19:25-27
For I know that my redeemer liveth, and that he shall stand at the latter day upon the earth: And though after my skin worms destroy this body, yet in my flesh shall I see God: Whom I shall see for myself, and mine eyes shall behold, and not another; though my reins be consumed within me.

(There may be many opinions but there is only one Way. Jesus is the way. Now ask the Lord to keep your heart and mind on Him.)

PRAYER OF INTERCESSION

FATHER – INSTRUCT: Psalm 27:4-5
One thing have I desired of the LORD, that will I seek after; that I may dwell in the house of the LORD all the days of my life, to behold the beauty of the LORD, and to enquire in his temple. For in the time of trouble he shall hide me in his pavilion: in the secret of his tabernacle shall he hide me; he shall set me up upon a rock.

MOTHER – TEACH: Isaiah 59:8-10
The way of peace they know not; and there is no judgment in their goings: they have made them crooked paths: whosoever goeth therein shall not know peace. Therefore is judgment far from us, neither doth justice overtake us: we wait for light, but behold obscurity; for brightness, but we walk in darkness. We grope for the wall like the blind, and we grope as if we had no eyes: we stumble at noon day as in the night; we are in desolate places as dead men.

SON(S) – LISTEN: John 8:10-12
When Jesus had lifted up himself, and saw none but the woman, he said unto her, Woman, where are those thine accusers? hath no man condemned thee? She said, No man, Lord. And Jesus said unto her, Neither do I condemn thee: go, and sin no more. Then spake Jesus again unto them, saying, I am the light of the world: he that followeth me shall not walk in darkness, but shall have the light of life.

DAUGHTER(S) – RESPOND: John 13:3-5
Jesus knowing that the Father had given all things into his hands, and that he was come from God, and went to God; He riseth from supper, and laid aside his garments; and took a towel, and girded himself. After that he poureth water into a bason, and began to wash the disciples' feet, and to wipe them with the towel wherewith he was girded.

(Let us follow the example of the true intercessor by showing mercy, not judgment. Now intercede for those whom you think as unworthy.)

PRAYER OF PERSONAL REQUEST

FATHER – INSTRUCT: 2 Timothy 2:10-13
Therefore I endure all things for the elect's sakes, that they may also obtain the salvation which is in Christ Jesus with eternal glory. It is a faithful saying: For if we be dead with him, we shall also live with him: If we suffer, we shall also reign with him: if we deny him, he also will deny us: If we believe not, yet he abideth faithful: he cannot deny himself.

MOTHER – TEACH: John 16:12-14
I have yet many things to say unto you, but ye cannot bear them now. Howbeit when he, the Spirit of truth, is come, he will guide you into all truth: for he shall not speak of himself; but whatsoever he shall hear, that shall he speak: and he will show you things to come. He shall glorify me: for he shall receive of mine, and shall show it unto you.

SON(S) – LISTEN: James 5:13-15
Is any among you afflicted? let him pray. Is any merry? let him sing psalms. Is any sick among you? let him call for the elders of the church; and let them pray over him, anointing him with oil in the name of the Lord: And the prayer of faith shall save the sick, and the Lord shall raise him up; and if he have committed sins, they shall be forgiven him.

DAUGHTER(S) – RESPOND: Matthew 8:7-8, 10
And Jesus saith unto him, I will come and heal him. The centurion answered and said, Lord, I am not worthy that thou shouldest come under my roof: but speak the word only, and my servant shall be healed.
When Jesus heard it, he marvelled, and said to them that followed, Verily I say unto you, I have not found so great faith, no, not in Israel.

(Now ask God to heal you of any sickness or affliction in your life today.)

PRAYER OF GUIDANCE

FATHER – INSTRUCT: Revelation 7:15-17
Therefore are they before the throne of God, and serve him day and night in his temple: and he that sitteth on the throne shall dwell among them. They shall hunger no more, neither thirst any more; neither shall the sun light on them, nor any heat. For the Lamb which is in the midst of the throne shall feed them, and shall lead them unto living fountains of waters: and God shall wipe away all tears from their eyes.

MOTHER – TEACH: Psalm 23:1-3
The LORD is my shepherd; I shall not want. He maketh me to lie down in green pastures: he leadeth me beside the still waters. He restoreth my soul: he leadeth me in the paths of righteousness for his name's sake.

SON(S) – LISTEN: John 16:28-30
I came forth from the Father, and am come into the world: again, I leave the world, and go to the Father. His disciples said unto him, Lo, now speakest thou plainly, and speakest no proverb. Now are we sure that thou knowest all things, and needest not that any man should ask thee: by this we believe that thou camest forth from God.

DAUGHTER(S) – RESPOND: Isaiah 48:17-18
Thus saith the LORD, thy Redeemer, the Holy One of Israel; I [am] the LORD thy God which teacheth thee to profit, which leadeth thee by the way [that] thou shouldest go. O that thou hadst hearkened to my commandments! then had thy peace been as a river, and thy righteousness as the waves of the sea.

(Christ led us to the fountains of living water rejoicing all the way. Now thank God for His Shepherd.)

DEDICATION AND CONSECRATION

FATHER – INSTRUCT: Job 5:6-9
Although affliction cometh not forth of the dust, neither doth trouble spring out of the ground; Yet man is born unto trouble, as the sparks fly upward. I would seek unto God, and unto God would I commit my cause: Which doeth great things and unsearchable; marvellous things without number.

MOTHER – TEACH: 2 Timothy 1:13-14
Hold fast the form of sound words, which thou hast heard of me, in faith and love which is in Christ Jesus. That good thing which was committed unto thee keep by the Holy Ghost which dwelleth in us.

SON(S) – LISTEN: 2 Corinthians 5:17-19
Therefore if any man be in Christ, he is a new creature: old things are passed away; behold, all things are become new. And all things are of God, who hath reconciled us to himself by Jesus Christ, and hath given to us the ministry of reconciliation; To wit, that God was in Christ, reconciling the world unto himself, not imputing their trespasses unto them; and hath committed unto us the word of reconciliation.

DAUGHTER(S) – RESPOND: Luke 12:40, 42-44
Be ye therefore ready also: for the Son of man cometh at an hour when ye think not. And the Lord said, Who then is that faithful and wise steward, whom his lord shall make ruler over his household, to give them their portion of meat in due season? Blessed is that servant, whom his lord when he cometh shall find so doing. Of a truth I say unto you, that he will make him ruler over all that he hath.

(Remember we shall reap if we faint not. Now renew your commitment to the ministry of reconciliation. This is going to be a great day.)

DAY 26
PRAYER OF PREPAREDNESS

FATHER – INSTRUCT: Romans 10:13-15
For whosoever shall call upon the name of the Lord shall be saved. How then shall they call on him in whom they have not believed? and how shall they believe in him of whom they have not heard? and how shall they hear without a preacher? And how shall they preach, except they be sent? as it is written, How beautiful are the feet of them that preach the gospel of peace, and bring glad tidings of good things!

MOTHER – TEACH: Exodus 19:8-9
And all the people answered together, and said, All that the LORD hath spoken we will do. And Moses returned the words of the people unto the LORD. And the LORD said unto Moses, Lo, I come unto thee in a thick cloud, that the people may hear when I speak with thee, and believe thee for ever. And Moses told the words of the people unto the LORD.

SON(S) – LISTEN: 1 Samuel 3:10-11
And the LORD came, and stood, and called as at other times, Samuel, Samuel. Then Samuel answered, Speak; for thy servant heareth. And the LORD said to Samuel, Behold, I will do a thing in Israel, at which both the ears of every one that heareth it shall tingle.

DAUGHTER(S) – RESPOND: John 6:43-45
Jesus therefore answered and said unto them, Murmur not among yourselves. No man can come to me, except the Father which hath sent me draw him: and I will raise him up at the last day. It is written in the prophets, And they shall be all taught of God. Every man therefore that hath heard, and hath learned of the Father, cometh unto me.

(It will forever be God's desire to prepare you to speak--in season--a word of comfort to the weary. Now ask Him to prepare you to spread the gospel message.)

WORSHIP AND PRAISE

FATHER – INSTRUCT: Psalm 145:1-3
I will extol thee, my God, O king; and I will bless thy name for ever and ever. Every day will I bless thee; and I will praise thy name for ever and ever. Great is the LORD, and greatly to be praised; and his greatness is unsearchable.

MOTHER – TEACH: Luke 1:41-43
And it came to pass, that, when Elisabeth heard the salutation of Mary, the babe leaped in her womb; and Elisabeth was filled with the Holy Ghost: And she spake out with a loud voice, and said, Blessed art thou among women, and blessed is the fruit of thy womb. And whence is this to me, that the mother of my Lord should come to me?

SON(S) – LISTEN: Luke 2:34-35
And Simeon blessed them, and said unto Mary his mother, Behold, this child is set for the fall and rising again of many in Israel; and for a sign which shall be spoken against; (Yea, a sword shall pierce through thy own soul also,) that the thoughts of many hearts may be revealed.

DAUGHTER(S) – RESPOND: Psalm 146:1-2, 10
Praise ye the LORD. Praise the LORD, O my soul. While I live will I praise the LORD: I will sing praises unto my God while I have any being. The LORD shall reign for ever, even thy God, O Zion, unto all generations. Praise ye the LORD.

(To be filled with the Holy Ghost for service and worship is the greatest high on earth. Now worship the Lord in the beauty of holiness.)

PRAYER OF CONFESSION

FATHER – INSTRUCT: 1 John 3:21-22
Beloved, if our heart condemn us not, *then* have we confidence toward God. And whatsoever we ask, we receive of him, because we keep his commandments, and do those things that are pleasing in his sight.

MOTHER – TEACH: Psalm 80:3-4, 14
Turn us again, O God, and cause thy face to shine; and we shall be saved. O LORD God of hosts, how long wilt thou be angry against the prayer of thy people? Return, we beseech thee, O God of hosts: look down from heaven, and behold, and visit this vine.

SON(S) – LISTEN: Job 40:6-8
Then answered the LORD unto Job out of the whirlwind, and said, Gird up thy loins now like a man: I will demand of thee, and declare thou unto me. Wilt thou also disannul my judgment? wilt thou condemn me, that thou mayest be righteous?

DAUGHTER(S) – RESPOND: 2 Corinthians 7:1-2
Having therefore these promises, dearly beloved, let us cleanse ourselves from all filthiness of the flesh and spirit, perfecting holiness in the fear of God. Receive us; we have wronged no man, we have corrupted no man, we have defrauded no man.

(The question was asked: "Will you condemn me that thou may be righteous?" Now confess any unholy acts committed in ignorance.)

PRAYER OF GRATITUDE

FATHER – INSTRUCT: 1 Timothy 4:4-6
For every creature of God *is* good, and nothing to be refused, if it be received with thanksgiving: For it is sanctified by the word of God and prayer. If thou put the brethren in remembrance of these things, thou shalt be a good minister of Jesus Christ, nourished up in the words of faith and of good doctrine, whereunto thou hast attained.

MOTHER – TEACH: Luke 8:17-18
For nothing is secret, that shall not be made manifest; neither *any thing* hid, that shall not be known and come abroad. Take heed therefore how ye hear: for whosoever hath, to him shall be given; and whosoever hath not, from him shall be taken even that which he seemeth to have.

SON(S) – LISTEN: Psalm 66:16-19
Come *and* hear, all ye that fear God, and I will declare what he hath done for my soul. I cried unto him with my mouth, and he was extolled with my tongue. If I regard iniquity in my heart, the Lord will not hear *me: But* verily God hath heard *me;* he hath attended to the voice of my prayer.

DAUGHTER(S) – RESPOND: Acts 2:7-8, 11
And they were all amazed and marvelled, saying one to another, Behold, are not all these which speak Galilaeans? And how hear we every man in our own tongue, wherein we were born? Cretes and Arabians, we do hear them speak in our tongues the wonderful works of God.

(Now be thankful for God's true nourishment, which is His uncut and uncensored Word.)

WISDOM AND UNDERSTANDING

FATHER – INSTRUCT: Job 36:5-7, 10-11
Behold, God *is* mighty, and despiseth not *any: he is* mighty in strength *and* wisdom. He preserveth not the life of the wicked: but giveth right to the poor. He withdraweth not his eyes from the righteous: but with kings *are they* on the throne; yea, he doth establish them for ever, and they are exalted. He openeth also their ear to discipline, and commandeth that they return from iniquity. If they obey and serve *him,* they shall spend their days in prosperity, and their years in pleasures.

MOTHER – TEACH: Proverbs 24:3-5
Through wisdom is an house builded; and by understanding it is established: And by knowledge shall the chambers be filled with all precious and pleasant riches. A wise man *is* strong; yea, a man of knowledge increaseth strength.

SON(S) – LISTEN: Luke 11:27-28, 31
And it came to pass, as he spake these things, a certain woman of the company lifted up her voice, and said unto him, Blessed *is* the womb that bare thee, and the paps which thou hast sucked. But he said, Yea rather, blessed *are* they that hear the word of God, and keep it. The queen of the south shall rise up in the judgment with the men of this generation, and condemn them: for she came from the utmost parts of the earth to hear the wisdom of Solomon; and, behold, a greater than Solomon *is* here.

DAUGHTER(S) – RESPOND: Romans 10:17-18, 20
So then faith *cometh* by hearing, and hearing by the word of God. But I say, Have they not heard? Yes verily, their sound went into all the earth, and their words unto the ends of the world. But Esaias is very bold, and saith, I was found of them that sought me not; I was made manifest unto them that asked not after me.

(The Lord placed emphasis on hearing the Word of God and keeping it. Now grasp this wisdom today. Pray believing.)

PRAYER OF SERENITY

FATHER – INSTRUCT: Romans 15:20-21
Yea, so have I strived to preach the gospel, not where Christ was named, lest I should build upon another man's foundation: But as it is written, To whom he was not spoken of, they shall see: and they that have not heard shall understand.

MOTHER – TEACH: Acts 2:17-19, 21
And it shall come to pass in the last days, saith God, I will pour out of my Spirit upon all flesh: and your sons and your daughters shall prophesy, and your young men shall see visions, and your old men shall dream dreams: And on my servants and on my handmaidens I will pour out in those days of my Spirit; and they shall prophesy: And I will show wonders in heaven above, and signs in the earth beneath; blood, and fire, and vapour of smoke: And it shall come to pass, *that* whosoever shall call on the name of the Lord shall be saved.

SON(S) – LISTEN: Matthew 10:27-28
What I tell you in darkness, *that* speak ye in light: and what ye hear in the ear, *that* preach ye upon the housetops. And fear not them which kill the body, but are not able to kill the soul: but rather fear him which is able to destroy both soul and body in hell.

DAUGHTER(S) – RESPOND: Luke 19:47-48
And he taught daily in the temple. But the chief priests and the scribes and the chief of the people sought to destroy him, And could not find what they might do: for all the people were very attentive to hear him.

(Search your heart today. Does the word of God have your undivided attention? Now pray for focus on God's Word.)

PRAYER OF INTERCESSION

FATHER – INSTRUCT: Psalm 143:6-8
I stretch forth my hands unto thee: my soul *thirsteth* after thee, as a thirsty land. Hear me speedily, O LORD: my spirit faileth: hide not thy face from me, lest I be like unto them that go down into the pit. Cause me to hear thy lovingkindness in the morning; for in thee do I trust: cause me to know the way wherein I should walk; for I lift up my soul unto thee.

MOTHER – TEACH: Romans 13:1-3
Let every soul be subject unto the higher powers. For there is no power but of God: the powers that be are ordained of God. Whosoever therefore resisteth the power, resisteth the ordinance of God: and they that resist shall receive to themselves damnation. For rulers are not a terror to good works, but to the evil. Wilt thou then not be afraid of the power? do that which is good, and thou shalt have praise of the same:

SON(S) – LISTEN: 1 Corinthians 3:9-11
For we are labourers together with God: ye are God's husbandry, *ye are* God's building. According to the grace of God which is given unto me, as a wise masterbuilder, I have laid the foundation, and another buildeth thereon. But let every man take heed how he buildeth thereupon. For other foundation can no man lay than that is laid, which is Jesus Christ.

DAUGHTER(S) – RESPOND: Psalm 146:5-6
Happy *is he* that *hath* the God of Jacob for his help, whose hope *is* in the LORD his God: Which made heaven, and earth, the sea, and all that therein *is:* which keepeth truth for ever:

(God made us the laborers, the husbandry, and the building. Now intercede for the fruits that need to be harvested today.)

PRAYER OF PERSONAL REQUEST

FATHER – INSTRUCT: Matthew 24:4-6
And Jesus answered and said unto them, Take heed that no man deceive you. For many shall come in my name, saying, I am Christ; and shall deceive many. And ye shall hear of wars and rumours of wars: see that ye be not troubled: for all *these things* must come to pass, but the end is not yet.

MOTHER – TEACH: 1 Thessalonians 5:3-5, 9
For when they shall say, Peace and safety; then sudden destruction cometh upon them, as travail upon a woman with child; and they shall not escape. But ye, brethren, are not in darkness, that that day should overtake you as a thief. Ye are all the children of light, and the children of the day: we are not of the night, nor of darkness. For God hath not appointed us to wrath, but to obtain salvation by our Lord Jesus Christ.

SON(S) – LISTEN: Mark 8:29-31
And he saith unto them, But whom say ye that I am? And Peter answereth and saith unto him, Thou art the Christ. And he charged them that they should tell no man of him. And he began to teach them, that the Son of man must suffer many things, and be rejected of the elders, and *of* the chief priests, and scribes, and be killed, and after three days rise again.

DAUGHTER(S) – RESPOND: Psalm 69:13-14
But as for me, my prayer *is* unto thee, O LORD, *in* an acceptable time: O God, in the multitude of thy mercy hear me, in the truth of thy salvation. Deliver me out of the mire, and let me not sink: let me be delivered from them that hate me, and out of the deep waters.

(The Light of the world keeps His children well informed. Now make your personal request as a child of the day.)

PRAYER OF GUIDANCE

FATHER – INSTRUCT: Psalm 142:3-5
When my spirit was overwhelmed within me, then thou knewest my path. In the way wherein I walked have they privily laid a snare for me. I looked on *my* right hand, and beheld, but *there was* no man that would know me: refuge failed me; no man cared for my soul. I cried unto thee, O LORD: I said, Thou *art* my refuge *and* my portion in the land of the living.

MOTHER – TEACH: Jeremiah 22:21, 29
I spake unto thee in thy prosperity; *but* thou saidst, I will not hear. This *hath been* thy manner from thy youth, that thou obeyedst not my voice. O earth, earth, earth, hear the word of the LORD.

SON(S) – LISTEN: Hosea 6:1-3
Come, and let us return unto the LORD: for he hath torn, and he will heal us; he hath smitten, and he will bind us up. After two days will he revive us: in the third day he will raise us up, and we shall live in his sight. Then shall we know, *if* we follow on to know the LORD: his going forth is prepared as the morning; and he shall come unto us as the rain, as the latter *and* former rain unto the earth.

DAUGHTER(S) – RESPOND: Psalm 143:10-12
Teach me to do thy will; for thou *art* my God: thy spirit *is* good; lead me into the land of uprightness. Quicken me, O LORD, for thy name's sake: for thy righteousness' sake bring my soul out of trouble. And of thy mercy cut off mine enemies, and destroy all them that afflict my soul: for I *am* thy servant.

(It has never taken God very long to heal us and put us on the right path. Now ask the Lord to guide your decisions today.)

DEDICATION AND CONSECRATION

FATHER – INSTRUCT: Romans 15:30-33
Now I beseech you, brethren, for the Lord Jesus Christ's sake, and for the love of the Spirit, that ye strive together with me in *your* prayers to God for me; That I may be delivered from them that do not believe in Judaea; and that my service which *I have* for Jerusalem may be accepted of the saints; That I may come unto you with joy by the will of God, and may with you be refreshed. Now the God of peace *be* with you all.

MOTHER – TEACH: John 11:40-43
Jesus saith unto her, Said I not unto thee, that, if thou wouldest believe, thou shouldest see the glory of God? Then they took away the stone *from the place* where the dead was laid. And Jesus lifted up *his* eyes, and said, Father, I thank thee that thou hast heard me. And I knew that thou hearest me always: but because of the people which stand by I said *it,* that they may believe that thou hast sent me. And when he thus had spoken, he cried with a loud voice, Lazarus, come forth.

SON(S) – LISTEN: Ephesians 4:29-30
Let no corrupt communication proceed out of your mouth, but that which is good to the use of edifying, that it may minister grace unto the hearers. And grieve not the holy Spirit of God, whereby ye are sealed unto the day of redemption.

DAUGHTER(S) – RESPOND: Jonah 2:1-4
Then Jonah prayed unto the LORD his God out of the fish's belly, And said, I cried by reason of mine affliction unto the LORD, and he heard me; out of the belly of hell cried I, *and* thou heardest my voice. For thou hadst cast me into the deep, in the midst of the seas; and the floods compassed me about: all thy billows and thy waves passed over me. Then I said, I am cast out of thy sight; yet I will look again toward thy holy temple.

(Paul desired to be refreshed. Jesus proved He had power to resurrect. We all await the day of redemption. Now dedicate this day to rereading the written Word.)

DAY 27
PRAYER OF PREPAREDNESS

FATHER – INSTRUCT: Romans 14:17-19
For the kingdom of God is not meat and drink; but righteousness, and peace, and joy in the Holy Ghost. For he that in these things serveth Christ *is* acceptable to God, and approved of men. Let us therefore follow after the things which make for peace, and things wherewith one may edify another.

MOTHER – TEACH: Psalm 22:27-30
All the ends of the world shall remember and turn unto the LORD: and all the kindreds of the nations shall worship before thee. For the kingdom *is* the LORD'S: and he *is* the governor among the nations. All *they that be* fat upon earth shall eat and worship: all they that go down to the dust shall bow before him: and none can keep alive his own soul. A seed shall serve him; it shall be accounted to the Lord for a generation.

SON(S) – LISTEN: Matthew 26:26-27
And as they were eating, Jesus took bread, and blessed *it,* and brake *it,* and gave *it* to the disciples, and said, Take, eat; this is my body. And he took the cup, and gave thanks, and gave *it* to them, saying, Drink ye all of it.

DAUGHTER(S) – RESPOND: John 21:12-14
Jesus saith unto them, Come *and* dine. And none of the disciples durst ask him, Who art thou? knowing that it was the Lord. Jesus then cometh, and taketh bread, and giveth them, and fish likewise. This is now the third time that Jesus showed himself to his disciples, after that he was risen from the dead.

(God in His infinite wisdom reduced everything to a seed. Now prepare your heart to meet your Savior.)

WORSHIP AND PRAISE

FATHER – INSTRUCT: Psalm 57:9-11
I will praise thee, O Lord, among the people: I will sing unto thee among the nations. For thy mercy *is* great unto the heavens, and thy truth unto the clouds. Be thou exalted, O God, above the heavens: *let* thy glory *be* above all the earth.

MOTHER – TEACH: Luke 1:30-33
And the angel said unto her, Fear not, Mary: for thou hast found favour with God. And, behold, thou shalt conceive in thy womb, and bring forth a son, and shalt call his name JESUS. He shall be great, and shall be called the Son of the Highest: and the Lord God shall give unto him the throne of his father David: And he shall reign over the house of Jacob for ever; and of his kingdom there shall be no end.

SON(S) – LISTEN: Ephesians 3:14-17
For this cause I bow my knees unto the Father of our Lord Jesus Christ, Of whom the whole family in heaven and earth is named, That he would grant you, according to the riches of his glory, to be strengthened with might by his Spirit in the inner man; That Christ may dwell in your hearts by faith; that ye, being rooted and grounded in love.

DAUGHTER(S) – RESPOND: Psalm 54:4, 6-7
Behold, God *is* mine helper: the Lord *is* with them that uphold my soul. I will freely sacrifice unto thee: I will praise thy name, O LORD; for *it is* good. For he hath delivered me out of all trouble: and mine eye hath seen *his desire* upon mine enemies.

(Now worship the Father for the eternal kingdom prepared for His people and Jesus, Lord of lords.)

PRAYER OF CONFESSION

FATHER – INSTRUCT: Psalm 52:1-2
Why boastest thou thyself in mischief, O mighty man? the goodness of God *endureth* continually. Thy tongue deviseth mischiefs; like a sharp razor, working deceitfully.

MOTHER – TEACH: Psalm 55:21-22
The words of his mouth were smoother than butter, but war *was* in his heart: his words were softer than oil, yet *were* they drawn swords. Cast thy burden upon the LORD, and he shall sustain thee: he shall never suffer the righteous to be moved.

SON(S) – LISTEN: Isaiah 6:3-5
And one cried unto another, and said, Holy, holy, holy, *is* the LORD of hosts: the whole earth *is* full of his glory. And the posts of the door moved at the voice of him that cried, and the house was filled with smoke. Then said I, Woe *is* me! for I am undone; because I *am* a man of unclean lips, and I dwell in the midst of a people of unclean lips: for mine eyes have seen the King, the LORD of hosts.

DAUGHTER(S) – RESPOND: John 9:1-3
And as *Jesus* passed by, he saw a man which was blind from *his* birth. And his disciples asked him, saying, Master, who did sin, this man, or his parents, that he was born blind? Jesus answered, Neither hath this man sinned, nor his parents: but that the works of God should be made manifest in him.

(In the face of God's glory, we are all men of unclean lips. Now confess any mischief or deceitful acts committed today. Then claim assurance of forgiveness.)

PRAYER OF GRATITUDE

FATHER – INSTRUCT: Romans 14:6-9
He that regardeth the day, regardeth *it* unto the Lord; and he that regardeth not the day, to the Lord he doth not regard *it*. He that eateth, eateth to the Lord, for he giveth God thanks; and he that eateth not, to the Lord he eateth not, and giveth God thanks. For none of us liveth to himself, and no man dieth to himself. For whether we live, we live unto the Lord; and whether we die, we die unto the Lord: whether we live therefore, or die, we are the Lord's. For to this end Christ both died, and rose, and revived, that he might be Lord both of the dead and living.

MOTHER – TEACH: Jonah 2:7-9
When my soul fainted within me I remembered the LORD: and my prayer came in unto thee, into thine holy temple. They that observe lying vanities forsake their own mercy. But I will sacrifice unto thee with the voice of thanksgiving; I will pay *that* that I have vowed. Salvation *is* of the LORD.

SON(S) – LISTEN: John 3:3-6
Jesus answered and said unto him, Verily, verily, I say unto thee, Except a man be born again, he cannot see the kingdom of God. Nicodemus saith unto him, How can a man be born when he is old? can he enter the second time into his mother's womb, and be born? Jesus answered, Verily, verily, I say unto thee, Except a man be born of water and *of* the Spirit, he cannot enter into the kingdom of God. That which is born of the flesh is flesh; and that which is born of the Spirit is spirit.

DAUGHTER(S) – RESPOND: 1 Thessalonians 2:13, 20
For this cause also thank we God without ceasing, because, when ye received the word of God which ye heard of us, ye received *it* not *as* the word of men, but as it is in truth, the word of God, which effectually worketh also in you that believe. For ye are our glory and joy.

(The Word of God is sufficient enough to be thankful for today. Now thank God with a grateful heart.)

WISDOM AND UNDERSTANDING

FATHER – INSTRUCT: Romans 15:4-7
For whatsoever things were written aforetime were written for our learning, that we through patience and comfort of the scriptures might have hope. Now the God of patience and consolation grant you to be likeminded one toward another according to Christ Jesus: That ye may with one mind *and* one mouth glorify God, even the Father of our Lord Jesus Christ. Wherefore receive ye one another, as Christ also received us to the glory of God.

MOTHER – TEACH: 1 Corinthians 3:16-18
Know ye not that ye are the temple of God, and *that* the Spirit of God dwelleth in you? If any man defile the temple of God, him shall God destroy; for the temple of God is holy, which *temple* ye are. Let no man deceive himself. If any man among you seemeth to be wise in this world, let him become a fool, that he may be wise.

SON(S) – LISTEN: 1 Corinthians 3:19-21
For the wisdom of this world is foolishness with God. For it is written, He taketh the wise in their own craftiness. And again, The Lord knoweth the thoughts of the wise, that they are vain. Therefore let no man glory in men. For all things are yours.

DAUGHTER(S) – RESPOND: Matthew 13:51-52
Jesus saith unto them, Have ye understood all these things? They say unto him, Yea, Lord. Then said he unto them, Therefore every scribe *which is* instructed unto the kingdom of heaven is like unto a man *that is* an householder, which bringeth forth out of his treasure *things* new and old.

(Our wisdom of the Scriptures has taught us that patience and comfort is the development of our hope. Now claim all things as yours.)

PRAYER OF SERENITY

FATHER – INSTRUCT: 1 John 5:1-3
Whosoever believeth that Jesus is the Christ is born of God: and every one that loveth him that begat loveth him also that is begotten of him. By this we know that we love the children of God, when we love God, and keep his commandments. For this is the love of God, that we keep his commandments: and his commandments are not grievous.

MOTHER – TEACH: John 9:24-27
Then again called they the man that was blind, and said unto him, Give God the praise: we know that this man is a sinner. He answered and said, Whether he be a sinner *or no,* I know not: one thing I know, that, whereas I was blind, now I see. Then said they to him again, What did he to thee? how opened he thine eyes? He answered them, I have told you already, and ye did not hear: wherefore would ye hear *it* again? will ye also be his disciples?

SON(S) – LISTEN: Revelation 3:20-22
Behold, I stand at the door, and knock: if any man hear my voice, and open the door, I will come in to him, and will sup with him, and he with me. To him that overcometh will I grant to sit with me in my throne, even as I also overcame, and am set down with my Father in his throne. He that hath an ear, let him hear what the Spirit saith unto the churches.

DAUGHTER(S) – RESPOND: Psalm 54:1-2
Save me, O God, by thy name, and judge me by thy strength. Hear my prayer, O God; give ear to the words of my mouth.

(We all have a birthday. It was the day that we believed Jesus was the Christ. Praise God for your miracle birth.)

PRAYER OF INTERCESSION

FATHER – INSTRUCT: Psalm 145:13-15
Thy kingdom *is* an everlasting kingdom, and thy dominion *endureth* throughout all generations. The LORD upholdeth all that fall, and raiseth up all *those that be* bowed down. The eyes of all wait upon thee; and thou givest them their meat in due season.

MOTHER – TEACH: Ephesians 3:10-12
To the intent that now unto the principalities and powers in heavenly *places* might be known by the church the manifold wisdom of God, According to the eternal purpose which he purposed in Christ Jesus our Lord: In whom we have boldness and access with confidence by the faith of him.

SON(S) – LISTEN: Hebrews 12:1-2
Wherefore seeing we also are compassed about with so great a cloud of witnesses, let us lay aside every weight, and the sin which doth so easily beset *us,* and let us run with patience the race that is set before us, Looking unto Jesus the author and finisher of *our* faith; who for the joy that was set before him endured the cross, despising the shame, and is set down at the right hand of the throne of God.

DAUGHTER(S) – RESPOND: 2 Thessalonians 3:11-13
For we hear that there are some which walk among you disorderly, working not at all, but are busybodies. Now them that are such we command and exhort by our Lord Jesus Christ, that with quietness they work, and eat their own bread. But ye, brethren, be not weary in well doing.

(Now intercede for all those who have failed to see God's eternal purpose for their lives.)

PRAYER OF PERSONAL REQUEST

FATHER – INSTRUCT: Psalm 142:1-2
I cried unto the LORD with my voice; with my voice unto the LORD did I make my supplication. I poured out my complaint before him; I showed before him my trouble.

MOTHER – TEACH: Mark 4:11-12
And he said unto them, Unto you it is given to know the mystery of the kingdom of God: but unto them that are without, all *these* things are done in parables: That seeing they may see, and not perceive; and hearing they may hear, and not understand; lest at any time they should be converted, and *their* sins should be forgiven them.

SON(S) – LISTEN: Daniel 7:26-27
But the judgment shall sit, and they shall take away his dominion, to consume and to destroy *it* unto the end. And the kingdom and dominion, and the greatness of the kingdom under the whole heaven, shall be given to the people of the saints of the most High, whose kingdom *is* an everlasting kingdom, and all dominions shall serve and obey him.

DAUGHTER(S) – RESPOND: Revelation 1:5-6
And from Jesus Christ, *who is* the faithful witness, *and* the first begotten of the dead, and the prince of the kings of the earth. Unto him that loved us, and washed us from our sins in his own blood, And hath made us kings and priests unto God and his Father; to him *be* glory and dominion for ever and ever.

(We are that people, the Saints of the Most High whose kingdom is everlasting. Who could ask for more? Just shout, "Glory!")

PRAYER OF GUIDANCE

FATHER – INSTRUCT: Psalm 70:1-2, 4
Make haste, O God, to deliver me; make haste to help me, O LORD. Let them be ashamed and confounded that seek after my soul: let them be turned backward, and put to confusion, that desire my hurt. Let all those that seek thee rejoice and be glad in thee: and let such as love thy salvation say continually, Let God be magnified.

MOTHER – TEACH: 2 Timothy 4:16-18
At my first answer no man stood with me, but all *men* forsook me: *I pray God* that it may not be laid to their charge. Notwithstanding the Lord stood with me, and strengthened me; that by me the preaching might be fully known, and *that* all the Gentiles might hear: and I was delivered out of the mouth of the lion. And the Lord shall deliver me from every evil work, and will preserve *me* unto his heavenly kingdom: to whom *be* glory for ever and ever.

SON(S) – LISTEN: 2 Corinthians 4:6-7, 10
For God, who commanded the light to shine out of darkness, hath shined in our hearts, to *give* the light of the knowledge of the glory of God in the face of Jesus Christ. But we have this treasure in earthen vessels, that the excellency of the power may be of God, and not of us. Always bearing about in the body the dying of the Lord Jesus, that the life also of Jesus might be made manifest in our body.

DAUGHTER(S) – RESPOND: Psalm 145:17-19
The LORD *is* righteous in all his ways, and holy in all his works. The LORD *is* nigh unto all them that call upon him, to all that call upon him in truth. He will fulfill the desire of them that fear him: he also will hear their cry, and will save them.

(Now pray for guidance and deliverance from every evil work facing you today.)

DEDICATION AND CONSECRATION

FATHER – INSTRUCT: 1 Corinthians 8:5-8
For though there be that are called gods, whether in heaven or in earth, (as there be gods many, and lords many,) But to us *there is but* one God, the Father, of whom *are* all things, and we in him; and one Lord Jesus Christ, by whom *are* all things, and we by him. Howbeit *there is* not in every man that knowledge: for some with conscience of the idol unto this hour eat *it* as a thing offered unto an idol; and their conscience being weak is defiled. But meat commendeth us not to God: for neither, if we eat, are we the better; neither, if we eat not, are we the worse.

MOTHER – TEACH: 2 Timothy 3:12-14
Yea, and all that will live godly in Christ Jesus shall suffer persecution. But evil men and seducers shall wax worse and worse, deceiving, and being deceived. But continue thou in the things which thou hast learned and hast been assured of, knowing of whom thou hast learned *them*.

SON(S) – LISTEN: 2 Timothy 3:15-17
And that from a child thou hast known the holy scriptures, which are able to make thee wise unto salvation through faith which is in Christ Jesus. All scripture *is* given by inspiration of God, and *is* profitable for doctrine, for reproof, for correction, for instruction in righteousness: That the man of God may be perfect, thoroughly furnished unto all good works.

DAUGHTER(S) – RESPOND: Titus 3:7-8
That being justified by his grace, we should be made heirs according to the hope of eternal life. *This is* a faithful saying, and these things I will that thou affirm constantly, that they which have believed in God might be careful to maintain good works. These things are good and profitable unto men.

(The Holy scriptures bring to us the wisdom of salvation to win the fight within us. Now consecrate your will today to study His holy Word.)

DAY 28
PRAYER OF PREPAREDNESS

FATHER – INSTRUCT: Ephesians 5:1-2, 6
Be ye therefore followers of God, as dear children; And walk in love, as Christ also hath loved us, and hath given himself for us an offering and a sacrifice to God for a sweetsmelling savour. Let no man deceive you with vain words: for because of these things cometh the wrath of God upon the children of disobedience.

MOTHER – TEACH: Romans 8:9-11
But ye are not in the flesh, but in the Spirit, if so be that the Spirit of God dwell in you. Now if any man have not the Spirit of Christ, he is none of his. And if Christ *be* in you, the body *is* dead because of sin; but the Spirit *is* life because of righteousness. But if the Spirit of him that raised up Jesus from the dead dwell in you, he that raised up Christ from the dead shall also quicken your mortal bodies by his Spirit that dwelleth in you.

SON(S) – LISTEN: Romans 8:12-14
Therefore, brethren, we are debtors, not to the flesh, to live after the flesh. For if ye live after the flesh, ye shall die: but if ye through the Spirit do mortify the deeds of the body, ye shall live. For as many as are led by the Spirit of God, they are the sons of God.

DAUGHTER(S) – RESPOND: Colossians 2:9-10
For in him dwelleth all the fulness of the Godhead bodily. And ye are complete in him, which is the head of all principality and power.

(Life is defined as growth; it is the Spirit of Christ that prepared and matured us for eternal life. Now praise God for the indwelling of the Spirit.)

WORSHIP AND PRAISE

FATHER – INSTRUCT: 1 Chronicles 16:23-25
Sing unto the LORD, all the earth; show forth from day to day his salvation. Declare his glory among the heathen; his marvellous works among all nations. For great is the LORD, and greatly to be praised: he also is to be feared above all gods.

MOTHER – TEACH: Psalm 51:10-12
Create in me a clean heart, O God; and renew a right spirit within me. Cast me not away from thy presence; and take not thy holy spirit from me. Restore unto me the joy of thy salvation; and uphold me *with thy* free spirit.

SON(S) – LISTEN: Psalm 104:30-33
Thou sendest forth thy spirit, they are created: and thou renewest the face of the earth. The glory of the LORD shall endure for ever: the LORD shall rejoice in his works. He looketh on the earth, and it trembleth: he toucheth the hills, and they smoke. I will sing unto the LORD as long as I live: I will sing praise to my God while I have my being.

DAUGHTER(S) – RESPOND: Ephesians 1:3-4
Blessed *be* the God and Father of our Lord Jesus Christ, who hath blessed us with all spiritual blessings in heavenly *places* in Christ: According as he hath chosen us in him before the foundation of the world, that we should be holy and without blame before him in love.

(Now worship and praise the Lord because you are seated in heavenly places in Christ.)

PRAYER OF CONFESSION

FATHER – INSTRUCT: 1 Corinthians 10:12-13
Wherefore let him that thinketh he standeth take heed lest he fall. There hath no temptation taken you but such as is common to man: but God *is* faithful, who will not suffer you to be tempted above that ye are able; but will with the temptation also make a way to escape, that ye may be able to bear *it*.

MOTHER – TEACH: Psalm 66:18-20
If I regard iniquity in my heart, the Lord will not hear *me:* But verily God hath heard *me;* he hath attended to the voice of my prayer. Blessed *be* God, which hath not turned away my prayer, nor his mercy from me.

SON(S) – LISTEN: Mark 2:15-17
And it came to pass, that, as Jesus sat at meat in his house, many publicans and sinners sat also together with Jesus and his disciples: for there were many, and they followed him. And when the scribes and Pharisees saw him eat with publicans and sinners, they said unto his disciples, How is it that he eateth and drinketh with publicans and sinners? When Jesus heard *it,* he saith unto them, They that are whole have no need of the physician, but they that are sick: I came not to call the righteous, but sinners to repentance.

DAUGHTER(S) – RESPOND: Romans 8:33-34
Who shall lay any thing to the charge of God's elect? *It is* God that justifieth. Who *is* he that condemneth? *It is* Christ that died, yea rather, that is risen again, who is even at the right hand of God, who also maketh intercession for us.

(Temptations are not sins. The yielding is the entrapment. Now confess any trespasses that may have overcome you today.)

PRAYER OF GRATITUDE

FATHER – INSTRUCT: Psalm 69:30-33
I will praise the name of God with a song, and will magnify him with thanksgiving. *This* also shall please the LORD better than an ox *or* bullock that hath horns and hoofs. The humble shall see *this, and* be glad: and your heart shall live that seek God. For the LORD heareth the poor, and despiseth not his prisoners.

MOTHER – TEACH: Colossians 2:6-7
As ye have therefore received Christ Jesus the Lord, *so* walk ye in him: Rooted and built up in him, and stablished in the faith, as ye have been taught, abounding therein with thanksgiving.

SON(S) – LISTEN: 1 Corinthians 4:20-21
For the kingdom of God *is* not in word, but in power. What will ye? shall I come unto you with a rod, or in love, and *in* the spirit of meekness?

DAUGHTER(S) – RESPOND: Colossians 3:15-16
And let the peace of God rule in your hearts, to the which also ye are called in one body; and be ye thankful. Let the word of Christ dwell in you richly in all wisdom; teaching and admonishing one another in psalms and hymns and spiritual songs, singing with grace in your hearts to the Lord.

(Now use your own song today to praise Him; make a joyful noise.)

WISDOM AND UNDERSTANDING

FATHER – INSTRUCT: Isaiah 11:2-4
And the spirit of the LORD shall rest upon him, the spirit of wisdom and understanding, the spirit of counsel and might, the spirit of knowledge and of the fear of the LORD; And shall make him of quick understanding in the fear of the LORD: and he shall not judge after the sight of his eyes, neither reprove after the hearing of his ears: But with righteousness shall he judge the poor, and reprove with equity for the meek of the earth: and he shall smite the earth with the rod of his mouth, and with the breath of his lips shall he slay the wicked.

MOTHER – TEACH: Matthew 3:15-17
And Jesus answering said unto him, Suffer *it to be so* now: for thus it becometh us to fulfil all righteousness. Then he suffered him. And Jesus, when he was baptized, went up straightway out of the water: and, lo, the heavens were opened unto him, and he saw the Spirit of God descending like a dove, and lighting upon him: And lo a voice from heaven, saying, This is my beloved Son, in whom I am well pleased.

SON(S) – LISTEN: 1 Corinthians 2:2, 4-6
For I determined not to know any thing among you, save Jesus Christ, and him crucified. And my speech and my preaching *was* not with enticing words of man's wisdom, but in demonstration of the Spirit and of power: That your faith should not stand in the wisdom of men, but in the power of God. Howbeit we speak wisdom among them that are perfect: yet not the wisdom of this world, nor of the princes of this world, that come to nought.

DAUGHTER(S) – RESPOND: Galatians 3:13-14
Christ hath redeemed us from the curse of the law, being made a curse for us: for it is written, Cursed *is* every one that hangeth on a tree: That the blessing of Abraham might come on the Gentiles through Jesus Christ; that we might receive the promise of the Spirit through faith.

(We have received the manifestation of the Father's love in the earth out of all His dominions in orbit. He used the earth to demonstrate this powerful love. Now pray for the wisdom of God to enlighten you today.)

PRAYER OF SERENITY

FATHER – INSTRUCT: Mark 14:36, 38-39
And he said, Abba, Father, all things are possible unto thee; take away this cup from me: nevertheless not what I will, but what thou wilt. Watch ye and pray, lest ye enter into temptation. The spirit truly is ready, but the flesh is weak. And again he went away, and prayed, and spake the same words.

MOTHER – TEACH: 1 John 4:1-2
Beloved, believe not every spirit, but try the spirits whether they are of God: because many false prophets are gone out into the world. Hereby know ye the Spirit of God: Every spirit that confesseth that Jesus Christ is come in the flesh is of God.

SON(S) – LISTEN: John 16:7-11
Nevertheless I tell you the truth; It is expedient for you that I go away: for if I go not away, the Comforter will not come unto you; but if I depart, I will send him unto you. And when he is come, he will reprove the world of sin, and of righteousness, and of judgment: Of sin, because they believe not on me; Of righteousness, because I go to my Father, and ye see me no more; Of judgment, because the prince of this world is judged.

DAUGHTER(S) – RESPOND: Psalm 55:16-17
As for me, I will call upon God; and the LORD shall save me. Evening, and morning, and at noon, will I pray, and cry aloud: and he shall hear my voice.

(Our consistency in prayer affirms the will of God for our lives. Now pray for contentment for your personal innermost desires.)

PRAYER OF INTERCESSION

FATHER – INSTRUCT: Isaiah 59:19, 21
So shall they fear the name of the LORD from the west, and his glory from the rising of the sun. When the enemy shall come in like a flood, the Spirit of the LORD shall lift up a standard against him. As for me, this is my covenant with them, saith the LORD; My spirit that is upon thee, and my words which I have put in thy mouth, shall not depart out of thy mouth, nor out of the mouth of thy seed, nor out of the mouth of thy seed's seed, saith the LORD, from henceforth and for ever.

MOTHER – TEACH: 1 John 2:27, 29
But the anointing which ye have received of him abideth in you, and ye need not that any man teach you: but as the same anointing teacheth you of all things, and is truth, and is no lie, and even as it hath taught you, ye shall abide in him. And now, little children, abide in him; that, when he shall appear, we may have confidence, and not be ashamed before him at his coming. If ye know that he is righteous, ye know that every one that doeth righteousness is born of him.

SON(S) – LISTEN: Romans 8:15-17
For ye have not received the spirit of bondage again to fear; but ye have received the Spirit of adoption, whereby we cry, Abba, Father. The Spirit itself beareth witness with our spirit, that we are the children of God: And if children, then heirs; heirs of God, and joint-heirs with Christ; if so be that we suffer with him, that we may be also glorified together.

DAUGHTER(S) – RESPOND: 1 Peter 1:11-12
Searching what, or what manner of time the Spirit of Christ which was in them did signify, when it testified beforehand the sufferings of Christ, and the glory that should follow. Unto whom it was revealed, that not unto themselves, but unto us they did minister the things, which are now reported unto you by them that have preached the gospel unto you with the Holy Ghost sent down from heaven; which things the angels desire to look into.

(Now intercede for loved ones by lifting up a standard against the wicked one holding them in various addictions and other vices that they may be caught up in.)

PRAYER OF PERSONAL REQUEST

FATHER – INSTRUCT: 1 Corinthians 15:45-47
And so it is written, The first man Adam was made a living soul; the last Adam was made a quickening spirit. Howbeit that was not first which is spiritual, but that which is natural; and afterward that which is spiritual. The first man is of the earth, earthy; the second man is the Lord from heaven.

MOTHER – TEACH: Ephesians 1:17-18
That the God of our Lord Jesus Christ, the Father of glory, may give unto you the spirit of wisdom and revelation in the knowledge of him: The eyes of your understanding being enlightened; that ye may know what is the hope of his calling, and what the riches of the glory of his inheritance in the saints.

SON(S) – LISTEN: Philippians 1:25-27
And having this confidence, I know that I shall abide and continue with you all for your furtherance and joy of faith; That your rejoicing may be more abundant in Jesus Christ for me by my coming to you again. Only let your conversation be as it becometh the gospel of Christ: that whether I come and see you, or else be absent, I may hear of your affairs, that ye stand fast in one spirit, with one mind striving together for the faith of the gospel.

DAUGHTER(S) – RESPOND: 1 Corinthians 12:3-7
Wherefore I give you to understand, that no man speaking by the Spirit of God calleth Jesus accursed: and that no man can say that Jesus is the Lord, but by the Holy Ghost. Now there are diversities of gifts, but the same Spirit. And there are differences of administrations, but the same Lord. And there are diversities of operations, but it is the same God which worketh all in all. But the manifestation of the Spirit is given to every man to profit withal.

(Now petition the Lord for the gifts He purposed for your life through the Holy Ghost.)

PRAYER OF GUIDANCE

FATHER – INSTRUCT: Isaiah 64:4-5
For since the beginning of the world men have not heard, nor perceived by the ear, neither hath the eye seen, O God, beside thee, what he hath prepared for him that waiteth for him. Thou meetest him that rejoiceth and worketh righteousness, those that remember thee in thy ways: behold, thou art wroth; for we have sinned: in those is continuance, and we shall be saved.

MOTHER – TEACH: Galatians 6:8-10
For he that soweth to his flesh shall of the flesh reap corruption; but he that soweth to the Spirit shall of the Spirit reap life everlasting. And let us not be weary in well doing: for in due season we shall reap, if we faint not. As we have therefore opportunity, let us do good unto all men, especially unto them who are of the household of faith.

SON(S) – LISTEN: 2 Timothy 1:6-7
Wherefore I put thee in remembrance that thou stir up the gift of God, which is in thee by the putting on of my hands. For God hath not given us the spirit of fear; but of power, and of love, and of a sound mind.

DAUGHTER(S) – RESPOND: Philippians 2:5-8
Let this mind be in you, which was also in Christ Jesus: Who, being in the form of God, thought it not robbery to be equal with God: But made himself of no reputation, and took upon him the form of a servant, and was made in the likeness of men: And being found in fashion as a man, he humbled himself, and became obedient unto death, even the death of the cross.

(The Lord guides our steps to walk in the Spirit that we may obtain an incorruptible crown. Now thank Him for His guidance today.)

DEDICATION AND CONSECRATION

FATHER – INSTRUCT: <u>1 John</u> 5:5-6
Who is he that overcometh the world, but he that believeth that Jesus is the Son of God? This is he that came by water and blood, even Jesus Christ; not by water only, but by water and blood. And it is the Spirit that beareth witness, because the Spirit is truth.

MOTHER – TEACH: <u>John</u> 15:26-27
But when the Comforter is come, whom I will send unto you from the Father, even the Spirit of truth, which proceedeth from the Father, he shall testify of me: And ye also shall bear witness, because ye have been with me from the beginning.

SON(S) – LISTEN: <u>1 Corinthians</u> 2:9-12
But as it is written, Eye hath not seen, nor ear heard, neither have entered into the heart of man, the things which God hath prepared for them that love him. But God hath revealed them unto us by his Spirit: for the Spirit searcheth all things, yea, the deep things of God. For what man knoweth the things of a man, save the spirit of man which is in him? even so the things of God knoweth no man, but the Spirit of God. Now we have received, not the spirit of the world, but the spirit which is of God; that we might know the things that are freely given to us of God.

DAUGHTER(S) – RESPOND: <u>Ephesians</u> 1:19-21
And what is the exceeding greatness of his power to us-ward who believe, according to the working of his mighty power, Which he wrought in Christ, when he raised him from the dead, and set him at his own right hand in the heavenly places, Far above all principality, and power, and might, and dominion, and every name that is named, not only in this world, but also in that which is to come.

(Jesus is the Son of God. The Holy Ghost is the Comforter. God has called us to be His own special people. Now, rededicate your life today.)

DAY 29
PRAYER OF PREPAREDNESS

FATHER – INSTRUCT: John 3:16-18
For God so loved the world, that he gave his only begotten Son, that whosoever believeth in him should not perish, but have everlasting life. For God sent not his Son into the world to condemn the world; but that the world through him might be saved. He that believeth on him is not condemned: but he that believeth not is condemned already, because he hath not believed in the name of the only begotten Son of God.

MOTHER – TEACH: Romans 8:1-2
There is therefore now no condemnation to them which are in Christ Jesus, who walk not after the flesh, but after the Spirit. For the law of the Spirit of life in Christ Jesus hath made me free from the law of sin and death.

SON(S) – LISTEN: 1 John 5:7-8
For there are three that bear record in heaven, the Father, the Word, and the Holy Ghost: and these three are one. And there are three that bear witness in earth, the Spirit, and the water, and the blood: and these three agree in one.

DAUGHTER(S) – RESPOND: Luke 18:1, 7-8
And he spake a parable unto them to this end, that men ought always to pray, and not to faint; And shall not God avenge his own elect, which cry day and night unto him, though he bear long with them? I tell you that he will avenge them speedily. Nevertheless when the Son of man cometh, shall he find faith on the earth?

(What a wonderful life! All of heaven got involved to save the saints of the eternal Father. Now praise Him for preparing your heart for His salvation.)

WORSHIP AND PRAISE

FATHER – INSTRUCT: Psalm 33:1-3
Rejoice in the LORD, O ye righteous: for praise is comely for the upright. Praise the LORD with harp: sing unto him with the psaltery and an instrument of ten strings. Sing unto him a new song; play skilfully with a loud noise.

MOTHER – TEACH: Psalm 100:1-5
Make a joyful noise unto the LORD, all ye lands. Serve the LORD with gladness: come before his presence with singing. Know ye that the LORD he is God: it is he that hath made us, and not we ourselves; we are his people, and the sheep of his pasture. Enter into his gates with thanksgiving, and into his courts with praise: be thankful unto him, and bless his name. For the LORD is good; his mercy is everlasting; and his truth endureth to all generations.

SON(S) – LISTEN: Psalm 23:1-6
The LORD is my shepherd; I shall not want. He maketh me to lie down in green pastures: he leadeth me beside the still waters. He restoreth my soul: he leadeth me in the paths of righteousness for his name's sake. Yea, though I walk through the valley of the shadow of death, I will fear no evil: for thou art with me; thy rod and thy staff they comfort me. Thou preparest a table before me in the presence of mine enemies: thou anointest my head with oil; my cup runneth over. Surely goodness and mercy shall follow me all the days of my life: and I will dwell in the house of the LORD for ever.

DAUGHTER(S) – RESPOND: Psalm 150:1-6
Praise ye the LORD. Praise God in his sanctuary: praise him in the firmament of his power. Praise him for his mighty acts: praise him according to his excellent greatness. Praise him with the sound of the trumpet: praise him with the psaltery and harp. Praise him with the timbrel and dance: praise him with stringed instruments and organs. Praise him upon the loud cymbals: praise him upon the high sounding cymbals. Let every thing that hath breath praise the LORD. Praise ye the LORD.

(Now worship the Lord. Today use everything at your disposal. He is worthy of all.)

PRAYER OF CONFESSION

FATHER – INSTRUCT: 1 John 3:18:21
My little children, let us not love in word, neither in tongue; but in deed and in truth. And hereby we know that we are of the truth, and shall assure our hearts before him. For if our heart condemn us, God is greater than our heart, and knoweth all things. Beloved, if our heart condemn us not, then have we confidence toward God.

MOTHER – TEACH: Psalm 71:7-9
I am as a wonder unto many; but thou art my strong refuge. Let my mouth be filled with thy praise and with thy honour all the day. Cast me not off in the time of old age; forsake me not when my strength faileth.

SON(S) – LISTEN: Ephesians 4:29-30
Let no corrupt communication proceed out of your mouth, but that which is good to the use of edifying, that it may minister grace unto the hearers. And grieve not the holy Spirit of God, whereby ye are sealed unto the day of redemption.

DAUGHTER(S) – RESPOND: John 11:32-35
Then when Mary was come where Jesus was, and saw him, she fell down at his feet, saying unto him, Lord, if thou hadst been here, my brother had not died. When Jesus therefore saw her weeping, and the Jews also weeping which came with her, he groaned in the spirit, and was troubled. And said, Where have ye laid him? They said unto him, Lord, come and see. Jesus wept.

(Let us not grieve the Holy Spirit with doubts or any root of bitterness against a brother. Now confess anything that hinders your growth in the Lord today.)

PRAYER OF GRATITUDE

FATHER – INSTRUCT: Psalm 33:12-15
Blessed is the nation whose God is the LORD; and the people whom he hath chosen for his own inheritance. The LORD looketh from heaven; he beholdeth all the sons of men. From the place of his habitation he looketh upon all the inhabitants of the earth. He fashioneth their hearts alike; he considereth all their works.

MOTHER – TEACH: Luke 13:16-17
And ought not this woman, being a daughter of Abraham, whom Satan hath bound, lo, these eighteen years, be loosed from this bond on the sabbath day? And when he had said these things, all his adversaries were ashamed: and all the people rejoiced for all the glorious things that were done by him.

SON(S) – LISTEN: Isaiah 61:1-2
The Spirit of the Lord GOD is upon me; because the LORD hath anointed me to preach good tidings unto the meek; he hath sent me to bind up the brokenhearted, to proclaim liberty to the captives, and the opening of the prison to them that are bound; To proclaim the acceptable year of the LORD, and the day of vengeance of our God; to comfort all that mourn.

DAUGHTER(S) – RESPOND: Luke 10:21-22
In that hour Jesus rejoiced in spirit, and said, I thank thee, O Father, Lord of heaven and earth, that thou hast hid these things from the wise and prudent, and hast revealed them unto babes: even so, Father; for so it seemed good in thy sight. All things are delivered to me of my Father: and no man knoweth who the Son is, but the Father; and who the Father is, but the Son, and he to whom the Son will reveal him.

(Rejoice today out of a grateful heart, just as Christ rejoiced in the Spirit.)

WISDOM AND UNDERSTANDING

FATHER – INSTRUCT: Isaiah 62:1-3
For Zion's sake will I not hold my peace, and for Jerusalem's sake I will not rest, until the righteousness thereof go forth as brightness, and the salvation thereof as a lamp that burneth. And the Gentiles shall see thy righteousness, and all kings thy glory: and thou shalt be called by a new name, which the mouth of the LORD shall name. Thou shalt also be a crown of glory in the hand of the LORD, and a royal diadem in the hand of thy God.

MOTHER – TEACH: Luke 13:18-21
Then said he, Unto what is the kingdom of God like? and whereunto shall I resemble it? It is like a grain of mustard seed, which a man took, and cast into his garden; and it grew, and waxed a great tree; and the fowls of the air lodged in the branches of it. And again he said, Whereunto shall I liken the kingdom of God? It is like leaven, which a woman took and hid in three measures of meal, till the whole was leavened.

SON(S) – LISTEN: 1 John 2:12-14
I write unto you, little children, because your sins are forgiven you for his name's sake. I write unto you, fathers, because ye have known him that is from the beginning. I write unto you, young men, because ye have overcome the wicked one. I write unto you, little children, because ye have known the Father. I have written unto you, fathers, because ye have known him that is from the beginning. I have written unto you, young men, because ye are strong, and the word of God abideth in you, and ye have overcome the wicked one.

DAUGHTER(S) – RESPOND: 1 John 2:15-17
Love not the world, neither the things that are in the world. If any man love the world, the love of the Father is not in him. For all that is in the world, the lust of the flesh, and the lust of the eyes, and the pride of life, is not of the Father, but is of the world. And the world passeth away, and the lust thereof: but he that doeth the will of God abideth for ever.

(The fathers, the young men, the children, all need the word of God in wisdom to overcome the wicked one. Now pray that you will become a crown of glory in God's hand.)

PRAYER OF SERENITY

FATHER – INSTRUCT: <u>Acts</u> 19:1-2, 6
And it came to pass, that, while Apollos was at Corinth, Paul having passed through the upper coasts came to Ephesus: and finding certain disciples, He said unto them, Have ye received the Holy Ghost since ye believed? And they said unto him, We have not so much as heard whether there be any Holy Ghost. And when Paul had laid his hands upon them, the Holy Ghost came on them; and they spake with tongues, and prophesied.

MOTHER – TEACH: <u>John</u> 6:61-63
When Jesus knew in himself that his disciples murmured at it, he said unto them, Doth this offend you? What and if ye shall see the Son of man ascend up where he was before? It is the spirit that quickeneth; the flesh profiteth nothing: the words that I speak unto you, they are spirit, and they are life.

SON(S) – LISTEN: <u>John</u> 7:37-38
In the last day, that great day of the feast, Jesus stood and cried, saying, If any man thirst, let him come unto me, and drink. He that believeth on me, as the scripture hath said, out of his belly shall flow rivers of living water.

DAUGHTER(S) – RESPOND: <u>Acts</u> 20:28-30
Take heed therefore unto yourselves, and to all the flock, over the which the Holy Ghost hath made you overseers, to feed the church of God, which he hath purchased with his own blood. For I know this, that after my departing shall grievous wolves enter in among you, not sparing the flock. Also of your own selves shall men arise, speaking perverse things, to draw away disciples after them.

(The Holy Ghost is promised to every believer, and especially to those who would be witnesses. Now pray for the indwelling of His Spirit in your life.)

PRAYER OF INTERCESSION

FATHER – INSTRUCT: Isaiah 65:1-3
I am sought of them that asked not for me; I am found of them that sought me not: I said, Behold me, behold me, unto a nation that was not called by my name. I have spread out my hands all the day unto a rebellious people, which walketh in a way that was not good, after their own thoughts; A people that provoketh me to anger continually to my face; that sacrificeth in gardens, and burneth incense upon altars of brick.

MOTHER – TEACH: Ephesians 2:1-4
And you hath he quickened, who were dead in trespasses and sins; Wherein in time past ye walked according to the course of this world, according to the prince of the power of the air, the spirit that now worketh in the children of disobedience: Among whom also we all had our conversation in times past in the lusts of our flesh, fulfilling the desires of the flesh and of the mind; and were by nature the children of wrath, even as others. But God, who is rich in mercy, for his great love wherewith he loved us.

SON(S) – LISTEN: Hebrews 9:13-14
For if the blood of bulls and of goats, and the ashes of an heifer sprinkling the unclean, sanctifieth to the purifying of the flesh: How much more shall the blood of Christ, who through the eternal Spirit offered himself without spot to God, purge your conscience from dead works to serve the living God?

DAUGHTER(S) – RESPOND: Hebrews 9:15-16
And for this cause he is the mediator of the New Testament, that by means of death, for the redemption of the transgressions that were under the first testament, they which are called might receive the promise of eternal inheritance. For where a testament is, there must also of necessity be the death of the testator.

(Now intercede for those who have been called to receive the eternal promise and inheritance.)

PRAYER OF PERSONAL REQUEST

FATHER – INSTRUCT: Hebrews 9:27-28
And as it is appointed unto men once to die, but after this the judgment: So Christ was once offered to bear the sins of many; and unto them that look for him shall he appear the second time without sin unto salvation.

MOTHER – TEACH: Luke 12:6-7
Are not five sparrows sold for two farthings, and not one of them is forgotten before God? But even the very hairs of your head are all numbered. Fear not therefore: ye are of more value than many sparrows.

SON(S) – LISTEN: Psalm 79:11-13
Let the sighing of the prisoner come before thee; according to the greatness of thy power preserve thou those that are appointed to die; And render unto our neighbours sevenfold into their bosom their reproach, wherewith they have reproached thee, O Lord. So we thy people and sheep of thy pasture will give thee thanks for ever: we will show forth thy praise to all generations.

DAUGHTER(S) – RESPOND: Psalm 14:1-2, 5
The fool hath said in his heart, There is no God. They are corrupt, they have done abominable works, there is none that doeth good. The LORD looked down from heaven upon the children of men, to see if there were any that did understand, and seek God. There were they in great fear: for God is in the generation of the righteous.

(Jesus overcame death. Now pray for that abundant life in Him today.)

PRAYER OF GUIDANCE

FATHER – INSTRUCT: Isaiah 66:22-24
For as the new heavens and the new earth, which I will make, shall remain before me, saith the LORD, so shall your seed and your name remain. And it shall come to pass, that from one new moon to another, and from one sabbath to another, shall all flesh come to worship before me, saith the LORD. And they shall go forth, and look upon the carcases of the men that have transgressed against me: for their worm shall not die, neither shall their fire be quenched; and they shall be an abhorring unto all flesh.

MOTHER – TEACH: Psalm 19:7-11
The law of the LORD is perfect, converting the soul: the testimony of the LORD is sure, making wise the simple. The statutes of the LORD are right, rejoicing the heart: the commandment of the LORD is pure, enlightening the eyes. The fear of the LORD is clean, enduring for ever: the judgments of the LORD are true and righteous altogether. More to be desired are they than gold, yea, than much fine gold: sweeter also than honey and the honeycomb. Moreover by them is thy servant warned: and in keeping of them there is great reward.

SON(S) – LISTEN: Luke 11:45-46, 49-50
Then answered one of the lawyers, and said unto him, Master, thus saying thou reproachest us also. And he said, Woe unto you also, ye lawyers! for ye lade men with burdens grievous to be borne, and ye yourselves touch not the burdens with one of your fingers. Therefore also said the wisdom of God, I will send them prophets and apostles, and some of them they shall slay and persecute: That the blood of all the prophets, which was shed from the foundation of the world, may be required of this generation.

DAUGHTER(S) – RESPOND: Psalm 68:6-8
God setteth the solitary in families: he bringeth out those which are bound with chains: but the rebellious dwell in a dry land. O God, when thou wentest forth before thy people, when thou didst march through the wilderness; Selah: The earth shook, the heavens also dropped at the presence of God: even Sinai itself was moved at the presence of God, the God of Israel.

(The Lord will guide us with His law, testimony, statutes, commandments, fear, and judgments, all tempered in His love. Now commit your decisions to Him today.)

DEDICATION AND CONSECRATION

FATHER – INSTRUCT: John 1:32-34
And John bare record, saying, I saw the Spirit descending from heaven like a dove, and it abode upon him. And I knew him not: but he that sent me to baptize with water, the same said unto me, Upon whom thou shalt see the Spirit descending, and remaining on him, the same is he which baptizeth with the Holy Ghost. And I saw, and bare record that this is the Son of God.

MOTHER – TEACH: John 10:15-17
As the Father knoweth me, even so know I the Father: and I lay down my life for the sheep. And other sheep I have, which are not of this fold: them also I must bring, and they shall hear my voice; and there shall be one fold, and one shepherd. Therefore doth my Father love me, because I lay down my life, that I might take it again.

SON(S) – LISTEN: John 11:25-26
Jesus said unto her, I am the resurrection, and the life: he that believeth in me, though he were dead, yet shall he live: And whosoever liveth and believeth in me shall never die. Believest thou this?

DAUGHTER(S) – RESPOND: John 6:27-29
Labour not for the meat which perisheth, but for that meat which endureth unto everlasting life, which the Son of man shall give unto you: for him hath God the Father sealed. Then said they unto him, What shall we do, that we might work the works of God? Jesus answered and said unto them, This is the work of God, that ye believe on him whom he hath sent.

(The Cross is shaped like a syringe used to inject the pure blood of Jesus to revive His creation. Now consecrate your life today to His service.)

DAY 30
PRAYER OF PREPAREDNESS

FATHER – INSTRUCT: John 1:43-47
The day following Jesus would go forth into Galilee, and findeth Philip, and saith unto him, Follow me. Now Philip was of Bethsaida, the city of Andrew and Peter. Philip findeth Nathanael, and saith unto him, We have found him, of whom Moses in the law, and the prophets, did write, Jesus of Nazareth, the son of Joseph. And Nathanael said unto him, Can there any good thing come out of Nazareth? Philip saith unto him, Come and see. Jesus saw Nathanael coming to him, and saith of him, Behold an Israelite indeed, in whom is no guile!

MOTHER – TEACH: John 10:34-38
Jesus answered them, Is it not written in your law, I said, Ye are gods? If he called them gods, unto whom the word of God came, and the scripture cannot be broken; Say ye of him, whom the Father hath sanctified, and sent into the world, Thou blasphemest; because I said, I am the Son of God? If I do not the works of my Father, believe me not. But if I do, though ye believe not me, believe the works: that ye may know, and believe, that the Father is in me, and I in him.

SON(S) – LISTEN: Hebrews 5:1-2
For every high priest taken from among men is ordained for men in things pertaining to God, that he may offer both gifts and sacrifices for sins: Who can have compassion on the ignorant, and on them that are out of the way; for that he himself also is compassed with infirmity.

DAUGHTER(S) – RESPOND: John 6:36-39
But I said unto you, That ye also have seen me, and believe not. All that the Father giveth me shall come to me; and him that cometh to me I will in no wise cast out. For I came down from heaven, not to do mine own will, but the will of him that sent me. And this is the Father's will which hath sent me, that of all which he hath given me I should lose nothing, but should raise it up again at the last day.

(Jesus found Philip; Philip found Nathaniel. Look for your friends today and bring them to Christ.)

WORSHIP AND PRAISE

FATHER—INSTRUCT: Ephesians 5:13-15
But all things that are reproved are made manifest by the light: for whatsoever doth make manifest is light. Wherefore he saith, Awake thou that sleepest, and arise from the dead, and Christ shall give thee light. See then that ye walk circumspectly, not as fools, but as wise.

MOTHER – TEACH: Colossians 2:13-15
And you, being dead in your sins and the uncircumcision of your flesh, hath he quickened together with him, having forgiven you all trespasses; Blotting out the handwriting of ordinances that was against us, which was contrary to us, and took it out of the way, nailing it to his cross; And having spoiled principalities and powers, he made a show of them openly, triumphing over them in it.

SON(S) – LISTEN: Psalm 86:3-5
Be merciful unto me, O Lord: for I cry unto thee daily. Rejoice the soul of thy servant: for unto thee, O Lord, do I lift up my soul. For thou, Lord, art good, and ready to forgive; and plenteous in mercy unto all them that call upon thee.

DAUGHTER(S) – RESPOND: Psalm 27:7-9
Hear, O LORD, when I cry with my voice: have mercy also upon me, and answer me. When thou saidst, Seek ye my face; my heart said unto thee, Thy face, LORD, will I seek. Hide not thy face far from me; put not thy servant away in anger: thou hast been my help; leave me not, neither forsake me, O God of my salvation.

(Think about it. All of the handwritten ordinances that were against us have been blotted out. Now confess everything. Hide nothing. Then claim His assurance of forgiveness.)

PRAYER OF CONFESSION

FATHER—INSTRUCT: Romans 8:1-4
There is therefore now no condemnation to them which are in Christ Jesus, who walk not after the flesh, but after the Spirit. For the law of the Spirit of life in Christ Jesus hath made me free from the law of sin and death. For what the law could not do, in that it was weak through the flesh, God sending his own Son in the likeness of sinful flesh, and for sin, condemned sin in the
flesh: That the righteousness of the law might be fulfilled in us, who walk not after the flesh, but after the Spirit.

MOTHER—TEACH: Colossians 2:13-15
And you, being dead in your sins and the uncircumcision of your flesh, hath he quickened together with him, having forgiven you all trespasses; Blotting out the handwriting of ordinances
that was against us, which was contrary to us, and took it out of the way, nailing it to his cross; And having spoiled principalities and powers, he made a shew of them openly, triumphing over
them in it.

SON(S)—LISTEN: Psalm 86:3-5
Be merciful unto me, O Lord: for I cry unto thee daily. Rejoice the soul of thy servant: for unto thee, O Lord, do I lift up my soul. For thou, Lord, art good, and ready to forgive; and plenteous in mercy unto all them that call upon thee.

DAUGHTER(S)—RESPOND: Psalm 27:7-9
Hear, O LORD, when I cry with my voice: have mercy also upon me, and answer me. When thou saidst, Seek ye my face; my heart said unto thee, Thy face, LORD, will I seek. Hide not thy face far from me; put not thy servant away in anger: thou hast been my help; leave me not, neither forsake me, O God of my salvation.

(The reason there is no condemnation is because we are in Christ Jesus. Now praise Him for your forgiveness.)

PRAYER OF GRATITUDE

FATHER – INSTRUCT: Psalm 147:5-7
Great is our Lord, and of great power: his understanding is infinite. The LORD lifteth up the meek: he casteth the wicked down to the ground. Sing unto the LORD with thanksgiving; sing praise upon the harp unto our God.

MOTHER – TEACH: Psalm 119:71-74
It is good for me that I have been afflicted; that I might learn thy statutes. The law of thy mouth is better unto me than thousands of gold and silver. Thy hands have made me and fashioned me: give me understanding, that I may learn thy commandments. They that fear thee will be glad when they see me; because I have hoped in thy word.

SON(S) – LISTEN: Ephesians 1:15-17
Wherefore I also, after I heard of your faith in the Lord Jesus, and love unto all the saints, Cease not to give thanks for you, making mention of you in my prayers; That the God of our Lord Jesus Christ, the Father of glory, may give unto you the spirit of wisdom and revelation in the knowledge of him.

DAUGHTER(S) – RESPOND: Romans 6:17-18
But God be thanked, that ye were the servants of sin, but ye have obeyed from the heart that form of doctrine which was delivered you. Being then made free from sin, ye became the servants of righteousness.

(We have many reasons to be grateful. One such is Christ who makes our faith accounted for righteousness. Praise the Lord.)

WISDOM AND UNDERSTANDING

FATHER – INSTRUCT: Matthew 12:31-32
Wherefore I say unto you, All manner of sin and blasphemy shall be forgiven unto men: but the blasphemy against the Holy Ghost shall not be forgiven unto men. And whosoever speaketh a word against the Son of man, it shall be forgiven him: but whosoever speaketh against the Holy Ghost, it shall not be forgiven him, neither in this world, neither in the world to come.

MOTHER – TEACH: Galatians 6:1-3
Brethren, if a man be overtaken in a fault, ye which are spiritual, restore such an one in the spirit of meekness; considering thyself, lest thou also be tempted. Bear ye one another's burdens, and so fulfil the law of Christ. For if a man think himself to be something, when he is nothing, he deceiveth himself.

SON(S) – LISTEN: 2 Corinthians 2:7-11
So that contrariwise ye ought rather to forgive him, and comfort him, lest perhaps such a one should be swallowed up with overmuch sorrow. Wherefore I beseech you that ye would confirm your love toward him. For to this end also did I write, that I might know the proof of you, whether ye be obedient in all things. To whom ye forgive any thing, I forgive also: for if I forgave any thing, to whom I forgave it, for your sakes forgave I it in the person of Christ; Lest Satan should get an advantage of us: for we are not ignorant of his devices.

DAUGHTER(S) – RESPOND: 2 Corinthians 2:14-17
Now thanks be unto God, which always causeth us to triumph in Christ, and maketh manifest the savour of his knowledge by us in every place. For we are unto God a sweet savour of Christ, in them that are saved, and in them that perish: To the one we are the savour of death unto death; and to the other the savour of life unto life. And who is sufficient for these things? For we are not as many, which corrupt the word of God: but as of sincerity, but as of God, in the sight of God speak we in Christ.

(Love for God and forgiveness of others is the wisdom from above. Now ask God to enlighten your heart to accept this wisdom.)

PRAYER OF SERENITY

FATHER – INSTRUCT: Matthew 18:15-18
Moreover if thy brother shall trespass against thee, go and tell him his fault between thee and him alone: if he shall hear thee, thou hast gained thy brother. But if he will not hear thee, then take with thee one or two more, that in the mouth of two or three witnesses every word may be established. And if he shall neglect to hear them, tell it unto the church: but if he neglect to hear the church, let him be unto thee as an heathen man and a publican. Verily I say unto you, Whatsoever ye shall bind on earth shall be bound in heaven: and whatsoever ye shall loose on earth shall be loosed in heaven.

MOTHER – TEACH: Matthew 18:19-22
Again I say unto you, That if two of you shall agree on earth as touching any thing that they shall ask, it shall be done for them of my Father which is in heaven. For where two or three are gathered together in my name, there am I in the midst of them. Then came Peter to him, and said, Lord, how oft shall my brother sin against me, and I forgive him? till seven times? Jesus saith unto him, I say not unto thee, Until seven times: but, Until seventy times seven.

SON(S) – LISTEN: 1 Peter 1:13-15
Wherefore gird up the loins of your mind, be sober, and hope to the end for the grace that is to be brought unto you at the revelation of Jesus Christ; As obedient children, not fashioning yourselves according to the former lusts in your ignorance: But as he which hath called you is holy, so be ye holy in all manner of conversation.

DAUGHTER(S) – RESPOND: Matthew 13:11, 15-16
He answered and said unto them, Because it is given unto you to know the mysteries of the kingdom of heaven, but to them it is not given. For this people's heart is waxed gross, and their ears are dull of hearing, and their eyes they have closed; lest at any time they should see with their eyes, and hear with their ears, and should understand with their heart, and should be converted, and I should heal them. But blessed are your eyes, for they see: and your ears, for they hear.

(The dispensation of grace barred condemnation from the scene for those who believe. Now any prayer in sincerity is accepted and approved in heaven.)

PRAYER OF INTERCESSION

FATHER – INSTRUCT: Psalm 143:1-2
Hear my prayer, O LORD, give ear to my supplications: in thy faithfulness answer me, *and* in thy righteousness. And enter not into judgment with thy servant: for in thy sight shall no man living be justified.

MOTHER – TEACH: Hebrews 9:27-28
And as it is appointed unto men once to die, but after this the judgment: So Christ was once offered to bear the sins of many; and unto them that look for him shall he appear the second time without sin unto salvation.

SON(S) – LISTEN: John 12:46-47
I am come a light into the world, that whosoever believeth on me should not abide in darkness. And if any man hear my words, and believe not, I judge him not: for I came not to judge the world, but to save the world.

DAUGHTER(S) – RESPOND: Colossians 1:12-15
Giving thanks unto the Father, which hath made us meet to be partakers of the inheritance of the saints in light: Who hath delivered us from the power of darkness, and hath translated *us* into the kingdom of his dear Son: In whom we have redemption through his blood, *even* the forgiveness of sins: Who is the image of the invisible God, the firstborn of every creature.

(Because of the Lord's faithfulness toward us, we can intercede for others with a faith that heals.)

PRAYER OF PERSONAL REQUEST

FATHER – INSTRUCT: Luke 13:34-35
O Jerusalem, Jerusalem, which killest the prophets, and stonest them that are sent unto thee; how often would I have gathered thy children together, as a hen doth gather her brood under her wings, and ye would not! Behold, your house is left unto you desolate: and verily I say unto you, Ye shall not see me, until the time come when ye shall say, Blessed is he that cometh in the name of the Lord.

MOTHER – TEACH: Matthew 9:2-3
And, behold, they brought to him a man sick of the palsy, lying on a bed: and Jesus seeing their faith said unto the sick of the palsy; Son, be of good cheer; thy sins be forgiven thee. And, behold, certain of the scribes said within themselves, This man blasphemeth.

SON(S) – LISTEN: John 5:7-9
The impotent man answered him, Sir, I have no man, when the water is troubled, to put me into the pool: but while I am coming, another steppeth down before me. Jesus saith unto him, Rise, take up thy bed, and walk. And immediately the man was made whole, and took up his bed, and walked: and on the same day was the sabbath.

DAUGHTER(S) – RESPOND: Matthew 20:30, 34
And, behold, two blind men sitting by the way side, when they heard that Jesus passed by, cried out, saying, Have mercy on us, O Lord, thou son of David. So Jesus had compassion on them, and touched their eyes: and immediately their eyes received sight, and they followed him.

(It doesn't matter if St. Luke or St. Matthew tells the story; the fact is that Christ has the power to forgive sins. Now make your personal requests with boldness today.)

PRAYER OF GUIDANCE

FATHER – INSTRUCT: Isaiah 30:21
And thine ears shall hear a word behind thee, saying, This is the way, walk ye in it, when ye turn to the right hand, and when ye turn to the left.

MOTHER – TEACH: Revelation 3:11
Behold, I come quickly: hold that fast which thou hast, that no man take thy crown.

SON(S) – LISTEN: Revelation 4:2
And immediately I was in the spirit: and, behold, a throne was set in heaven, and one sat on the throne.

DAUGHTER(S) – RESPOND: Hebrews 4:15-16
For we have not an high priest which cannot be touched with the feeling of our infirmities; but was in all points tempted like as we are, yet without sin. Let us therefore come boldly unto the throne of grace, that we may obtain mercy, and find grace to help in time of need.

(The Holy Ghost is our teacher. Jesus is our high priest. The deck is stacked in your favor. Now trust all your decisions to Christ's guidance today.)

DEDICATION AND CONSECRATION

FATHER – INSTRUCT: Genesis 3:15-16
And I will put enmity between thee and the woman, and between thy seed and her seed; it shall bruise thy head, and thou shalt bruise his heel. Unto the woman he said, I will greatly multiply thy sorrow and thy conception; in sorrow thou shalt bring forth children; and thy desire shall be to thy husband, and he shall rule over thee.

MOTHER – TEACH: Deuteronomy 18:17-19
And the LORD said unto me, They have well spoken that which they have spoken. I will raise them up a Prophet from among their brethren, like unto thee, and will put my words in his mouth; and he shall speak unto them all that I shall command him. And it shall come to pass, that whosoever will not hearken unto my words which he shall speak in my name, I will require it of him.

SON(S) – LISTEN: Isaiah 7:11, 14
Ask thee a sign of the LORD thy God; ask it either in the depth, or in the height above. Therefore the Lord himself shall give you a sign; Behold, a virgin shall conceive, and bear a son, and shall call his name Immanuel.

DAUGHTER(S) – RESPOND: 1 Corinthians 15:45-47
And so it is written, The first man Adam was made a living soul; the last Adam was made a quickening spirit. Howbeit that was not first which is spiritual, but that which is natural; and afterward that which is spiritual. The first man is of the earth, earthy: the second man is the Lord from heaven.

(God started with a seed, a seer, a sign. He ended with a quickening Spirit. Now, rededicate your life anew.)

INDEX

MY SERVICE UNTO THE LORD

St. John 4:36: "And he that reapeth receiveth wages, and gathereth fruit unto life eternal: that both he that soweth and he that reapeth may rejoice together." List the names of your prayer partners who completed the 30-day 24 Minute Ministry Session with you.

Names:_____

_____

_____

_____

_____

_____

_____

_____

_____

_____

_____

_____

_____

_____

_____

_____

_____

My daily spiritual meditation and prayer journal sheet
Copy Sheet for daily journaling

My source for meditation and devotion today_____

What did the spirit say to me today?
_____
_____
_____
_____
_____
_____

My personal requests:
_____
_____
_____
_____
_____
_____

My testimony:
_____
_____
_____
_____
_____
_____
_____

My prayer today:
_____
_____
_____
_____
_____
_____

All Faith Chapel Ministry
Presents
"THE 24 MINUTE MINISTRY FEDERAL PRISON PRAYER GROUP"
For All Members

The following is a list of "Prayer Partners" who are currently members of the 24 Minute Ministry. Choose a prayer partner and begin to experience what GOD intended for His sons. Each person is committed to helping you grow spiritually and to teach you how to be in fellowship with GOD daily.

Ambrose	Allen	Benard	Derek
Anthony	Greg	Will	Leroy
Dedrick	Eugene	Willie	Johnnie
Vidales	Timothy	Donnie	Wayne
Mack	Dexter	Ocie	Chris
Chester	Timothy	Jerome	Charles
Quinten	Willie	Clifton	Derell
Gary	Jordan	Keith	Rufus
Tim	Damon	Damon	Michael
Edward	Steve	Barry	William
Ervin	Melvin		

God Bless and Keep You. Amen

Elder Bond

This is the flyer that was posted in every dormitory of the prison camp. Only the first names are mentioned to protect the identity of each prayer partner.

CREED OF CONSECRATION

God has set me apart — Exodus 32:29
He has declared me holy — Luke 2:23
I have been purchased with a price — Acts 20:28
This price was paid by God — 1 Corinthians 6:20
Who sacrificed His only Son, Jesus — John 3:16
Whose blood poured forth to wash me clean — Colossians 1:14
God has made me a student of His Word — Acts 6:4
God has made me a judge of myself, not others — 1 Corinthians 11:31-32
I will rebuke all thoughts contrary to God's will before they become strongholds — 2 Corinthians 10:5
I am an honored vessel — Jude 1
Therefore, I will honor God with my life — Romans 12:1
I am consecrated — Romans 8:1

THE PRAYER OF A SHEEP
By Johnnie D. Bond, Sr.

Lord, I want to be sacrificed for my brothers,
To give to the needs and benefits of others,
to never complain about my personal abuses.
Lord, please make me a sheep.

Lord, I want to appease the shepherd's appetite,
To be led to the slaughter in yonder sight,
To be cold that others may be covered.
Lord, please make me a sheep.

Lord, I know I must be brutally bruised.
This is a role I desire to choose.
No greater joy for any master to reap—
Lord, please answer my prayer and make me a sheep.

Lord, without a mumbling word I will go
To reconcile your sons, to defeat your foe,
To warn your loved ones to avoid the deep.
Lord, grant my desire and make me a sheep.

www.ingramcontent.com/pod-product-compliance
Lightning Source LLC
Chambersburg PA
CBHW071853290426
44110CB00013B/1134